How to Probate and Settle an Estate in Texas

Third Edition

Karen Ann Rolcik
Attorney at Law

SPHINX® PUBLISHING
AN IMPRINT OF SOURCEBOOKS, INC.®
NAPERVILLE, ILLINOIS

Copyright © 1995, 1999, 2002 by Karen Ann Rolcik

All rights reserved. No part of this book may be reproduced in any form or by any electronic or mechanical means including information storage and retrieval systems—except in the case of brief quotations embodied in critical articles or reviews—without permission in writing from its publisher, Sourcebooks, Inc. Purchasers of the book are granted a license to use the forms contained herein for their own personal use. No claim of copyright is made in any government form reproduced herein.

Third Edition, 2002

Published by: **Sphinx® Publishing, An Imprint of Sourcebooks, Inc.®**

<u>Naperville Office</u>
P.O. Box 4410
Naperville, Illinois 60567-4410
630-961-3900
Fax: 630-961-2168
http://www.sourcebooks.com
http://www.sphinxlegal.com

This publication is designed to provide accurate and authoritative information in regard to the subject matter covered. It is sold with the understanding that the publisher is not engaged in rendering legal, accounting, or other professional service. If legal advice or other expert assistance is required, the services of a competent professional person should be sought.

*From a Declaration of Principles Jointly Adopted by a Committee of the
American Bar Association and a Committee of Publishers and Associations*

This product is not a substitute for legal advice.

Disclaimer required by Texas statutes

Library of Congress Cataloging-in-Publication Data

Rolcik, Karen Ann.
    How to probate and settle an estate in Texas / Karen Ann Rolcik.-- 3rd ed.
      p. cm. -- (Legal survival guides)
    Includes index.
    ISBN 1-57248-214-1 (alk. paper)
    1. Probate law and practice--Texas--Popular works. I. Title. II. Series.
Title. III. Series.

KFT1344.Z9 R654 2002
346.76405'2--dc21

                                                    2002017384

Printed and bound in the United States of America.

VHG Paperback — 10 9 8 7 6 5 4 3 2 1

Contents

Using Self-Help Law Books v

Introduction ix

Chapter 1: Understanding Probate 1
    When Probate Is Required
    Types of Probate Procedures
    Property Subject to Probate
    Who May Represent an Estate
    Estate and Inheritance Taxes
    When the Decedent was not a Resident of Texas
    Filing Fees
    Signing Documents
    Duration of the Probate Process
    The Simplest Form of Probate
    Needing an Attorney
    General Things to Do

Chapter 2: Independent Administration 15
    Application for Probate of Will and Issuance of Letters Testamentary
    Appointment of Resident Agent
    Proof of Subscribing Witness
    Proof of Death and Other Facts
    Order Admitting Will to Probate and Authorizing Letters Testamentary
    Oath
    Bond
    Notice to Creditors
    Administering the Estate
    IRS Form SS-4
    Inventory, Appraisement, and List of Claims
    Homestead, Exempt Personal Property, and Family Allowance
    Payment of Debts and Expenses
    Tax Returns
    Distribution of the Estate Assets
    Affidavit Regarding Debts and Taxes
    Texas Probate Checklist—Independent Administration with Will

CHAPTER 3: DEPENDENT ADMINISTRATION 31
    Administration with Will Annexed (AWA)
    Administration with Dependent Executor (ADE)
    Regular Dependent Administration (RDA)
    Filing the Application
    Appointment of Resident Agent
    Proof of Subscribing Witness
    Filing Fees
    Proof of Death and Other Facts
    Order Admitting Will to Probate and Authorizing Letters Testamentary
        or Letters of Administration
    Oath of Administrator or Executor
    Bond
    Notice to Creditors
    Administering the Estate
    IRS Form SS-4
    Inventory, Appraisement, and List of Claims
    Homestead, Exempt Personal Property, and Family Allowance
    Annual Accountings
    Payment of Debts and Expenses
    Tax Returns
    Distribution of the Estate Assets
    Final Account and Application for Discharge
    Texas Probate Checklist—Administration with Will Annexed (AWA)
    Texas Probate Checklist—Administration with Dependent Executor (ADE)
    Texas Probate Checklist—Regular Dependent Administration (RDA)

CHAPTER 4: PROCEDURES IN LIEU OF ADMINISTRATION 55
    Muniment of Title
    Proceedings to Determine Heirship
    Small Estates
    Affidavit of Heirship
    Texas Probate Checklist—Muniment of Title
    Texas Probate Checklist—Heirship Determination
    Texas Probate Checklist—Small Estates

GLOSSARY 65

APPENDIX A: TEXAS PROBATE CODE 71

APPENDIX B: BLANK FORMS 99

INDEX 217

Using Self-Help Law Books

Before using a self-help law book, you should realize the advantages and disadvantages of doing your own legal work and understand the challenges and diligence that this requires.

The Growing Trend

Rest assured that you won't be the first or only person handling your own legal matter. For example, in some states, more than seventy-five percent of divorces and other cases have at least one party representing him or herself. Because of the high cost of legal services, this is a major trend and many courts are struggling to make it easier for people to represent themselves. However, some courts are not happy with people who do not use attorneys and refuse to help them in any way. For some, the attitude is, "Go to the law library and figure it out for yourself."

We at Sphinx write and publish self-help law books to give people an alternative to the often complicated and confusing legal books found in most law libraries. We have made the explanations of the law as simple and easy to understand as possible. Of course, unlike an attorney advising an individual client, we cannot cover every conceivable possibility.

Cost/Value Analysis

Whenever you shop for a product or service, you are faced with various levels of quality and price. In deciding what product or service to buy, you make a cost/value analysis on the basis of your willingness to pay and the quality you desire.

When buying a car, you decide whether you want transportation, comfort, status, or sex appeal. Accordingly, you decide among such choices as a Neon, a Lincoln, a Rolls Royce, or a Porsche. Before making a decision, you usually weigh the merits of each option against the cost.

When you get a headache, you can take a pain reliever (such as aspirin) or visit a medical specialist for a neurological examination. Given this choice, most people, of course, take a pain reliever, since it costs only pennies; whereas a medical examination costs hundreds of dollars and takes a lot of time. This is usually a logical choice because it is rare to need anything more than a pain reliever for a headache. But in some cases, a headache may indicate a brain tumor and failing to see a specialist right away can result in complications. Should everyone with a headache go to a specialist? Of course not, but people treating their own illnesses must realize that they are betting on the basis of their cost/value analysis of the situation. They are taking the most logical option.

The same cost/value analysis must be made when deciding to do one's own legal work. Many legal situations are very straight forward, requiring a simple form and no complicated analysis. Anyone with a little intelligence and a book of instructions can handle the matter without outside help.

But there is always the chance that complications are involved that only an attorney would notice. To simplify the law into a book like this, several legal cases often must be condensed into a single sentence or paragraph. Otherwise, the book would be several hundred pages long and too complicated for most people. However, this simplification necessarily leaves out many details and nuances that would apply to special or unusual situations. Also, there are many ways to interpret most legal questions. Your case may come before a judge who disagrees with the analysis of our authors.

Therefore, in deciding to use a self-help law book and to do your own legal work, you must realize that you are making a cost/value analysis. You have decided that the money you will save in doing it yourself outweighs the chance that your case will not turn out to your satisfaction. Most people handling their own simple legal matters never have a problem, but occasionally people find that it ended up costing them more to have an attorney straighten out the situation than it would have if they had hired an attorney in the beginning. Keep this in mind if you decide to handle your own case, and be sure to consult an attorney if you feel you might need further guidance.

LOCAL RULES

The next thing to remember is that a book which covers the law for the entire nation, or even for an entire state, cannot possibly include every procedural difference of every county court. Whenever possible, we provide the exact form needed; however, in some areas, each county, or even each judge, may require unique forms and procedures. In our *state* books, our forms usually cover the majority of counties in the state, or provide examples of the type of form that will be required. In our *national* books, our forms are sometimes even more general in nature but are designed to give a good idea of the type of form that will be needed in most locations. Nonetheless, keep in mind that your *state*, county, or judge may have a requirement, or use a form, that is not included in this book.

You should not necessarily expect to be able to get all of the information and resources you need solely from within the pages of this book. This book will serve as your guide, giving you specific information whenever possible and helping you to find out what else you will need to know. This is just like if you decided to build your own backyard deck. You might purchase a book on how to build decks. However, such a book would not include the building codes and permit requirements of every city, town, county, and township in the nation; nor would it include the lumber, nails, saws, hammers, and other materials and tools you would need to actually build the deck. You would use the book as your guide, and then do some work and research involving such matters as whether you need a permit of some kind, what type and grade of wood are available in your area, whether to use hand tools or power tools, and how to use those tools.

Before using the forms in a book like this, you should check with your court clerk to see if there are any local rules of which you should be aware, or local forms you will need to use. Often, such forms will require the same information as the forms in the book but are merely laid out differently, use slightly different language, or use different color paper so the clerks can easily find them. They will sometimes require additional information.

CHANGES IN THE LAW

Besides being subject to state and local rules and practices, the law is subject to change at any time. The courts and the legislatures of all fifty states are constantly revising the laws. It is possible that while you are reading this book, some aspect of the law is being changed or that a court is interpreting a law in a different way. You should always check the most recent statutes, rules and regulations to see what, if any changes have been made.

In most cases, the change will be of minimal significance. A form will be redesigned, additional information will be required, or a waiting period will be extended. As a result, you might need to revise a form, file an extra form, or wait out a longer time period; these types of changes will not usually affect the outcome of your case. On the other hand, sometimes a major part of the law is changed, the entire law in a particular area is rewritten, or a case that was the basis of a central legal point is overruled. In such instances, your entire ability to pursue your case may be impaired.

Again, you should weigh the value of your case against the cost of an attorney and make a decision as to what you believe is in your best interest.

Introduction

Joint ownership of property, living trusts, beneficiary accounts, Totten trusts, and other estate planning devices have eliminated the need for most property to go through probate. With some basic estate planning, probate can be avoided for most estates. However, many people prefer not to think about death and never plan for it, and those who do plan sometimes end up with property that is still subject to probate.

This is not a law school course, but a practical guide to get you through the probate process as easily as possible.

The first chapter of this book gives you an overview of the probate process. This will help you determine which of the various probate procedures you will need to follow, and provide you with essential information, regardless of the procedure you use.

The remaining three chapters will describe the various probate procedures in detail, including an explanation of the forms you will need. Checklists are found at the end of each chapter, to help you through the procedure in a logical manner.

Appendix A contains selected portions of the Texas Probate Code. Appendix B contains the forms you will need.

NOTE: *In Texas there is no formal rule or statute prohibiting an individual from representing himself individually or in his role as an executor of an estate. In most counties in Texas, the judges will permit an individual to represent himself in a probate matter. However, there are a few judges who have established rules in their own court that prohibit such representation. (Such rules are the exception to the prevailing practice. You should check with the probate court where you wish to file the papers to determine whether the judge requires that an attorney be used in probate proceedings.)*

Understanding Probate 1

Probate is a legal process to transfer property of a deceased person (called a *decedent*) to the *heirs* or *beneficiaries*. Heirs are persons entitled by law to receive a decedent's property if the decedent died without a will. Beneficiaries are persons named in a decedent's will.

The process basically involves five steps:

- Prepare certain forms and file them (along with the will if there is one) with the probate court. The court will then appoint someone to represent the estate. This will either be a person named in the will to be the *executor*, or someone the judge appoints as the *administrator* (typically the person who is filing the probate case). The executor or administrator is then responsible for carrying out the following steps.

- Notify the decedent's heirs and beneficiaries of the probate.

- Notify the decedent's creditors of the deadline for submitting claims.

- Pay any claims owed by the decedent or the estate, including estate or inheritance taxes, and collect any amounts owed to the decedent or the estate.

- Distribute property to the heirs or beneficiaries.

In most cases, especially where there is not a will, the probate process is a fairly simple matter. Unless there is a delay in selling or collecting some of the decedent's assets, the probate process many times can be concluded shortly after the six-month period for claims expires.

While many executors and administrators hire an attorney, a probate can be handled without a lawyer, which can save a lot of money in attorneys fees. However, if there is a will that leaves property to someone who would not be an heir if there had not been a will, particularly if there is a large estate, heirs and beneficiaries may have conflicting interests. This can make the probate process emotional and sometimes very bitter. In the case of such conflicting claims, there will usually be attorneys to represent the executor, as well as various beneficiaries and heirs. If you are the executor or administrator, and find yourself involved in a contested probate case, you will need to hire an attorney. If you are an heir or beneficiary, and find yourself involved in a contested probate case, you should also seriously consider hiring an attorney.

When Probate Is Required

Probate is required if the decedent owned property that is subject to probate at the time of his or her death. There are certain types of property ownership that allow the property to be transferred upon death without going through the probate process. Types of property ownership are discussed more fully in the section of this chapter titled "Property Subject to Probate."

Probate may be necessary whether a decedent had a will or not. A will does not eliminate the need for probate, but becomes the primary document used in the probate process.

If a decedent died without a will (called dying *intestate*), property passes to the decedent's heirs as determined by the Texas Probate Code, which lists the classes of heirs and the order in which they will inherit. If a decedent died with a will (called dying *testate*), the property passes to those persons named in the will (the beneficiaries). If a person challenges the validity of the will, often called *contesting the will*, the probate court will determine whether the will is valid and who is legally entitled to receive the decedent's property.

Types of Probate Procedures

Texas has several different probate procedures. Which procedure to use depends upon the size of the estate, the type of property involved, and whether the decedent died testate or intestate. Each of these types of procedures is explained in detail in later chapters. The following provides some basic information about each type, to assist you in determining which type of procedure you will need to use.

Summaries of Types of Probate

Independent Administration. This procedure is available when there is a will that specifically provides for independent administration, or if all of the beneficiaries and the court agree that an independent administration is appropriate. This is a relatively simple procedure that is not closely supervised by the court. This procedure is explained in Chapter 2.

Administration with Dependent Executor **(ADE).** This procedure is used when there is a will that does *not* specifically provide for independent administration. This procedure is explained in Chapter 3.

Administration with Will Annexed **(AWA).** This procedure is used if there is a will, but the will either does not name an executor or names an executor who has died or is unable to serve as the executor (and there is no alternate executor named in the will). This procedure is explained in Chapter 3.

Regular Dependent Administration **(RDA).** This procedure is used if there is not a will and there are debts that are *not* secured by a lien on real estate. This procedure is explained in Chapter 3.

Muniment of Title. This procedure may used if there is a will, and there are no unpaid debts, except those secured by a lien on real estate. See Chapter 4 for an explanation of this procedure.

NOTE: *If the only debts are those secured by real estate, you may want to consider the Muniment of Title procedure.*

Proceeding to Determine Heirship. This procedure is available if there is not a will, or if there is property that was not disposed of by a will. See Chapter 4 for an explanation of this procedure.

Small Estates. This procedure is available if the gross value (not subtracting any liabilities) of the decedent's property is less than $50,000; and the value of property other than homestead and exempt property is greater than the liabilities. This procedure is explained in Chapter 4.

Property Subject to Probate

In order to understand what property is subject to probate, it is necessary to understand the various types of property ownership. There are four common types of ownership of property: sole ownership, joint tenancy, tenancy by the entireties, and tenancy in common.

Types of Property Ownership

Sole ownership. *Sole ownership* is where one person owns the entire property in his or her name alone.

Joint tenancy with rights of survivorship. If two or more persons own property as *joint tenants with rights of survivorship*, the survivor will automatically own all of the property upon the death of the other co-owner. The property does not have to go through probate.

Tenancy by the entireties. A *tenancy by the entireties* is a special type of joint tenancy that can only exist between a husband and wife. Title to real estate would specifically state that the husband and wife owned the property "as tenants by the entireties." This means that the husband and wife own the property as one entity. If one spouse dies, the survivor gets the property without the property going through probate.

NOTE: *Tenancies by the entireties are rarely, if ever, used in Texas.*

Tenancy in common. If two or more persons own property as *tenants in common*, each co-owner owns his or her share of the property independently. Upon the death of a co-owner, his or her share goes to his or her heirs or beneficiaries—not to the other co-owners. The heirs or beneficiaries become tenants in common with the surviving tenants or owners. Unless title to the property specifically designates that the parties own the property as joint tenants with rights of survivorship, it will be presumed that the parties own it as tenants in common. Tenancy in common property will need to go through probate.

SEPARATE AND
COMMUNITY
PROPERTY

Texas characterizes property possessed by either spouse during marriage as *community property* or *separate property*. Separate property is property owned by a spouse before marriage, property acquired during marriage by gift or inheritance, and funds recovered by the spouse for personal injuries.

All other property of the spouses is community property. Each spouse automatically owns one-half of the community property. Community property is subject to the probate process. If the decedent has a will, it only controls his or her one-half interest in the community property. However, all of the community property, not just the decedent's one-half, is subject to probate administration.

PROBATE
PROPERTY

Only property that is classified as *probate property* is subject to the probate process. Probate property includes:

- sole property and

- tenancy in common property (i.e., ownership that does *not* have survivorship rights).

For example, if two people owned property as *joint tenants with rights of survivorship*, the property passes automatically to the survivor. A certified copy of the decedent's death certificate generally is all that is required to show that the entire property interest is now held by the surviving owner.

Example: If the total property a husband and wife owned were a home as joint tenants with rights of survivorship, a car titled in both names, and a joint bank account, probate would be unnecessary because none of the property is subject to probate.

A death certificate and the original deed are all that are required for the survivor to prove ownership of the house. The county tax collector-assessor's office will explain what papers need to be filed with it to transfer title to the car. A certified copy of the death certificate would be sufficient to present to the bank to have the decedent's name removed from the account. Certified copies of the death certificate can be obtained from the funeral home.

To determine whether probate is necessary, and what type of probate procedure can be used, you must first collect information regarding all of the assets owned by the decedent and determine whether the property passed automatically at death or must be probated.

One other type of property that is not subject to probate is proceeds from a life insurance policy on the life of the decedent. The only exceptions would be where the policy does not name a beneficiary, names a beneficiary who is dead (and does not name a living alternate beneficiary), or names the decedent or the decedent's estate as beneficiary. In such cases, the life insurance proceeds would become part of the estate and would be subject to probate.

Who May Represent an Estate

In Texas, the person responsible for probating the estate of the decedent is the *executor* (if the person is appointed in a will) or *administrator* (if the person is appointed by the court). (In other states, the executor or administrator may be referred to as the *personal representative*.) If the named executor in the will is unable or unwilling to serve as executor, the alternate person named in the will usually serves as executor. However, if there is no alternate executor named in the will, or if the decedent died without a will, then an administrator will be appointed by the probate court.

The following persons who are qualified, in the order of preference, will be considered by the court for appointment as administrator:

1. the surviving spouse;

2. the primary devisee or legatee of the decedent (A *devisee* is a person who inherits real estate under the terms of a will. A *legatee* is a person who inherits personal property under a will.);

3. any devisee or legatee of the decedent;

4. the next of kin of the decedent;

5. a creditor of the decedent;

6. any person of good character living in the county where the decedent resided; or,

7. any other person who is not disqualified to serve by reason of being a minor, mentally incompetent, a convicted felon, a person who is not a resident of Texas and who has not appointed a person in Texas to act as resident agent, a corporation that is not authorized to serve as an executor, or a person whom the court finds unsuitable.

In Texas, it is possible that a person with whom the decedent had no contact or who was never acquainted with the decedent, might be appointed by the court to serve as administrator.

Many times a person making a will wants to name a person who does not live in Texas as executor of his estate. Texas law permits a person who is not a resident of Texas to serve as executor, provided that person has appointed a *resident agent*. A resident agent is a person or corporation (namely a bank or trust company) who can accept service of process (notice of lawsuits) in all actions or proceedings involving the estate.

Estate and Inheritance Taxes

Texas does not impose either an estate or inheritance tax on an estate unless the size of the estate is large enough to deduct the amount of such tax from its federal estate tax bill.

The federal government imposes a tax on estates greater than $1,000,000 in value. In determining if the estate is over this federal tax limit, you must include all of the property owned by the decedent at the time of death (but only the decedent's one-half of any community property). Therefore, probate and non-probate property such as life insurance benefits, joint property, retirement accounts, and trust interests must be added together to determine if this limit is met. If you have any question whether the estate is subject to estate tax, you should consult with a probate attorney or an accountant.

There is an income tax imposed on the estate of a decedent. If $600.00 or more in income will be received by the estate before December 31, the executor will have to file a U.S. Income Tax Return for Estates and Trusts (IRS Form 1041) and also file a **Notice Concerning Fiduciary Relationship (IRS Form 56)** with the IRS that he is serving as the representative of the estate. (see form 46, p.211.) Income to the estate includes such things as interest, dividends, royalties, and rents. Income does not include money received from the sale of property. An accountant or probate attorney should be consulted if you have any questions about this.

If the decedent received over $5,900 of income between January 1 and the date of death, a final **U.S. Individual Income Tax Return (IRS Form 1040)** must be filed for that period. (see form 48, p.215.) This limit increases if the decedent was married and/or over the age of sixty-five. Again, contact an accountant or probate attorney about this. Of course, you would also file a return if the decedent is entitled to a refund, regardless of whether the $5,900 limit is met.

When the Decedent was not a Resident of Texas

If the decedent was not a resident of Texas but left Texas property, the property may be probated through a process called *ancillary administration*. Typically in this situation, the primary probate proceeding is handled in the state where the decedent had his or her primary residence. A second proceeding is handled in the Texas county where the property is located in order to pass title to the property to the heirs or beneficiaries.

> *Warning*: If you have a need for an ancillary administration in Texas, you should consult with a probate attorney.

Filing Fees

When a probate case is started, a fee must be paid to the county clerk. It is important to check with your local probate court clerk, as the amount of the fee may vary depending upon the county. The county clerk will not open an estate without the fee. If the estate does not have money available to pay the fee, the executor (or applicant if there is no will) can pay the fee and be reimbursed from the estate assets later.

Signing Documents

A majority of the probate documents are signed by the applicant (usually the executor if there is a will). Most of the documents do not have to be notarized, but on those that have to be notarized, the date of the expiration of the notary public's commission must be included.

DURATION OF THE PROBATE PROCESS

The amount of time that probate takes depends on a variety of factors. The number of assets, the size of the assets, the number of creditors, and the number of beneficiaries all have a bearing on how long the probate can take. If there are only a few small assets, no creditors, and all of the beneficiaries are known and can be located, an estate can be settled in a few weeks. If there are a lot of assets, debts, and beneficiaries, an estate could drag on for several years.

THE SIMPLEST FORM OF PROBATE

The basic steps for the different forms of probate proceedings are included in the various chapters of this book. As you will see from the checklists at the end of each chapter, the procedures in Chapter 4 have the fewest steps. All of the procedures can be fairly simple if the steps are followed closely and there are no objections by any creditors, heirs, or beneficiaries. The steps are explained as simply and concisely as possible. However, not every situation can be covered in a book like this.

Warning: You should contact an experienced probate attorney in any of the following situations:

- if the estate has assets close to $1,000,000 in value;
- if the estate has assets with unique characteristics such as royalty interests, partnership interests, or interests in trusts or annuities;
- if the will is not clear with regard to the distribution of the assets;
- if the beneficiaries or heirs are difficult to locate or determine;
- if there are significant claims against the estate; or,
- if someone is contesting the will.

Needing an Attorney

One of the first questions you will want to consider, and most likely the reason you are reading this book is: how much will an attorney cost? As a very rough estimate, probate attorneys will charge anywhere from $75 to $300 per hour.

There are some advantages to hiring a lawyer. First, an attorney will be familiar with all of the local court rules and this will save you the time of finding them yourself. In case the estate suddenly becomes complicated, because someone contests the will or a creditor files a claim against the estate, it is an advantage to have an attorney who is familiar with the estate. It may also be comforting to have an attorney to turn to for advice and to get your questions answered.

There are also advantages to representing yourself besides saving legal fees. The procedure may be faster. Two of the most frequent complaints about lawyers are delay in completing the estate and failure to return phone calls. Most lawyers have heavy caseloads that sometimes results in cases being neglected for various periods of time. If you are following the progress of your own case, you will be able to push it along in the system.

A middle ground would be to find an attorney who will be willing to accept an hourly fee to answer your questions and give you help as you need it. This way you will save some legal costs but still get professional assistance. Selecting an attorney is not easy. As the next section shows, it is hard to know whether you are selecting an attorney that will make you happy.

Selecting an Attorney

A common, and frequently the best, way to find an attorney is to ask friends or acquaintances to recommend one to you. You can also contact a lawyer referral service. This is a service, usually operated by a bar association, that is designed to match a client with a lawyer who actively handles cases in the area of law that the client needs. Lawyer referral services are usually listed in the yellow pages under "Attorneys."

You may also look under "Attorneys" in the yellow pages, where many lawyers list their areas of practice, and some yellow pages list attorneys under various sub-headings such as probate, personal injury, tax, etc.

However you find an attorney, you should have a clear understanding with the attorney regarding the amount of the *fee*, how the fee will be calculated, and exactly what will be done for the fee. For instance, does the attorney charge a set fee and if so, what does that set fee include? If the attorney charges on an hourly basis, find out how much the hourly rate is and how many hours the attorney estimates will be required to complete the matter. What court papers are to be prepared and filed? This fee understanding should be reached before you actually hire the lawyer.

Attorneys will distinguish their fees from the *costs*. Costs are items such as filing fees, mailing charges, duplication charges, certification costs, cost of publication, etc. These costs can add considerably to the total expense. The attorney should be able to give you a fairly accurate estimate of the costs.

General Things to Do

In addition to filing the proper papers with the court to initiate the probate of an estate, several other matters must be handled.

Safe Deposit Boxes

Any safe deposit box registered in the name of the decedent must be opened. Often, the decedent's original will has been placed in the safe deposit box. A safe deposit box can be opened without court order and examined in front of a bank official by the decedent's spouse, parents, descendants who are over age eighteen, or the executor named in the will. The bank will permit removal of only the following documents:

- the decedent's will, as long as it is delivered to the executor or to the county clerk;

- deed to a burial plot or burial instructions to the person requesting that the box be opened; or,

- a life insurance policy to the beneficiary of the policy.

An inventory of the contents of the box should be made in the presence of the bank officer. Sometimes you will need to get a court's permission to open a safe deposit box. If so, use the **MOTION TO OPEN SAFE DEPOSIT BOX AND TO EXAMINE PAPERS AND ORDER**. (see form 25, p.157.) An order for the judge to sign, approving your request to open the box, is included as part of this form.

SOCIAL SECURITY ADMINISTRATION

The Social Security Administration should be notified of the decedent's death immediately. If the decedent was receiving Social Security, and a Social Security check was received at any time during the month in which the decedent died or if checks are received in months after the decedent's death, the full amount of the checks or the checks themselves must be returned. When the checks are returned or a reimbursement check is made by the executor, a letter should be included explaining that the return or reimbursement is being made because of the decedent's death.

Social Security also provides a death benefit to help cover funeral expenses and may provide survivor's benefits to the spouse and minor children. The local office of the Social Security Administration should be contacted to claim these benefits.

U.S. MAIL

Mail addressed to the decedent should be collected and sorted, which will assist in identifying the decedent's assets and liabilities. Once you are appointed executor or administrator, file a change of address for the decedent with the local post office. The forwarding address should be the address of the executor. (Of course, if the decedent was married, his or her mail should continue to be sent to the surviving spouse.)

CREDIT CARDS AND CREDITORS

All of the decedent's credit cards should be cancelled or the decedent should be removed as an authorized signer if the credit card account is a joint account. The credit card companies should be sent a letter cancelling the card. The date of death should be given to avoid any unauthorized charges. Newspaper and magazine vendors should be notified and subscriptions cancelled. Creditors with whom the decedent had automobile loans, student loans, etc., should be notified.

EMPLOYER
PROVIDED
BENEFITS
The decedent's employer should be contacted to find out whether the employer's insurance provides any death benefits. Additional company benefits, such as a profit-sharing plan or pension plan, may be provided, so you must contact the employer to ask about those benefits.

MILITARY
SERVICE
BENEFITS
If the decedent was a veteran, Veteran's Benefits may be available to the decedent's dependents. This may also include some burial expenses, such as grave headstones. This information can be obtained from the local Veterans Administration Office.

OTHER
GOVERNMENT
BENEFITS
In addition to Social Security and Veteran's Benefits, if the decedent was an employee of the federal government, the decedent's family or beneficiaries may be entitled to benefits. There may also be benefits available through the Medicare program.

OTHER
BENEFITS
Benefits may be available through worker's compensation if the death was related to the decedent's employment. Some credit card companies or travel clubs such as AAA offer accidental death benefits to their members.

Independent Administration 2

Independent administration is the administration of an estate without the supervision of the probate court. Usually, this is more convenient, efficient, and much less expensive than a dependent, court supervised administration. There is more flexibility in the management of the estate and there are usually far fewer court costs and attorney's fees. However, if the estate has more liabilities than assets, it is generally better to use a dependent administration.

In Texas, an independent administration may be provided for in a decedent's will. Texas Probate Code, Section 145(b), allows a person to name an independent executor in his or her will, and provides that "no other action shall be had in the county court in relation to the settlement of his estate than the probating and recording of his will, and the return of an inventory, appraisement and list of claims of the estate." Only the person named in the will as independent executor may qualify and act as such. If the will provides for an independent executor but the person does not qualify, an independent administration cannot be used.

After the will has been probated and the independent executor has qualified by taking the oath, the executor must file an inventory, appraisement, and list of claims to be approved by the court. Once the inventory, appraisement, and list of claims has been approved by the court, as long as the estate is represented by the independent executor, there is no further action to be taken in court.

Section 145(c) of the Texas Probate Code allows the court, in its discretion, to create an independent administration where all of the distributees of the decedent agree on independent administration even where dependent administration is normally used. (However, since courts are reluctant to order independent administrations in these situations, that procedure is not covered in this book.)

Independent administration is the estate administration most commonly used in Texas. At the end of this chapter is a checklist of the steps for an independent administration.

APPLICATION FOR PROBATE OF WILL AND ISSUANCE OF LETTERS TESTAMENTARY

The Texas Probate Code, Section 81, provides that the APPLICATION FOR PROBATE OF WILL AND ISSUANCE OF LETTERS TESTAMENTARY should include the following information (see form 1, p.103):

- name and domicile of each applicant;
- name, age if known, and domicile (street, city, and county) of the decedent and the fact, time, and place of death;
- facts showing that the court has venue;
- that decedent owned real or personal property, or both, describing the property generally and stating an estimated value;
- the date of the will, the name and address (street, city, and county) of the executor named in the will, and the names and current addresses (street, city, and county) of the witnesses, if known;
- whether a child or children were born or adopted by decedent after the will was signed, and the name of each such child who is alive;
- that the executor is not disqualified from serving as executor;

- whether decedent was ever divorced, and if so, when and from whom; and,

- whether the state, governmental agency of the state or charitable organization is named in the will as a beneficiary.

WHERE TO FILE The APPLICATION FOR PROBATE OF WILL AND ISSUANCE OF LETTERS TESTAMENTARY (form 1) should be filed with the Probate Court in the county in which the decedent was *domiciled* (had primary residence) at the time of his or her death.

FILING FEES The filing fee to probate the estate may vary somewhat from county to county. The filing fee must be paid at the time that the APPLICATION FOR PROBATE OF WILL AND ISSUANCE OF LETTERS TESTAMENTARY (form 1) is filed. This amount should be paid from the probate estate, or by the executor and reimbursed from the estate upon appointment. Be sure to check with the court clerk about the amount before filing.

APPOINTMENT OF RESIDENT AGENT

If the executor is not a resident of Texas, he or she must appoint a *resident agent* (a person who is both a resident of Texas and of the county in which the estate is probated) for the purpose of accepting any notice of a lawsuit or service of a summons. Often an attorney will act as the resident agent. However, any adult residing in Texas may act as resident agent. The APPOINTMENT OF RESIDENT AGENT must be signed in the presence of a notary public. (see form 26, p.159.)

PROOF OF SUBSCRIBING WITNESS

Self-proved wills signed as required under Texas law may be admitted to probate without additional documentation. *Self-proved* means that the testator (the person whose will it is) and witnesses took an oath at the time the will was signed. The statement is included with the will and notarized by a notary public.

If the will is not self-proved, the will may be admitted to probate only after one of the witnesses appears in court to give testimony regarding the signing of the will. This can be done by completing the PROOF OF SUBSCRIBING WITNESS. (see form 27, p.161.) This testimony must be included in written form and signed in the presence of the judge or the judge's clerk. This means that you must contact one of the witnesses and ask that they appear at the courthouse to give testimony to the judge and to sign the PROOF OF SUBSCRIBING WITNESS.

If the witnesses cannot appear in court to take the oath, one or more of them may give testimony in the form of a deposition. If this procedure must be used, you should talk to the judge's clerk for assistance.

PROOF OF DEATH AND OTHER FACTS

The court cannot have a hearing on the APPLICATION FOR PROBATE OF WILL AND ISSUANCE OF LETTERS TESTAMENTARY (form 1) until after the first Monday following ten days from the date the is posted. (See Texas Probate Code, Section 33.) When the APPLICATION FOR PROBATE OF WILL is filed, the court will post a notice on the courthouse that it has been filed. When you file the APPLICATION FOR PROBATE OF WILL, you can ask the clerk when you can have a hearing.

The applicant must appear before the court and prove the facts listed in the APPLICATION FOR PROBATE OF WILL and also the following (See Texas Probate Code, Section 88):

- that the person is dead and four years have not elapsed since the date of death;
- that the court has jurisdiction and venue;
- that the executor is not disqualified from serving; and,
- that a necessity exists for an administration of the estate.

The applicant must sign the PROOF OF DEATH AND OTHER FACTS in the presence of the judge. (see form 2, p.105.)

Order Admitting Will to Probate and Authorizing Letters Testamentary

The judge will sign an ORDER ADMITTING WILL TO PROBATE AND AUTHORIZING LETTERS TESTAMENTARY. (see form 3, p.107.) You will provide this form to the judge at the hearing. The ORDER ADMITTING WILL TO PROBATE AND AUTHORIZING LETTERS TESTAMENTARY must include the name of the decedent, the name of the executor, the amount of bond (which will be set by the court), if any, and that the clerk will issue letters when the executor qualifies. (See Texas Probate Code, Section 181.) The executor qualifies when he or she takes the OATH (form 4) and posts the bond, if any, with the court.

When the Letters Testamentary are issued, the independent executor will have the power to perform any act necessary for the full and complete settlement of the estate. (The court will prepare Letters Testamentary.) Texas Probate Code, Section 232, provides that the executor shall collect and take into possession all of the decedent's personal property, records, books, claims, debts due, title papers and business papers.

Oath

After the probate court has signed the ORDER ADMITTING WILL TO PROBATE AND AUTHORIZING LETTERS TESTAMENTARY (form 3), the executor must sign and file an OATH (form 4), whereupon the judge will issue Letters Testamentary (a document authorizing the executor to act on behalf of the estate). This OATH must be signed in the presence of a notary public and delivered to the court within twenty days after the ORDER ADMITTING WILL TO PROBATE AND AUTHORIZING LETTERS TESTAMENTARY is signed by the judge. In the OATH the executor states that the decedent's will has been presented to probate and that the executor will perform all of the duties of an independent executor. (Texas Probate Code, Section 192.)

BOND

Even if bond is waived in the will, the court may still require the executor to obtain a bond. (Texas Probate Code, Section 194.) A *bond* is a guaranty by a bonding or insurance company that the executor will perform his or her required duties properly and will not misuse the estate funds. The clerk of the probate court may be able to find out what amount of bond the judge will require or whether the bond will be waived. If a bond is required, the probate court can usually provide the forms it will require for the bond.

NOTICE TO CREDITORS

As executor, you not only have a duty to the beneficiaries of the estate, but also to the creditors of the decedent. This requires you to do certain things to attempt to give creditors notice of the estate so they can submit claims. Creditors must be notified within one month after the executor has received Letters Testamentary. However, if there is a *secured creditor* (a creditor who may take certain property to satisfy the debt; most commonly a mortgage on a home, or a car loan), notice is to be given within two months after receiving Letters Testamentary.

Notice should be given to:

- comptroller of Public Accounts, by certified mail if the decedent paid or owed taxes administered by the Comptroller (for example, if the decedent owned a business and was required to pay sales or franchise tax);

- unsecured creditors, by publication in a newspaper printed in the county where the will has been probated. A NOTICE TO CREDITORS should be used for this purpose. (see form 28, p.163.) There will be a fee for publishing this notice and this will vary from newspaper to newspaper;

- secured creditors, by certified or registered mail (return receipt requested); and,

- all persons having an unpaid claim against the estate if the executor has knowledge of the claim. Although not legally required, this should be done by certified or registered mail (return receipt requested).

A copy of the notice to secured creditors together with the return receipt and PROOF OF SERVICE OF NOTICE UPON CLAIMANTS AGAINST ESTATE stating that notice was made by certified or registered mail shall be filed with the court. (see form 29, p.165.)

A copy of the published notice to unsecured creditors, together with the PUBLISHER'S AFFIDAVIT that notice was published, shall be filed with the court. (see form 30, p.167.) The actual newspaper clipping should be attached to the PUBLISHER'S AFFIDAVIT. Sometimes the newspaper will prepare and file the PUBLISHER'S AFFIDAVIT directly with the court. You should check with the particular newspaper.

If the decedent left property to a charity, governmental agency, or the State of Texas, the executor must give written notice within thirty days after the will has been probated. The notice must state the county in which the will is probated and must include a copy of the will. This notice must be given by registered or certified mail, return receipt requested. The executor must file proof with the court (an affidavit and the green return receipt card) that notice was given.

ADMINISTERING THE ESTATE

Once the Letters Testamentary have been issued, the executor can begin administering the estate. This means that assets must be collected and legitimate claims against the estate must be paid.

One of the first things you must do is open a checking account in the name of the estate with you as the executor authorized to sign on the account. For example, "Bob Smith as Independent Executor of the Estate of Jane Doe." You will need a taxpayer identification number to open the account. This is explained in the next section.

One of the duties of the executor is to convert the assets of the estate into cash so that it may be divided among the beneficiaries. If the beneficiaries of the estate prefer to receive certain items in the estate, such as personal items, real estate, or stocks and bonds, these items can be distributed to them. However, you should take certain precautions.

First, you must make certain that you are following the terms of the will. The will may give certain things to certain beneficiaries. Second, you should discuss the distribution with all of the beneficiaries. Ask them how they would like the assets distributed. Do they want the property sold and the cash proceeds divided? Do they want to receive some or all of the property instead?

If property is to be distributed instead of sold, be certain the beneficiaries are comfortable with the distribution plans. You do not want them fighting over such things as valuation and who should get what item of property.

Some of the things you may have to do in administering the estate are to close out bank accounts, sell or distribute personal belongings such as clothing and furniture, and sell stocks and bonds.

IRS Form SS-4

In the event a fiduciary tax return is required (explained below), the estate must obtain a federal taxpayer identification number. A federal identification number will also be required by the bank when you open an estate checking account. The **Application for Employer Identification Number (IRS Form SS-4)** must be completed and sent by the executor to the Internal Revenue Service Center in Austin, Texas. (see form 31, p.169.) The IRS will assign a taxpayer identification number to the estate and the executor will be notified by mail within approximately three to four weeks.

The executor may also obtain the taxpayer identification number by telephone by calling 512-462-7843. However, you must have the completed form in front of you when you call because the IRS officer asks how the questions are completed on the form. The IRS officer will give you a number and then you must mail in the form along with the assigned number written in the upper-right hand corner. You may be permitted to fax the completed form. Just follow the instructions given by the IRS when you call them.

Inventory, Appraisement, and List of Claims

An INVENTORY, APPRAISEMENT AND LIST OF CLAIMS (which will be referred to as the "INVENTORY") protects creditors and persons interested in the estate by identifying the estate assets that are available to pay debts and taxes. (see form 32, p.177.) An INVENTORY also assists in determining the proper amount of bond and affects the compensation of the executor.

When to File the Inventory

Within ninety days after the executor is appointed, an INVENTORY must be filed with the probate court. If necessary, the executor may ask the court for an extension of time to file, in order to gather all of the necessary information to prepare an accurate and complete INVENTORY.

What the Inventory Should Include

The INVENTORY, APPRAISEMENT, AND LIST OF CLAIMS should include a list of all of the decedent's probate property, including all real estate in Texas and all personal property wherever it is located. Real estate in other states and property passing to beneficiaries outside of the will (such as proceeds from life insurance, employee benefit plans, trust assets, and survivorship property) should not be included in the INVENTORY. The value of the assets on the date the decedent died should be listed on the INVENTORY.

Claims owed to the estate, not claims against the estate, should be listed. The description of the claims should include the name of the person who owes the estate money, the amount and type of the debt, interest rate, date the claim is due, and date the claim was originally made.

When listing the assets and claims, the executor must indicate whether the asset or claim is separate, community, or joint tenancy property. If the property is joint tenancy, the name of the co-owner must be included.

Amending the Inventory

If the executor later learns of additional property, the INVENTORY should be amended or supplemented. This can be done by preparing a new INVENTORY, which will be titled *Amended Inventory*, that includes the new items in addition to what was on the original INVENTORY.

Signing the Inventory

The executor should sign the affidavit included as part of the INVENTORY (form 32). This affidavit states that the INVENTORY is true, accurate, and complete.

Court Review

After reviewing the INVENTORY, the court will either approve or disapprove it. If disapproved, the executor must file a revised INVENTORY within the time specified by the court. If the INVENTORY is approved, the court will sign an ORDER APPROVING INVENTORY AND APPRAISEMENT, which you will supply to the court in advance. (see form 33, p.181.)

Homestead, Exempt Personal Property, and Family Allowance

Homestead

The real estate used by the decedent as his or her primary residence is called the *homestead*. The homestead is either:

- one or more parcels totalling no more than 200 acres outside of a city, town, or village or

- one or more lots in a city, town, or village totalling no more than one acre, with improvements.

There is no dollar limit on the value of the property that may be claimed as the homestead.

If there is a surviving spouse, minor children, or an unmarried adult child living in the homestead, the homestead passes to the spouse or children free of any creditor claims against the estate, other than for taxes or mortgages on the property.

EXEMPT
PERSONAL
PROPERTY

Exempt personal property includes certain types of personal property, such as household furnishings and vehicles, totalling no more than $30,000 per decedent. This property is generally free from the claims of creditors. However, it can be used to pay claims for funeral expenses and expenses of the decedent's last illness. If the estate is *solvent* (assets are greater than debts), the exempt property is distributed when the executor distributes the other estate assets. If the estate is *insolvent* (debts are greater than assets), title to the exempt property passes to the spouse and children immediately.

Distribution of exempt assets can be requested by filing an APPLICATION TO SET ASIDE EXEMPT PROPERTY, along with an ORDER TO SET ASIDE EXEMPT PROPERTY, with the court. (see form 34, p.183 and form 35, p.185.) The exempt assets, including the homestead, should be described in the APPLICATION TO SET ASIDE EXEMPT PROPERTY and in the ORDER TO SET ASIDE EXEMPT PROPERTY. The ORDER TO SET ASIDE EXEMPT PROPERTY should also contain a list of the people to whom the exempt property should be delivered.

FAMILY
ALLOWANCE

The surviving spouse and minor children are entitled to receive a *family allowance* sufficient to support them for one year. (Texas Probate Code, Sections 286 and 287.) The family allowance will not be paid if the surviving spouse has separate property adequate to support her during the year or when the minor children have sufficient property to support themselves. The amount of the family allowance will be determined by the executor after reviewing all of the facts. The executor may pay the allowance in lump sum or in installments. Use the APPLICATION FOR FAMILY ALLOWANCE, and the ORDER FOR FAMILY ALLOWANCE, to request payment of the family allowance from the court. (see form 36, p.187 and form 37, p.189.)

Payment of Debts and Expenses

The executor must pay the decedent's debts and expenses as provided in Texas Probate Code, Section 322. The following is the order in which claims should be paid if the estate has sufficient funds:

1. funeral expenses and expenses of last illness up to $5,000, if the claims were presented to the executor within sixty days after the Letters Testamentary have been issued;
2. allowances to the surviving spouse and children;
3. expenses of administering the estate and expenses incurred to preserve, safekeep, and manage the estate;
4. secured claims up to the value of the property subject to the debt;
5. taxes, penalties, and interest due to the State of Texas;
6. claims for the costs of confinement in prison;
7. claims for the repayment of medical assistance made by the State of Texas;
8. claims made within six months after the Letters Testamentary have been issued; and,
9. claims made after six months after the Letters Testamentary have been issued.

If there is not sufficient money left in the estate after a certain priority of debts are paid, then the creditors in the next priority will be paid a pro rata share of their claim.

The executor must either approve or reject a claim presented by a creditor within thirty days of when it was presented, otherwise it will be deemed to be rejected. The executor must establish that the claim is valid and legal before he or she may approve it. (Texas Probate Code, Section 310.)

If the claim is approved, the executor should notify the creditor. The executor must show good cause for failing to approve and pay any valid claims. If the executor does not pay a valid claim, the executor may be required to pay the amount of the claim plus interest, costs and damages of 5% per month. (Texas Probate Code, Section 328.)

The executor is responsible for paying federal income taxes for the decedent and for the estate, and for paying federal estate taxes and Texas inheritance taxes.

Tax Returns

The executor is responsible for filing all tax returns, which may include one or more of the following:

- decedent's last federal income tax return;
- annual federal income tax returns for the estate;
- federal gift tax return for the decedent;
- federal estate tax return; and/or,
- Texas inheritance tax return.

IRS FORM 1040   If it is necessary to file a federal income tax return on behalf of a decedent who is single, a **U.S. INDIVIDUAL INCOME TAX RETURN (IRS FORM 1040)** will be signed by the executor as "[*Executor's name*], Executor of the Estate of [*decedent's name*]." For example, "Jane Doe, Executor of the Estate of Jim Smith." (see form 48, p.215.)

The name of the decedent should be followed by the word "Deceased" and the date of death. For example, "Jim Smith, Deceased 10-31-02." "DECEASED" should be written across the top of the form.

If the decedent has a surviving spouse, the final joint return should be signed by the executor and the surviving spouse.

A copy of the current IRS publication explaining this subject can be obtained by going to the IRS local office or calling 800-829-1040. IRS publications can also be found on the Internet at:

http://www.irs.gov

IRS FORM 1041

Income on the assets of the decedent is also taxable and must be shown on IRS Form 1041. The executor must report any income from the assets prior to distribution to the beneficiaries. This form can be obtained from the IRS.

FEDERAL ESTATE TAX RETURN IRS FORM 706

The federal estate tax return must be filed within nine months of the decedent's death if the value of the gross estate exceeds $1,000,000. A tax return must be filed if the estate is above this amount, even if there is no tax due. If any tax is due, it must be paid when the return is filed.

TEXAS INHERITANCE TAX AND OTHER TAX RETURNS

The Texas inheritance tax return will only be filed if a federal estate tax return is filed. There may be other tax returns due, such as partnership returns, corporate returns, sales tax returns, etc. It is important to contact an accountant who is familiar with the decedent's financial affairs to assist with the preparation of these returns.

DISTRIBUTION OF THE ESTATE ASSETS

After the debts, expenses, and taxes have been paid, the executor must distribute the property remaining in the estate as provided in the decedent's will. If real estate is to be distributed, a deed of distribution should be prepared. To avoid problems, especially if homestead property is involved, an attorney familiar with real estate should be contacted to prepare this deed.

Affidavit Regarding Debts and Taxes

After all of the property has been distributed, and taxes, expenses and debts have been paid, the executor may file an AFFIDAVIT REGARDING DEBTS AND TAXES with the probate court stating that all taxes, debts, and expenses have been paid. (see form 38, p.191.) This gives third parties notice that the estate administration is completed and that they must deal directly with the beneficiaries. Unlike dependent estate administrations, independent estate administrations are not formally closed with the probate court. This is generally because in the event estate assets are later located, the estate administration does not have to be reopened. Instead, the probate court can be requested to issue updated Letters Testamentary.

Texas Probate Checklist—Independent Administration with Will

- ❑ Gather information required for APPLICATION FOR PROBATE AND ADMINISTRATION OF ESTATE
  - original will and any codicils
  - decedent's social security number
  - applicant's social security number
  - names and addresses of beneficiaries
  - names and addresses of witnesses to will
  - list of assets and approximate value
  - amount of bond, if any
- ❑ Prepare the following documents:
  - APPLICATION FOR PROBATE OF WILL AND ISSUANCE OF LETTERS TESTAMENTARY (form 1).
  - OATH (form 4).
  - ORDER ADMITTING WILL TO PROBATE AND AUTHORIZING LETTERS TESTAMENTARY (form 3).
- ❑ If the will is not self-proved, prepare PROOF BY SUBSCRIBING WITNESS (form 27).
- ❑ If a bond is required, obtain forms from the probate court, bonding agency, or insurance company.
- ❑ If out of state executor, prepare APPOINTMENT OF RESIDENT AGENT (form 26).
- ❑ File APPLICATION FOR PROBATE, along with original will, any codicils, and filing fee.
- ❑ Attend "Prove-up" hearing at probate court. Applicant must testify to facts contained in PROOF OF DEATH AND OTHER FACTS (form 2) and sign the PROOF OF DEATH AND OTHER FACTS in presence of court clerk or judge. Judge will sign ORDER ADMITTING WILL TO PROBATE AND AUTHORIZING LETTERS TESTAMENTARY (form 3).
- ❑ File OATH (form 4).
- ❑ Wait for Letters Testamentary to be issued by court (usually the day of hearing).
- ❑ Publish NOTICE TO CREDITORS (form 28).
- ❑ Prepare and file IRS forms: NOTICE CONCERNING FIDUCIARY RELATIONSHIP (IRS FORM 56) (form 46) and APPLICATION FOR TAXPAYER IDENTIFICATION NUMBER (IRS FORM SS-4) (form 31).
- ❑ Open checking account for estate.
- ❑ File change of address notice for decedent at post office.
- ❑ Gather the assets and asset records of the estate. These include:

deeds	mortgages owned	savings bonds	coins; stamps; antiques
stocks and bonds	bank books	car and boat titles	promissory notes
mutual funds	contracts	insurance policies	personal property

- ❑ Prepare and file INVENTORY, APPRAISEMENT AND LIST OF CLAIMS (form 32).
- ❑ Provide the court with ORDER APPROVING INVENTORY AND APPRAISEMENT (form 33).
- ❑ Sell any assets necessary to settle the estate.
- ❑ Distribute assets to beneficiaries, leaving sufficient amount to pay taxes, if any.
- ❑ File federal and Texas estate tax returns, if necessary.
- ❑ File AFFIDAVIT REGARDING DEBTS AND TAXES (form 38).
- ❑ Close checking account.
- ❑ File final IRS Form 1041 (obtain form from IRS).
- ❑ Cancel bond.
- ❑ File TERMINATION (IRS FORM 56), with box for "termination" checked (form 46).

Dependent Administration 3

In a *dependent administration*, the probate judge is responsible for making sure that the executor or administrator of the estate performs his or her duties in strict compliance with the court's orders. To do this, the judge will often require that the executor or administrator post a bond with the court, file annual and final accounts with the court, and obtain the court's permission for almost everything the executor or administrator does.

The Texas Probate Code provides that a dependent administration will be appropriate in the following instances:

- when the decedent died *intestate* (without a will);
- when the decedent's will does not name an executor;
- when the decedent's will names an executor who has predeceased the decedent and no successor executor is named;
- when the executor named in the will fails to qualify; or,
- when the executor named in the will does not present will for probate within thirty days after the testator's death.

If the decedent died intestate (without a will), the procedure that must be used is called *Regular Dependent Administration* (RDA). If the decedent died *testate* (with a will), there are two types of dependent administration:

1. Administration with Will Annexed (AWA) and
2. Administration with a Dependent Executor (ADE).

In both of these types of dependent administration, after the will is admitted to probate and the administrator or executor is appointed, the estate administration will proceed in the same manner as a Regular Dependent Administration (RDA). At the end of this chapter are checklists for each type of dependent administration

ADMINISTRATION WITH WILL ANNEXED (AWA)

This procedure is used when an administration is necessary for the estate of a decedent who has a will, but the will does not name an executor, or names an executor who is dead or unable to act, and does not name an alternate executor. The person appointed by the court will be called the *administrator* instead of an *executor*, and will receive Letters of Administration instead of Letters Testamentary.

An APPLICATION FOR PROBATE OF WILL AND ISSUANCE OF LETTERS OF ADMINISTRATION WITH WILL ANNEXED (which will also be called simply the APPLICATION) should be filed with the court and should include the following information (see form 9, p.119):

- name and domicile (street, city, and county) of each applicant;
- name, age (if known), and domicile (street, city, and county) of the decedent and the fact, time, and place of death;
- facts showing that the court has venue;
- that the decedent owned real or personal property, or both, describing the property generally and stating an estimated value;
- the date of the will, the name, and address (street, city, and county) of the administrator, and the names and current addresses (street, city, and county) of the witnesses, if known;

- a statement that the applicant is requesting administration with will annexed;

- whether a child or children were born or adopted by the decedent after the will was signed and the name of each such child who is alive;

- that the executor named in the will is unable or disqualified from serving;

- whether the decedent was ever divorced, and if so, when and from whom; and,

- whether the state, governmental agency of the state, or charitable organization is named in the will as beneficiary.

ADMINISTRATION WITH DEPENDENT EXECUTOR (ADE)

This procedure is used when an administration is necessary for the estate of a decedent who has a will, but the will does not name an independent executor, or does not provide for an independent administration, even though the executor is able and qualified to serve as an independent executor. The person appointed by the court will be called an *executor* and will receive Letters Testamentary.

An APPLICATION FOR PROBATE OF WILL AND ISSUANCE OF LETTERS TESTAMENTARY (which will also be called simply the APPLICATION) should be filed with the court and should include the following information (see form 13, p.127):

- name and domicile (street, city, and county) of each applicant;

- name, age if known, and domicile (street, city, and county) of the decedent and the fact, time, and place of death;

- facts showing that the court has venue;

- that the decedent owned real or personal property, or both, describing the property generally and stating an estimated value;

- the date of the will, the name and address (street, city, and county) of the executor, and the names and current addresses (street, city, and county) of the witnesses, if known;

- a statement that the applicant seeks dependent administration;

- whether a child or children were born or adopted by the decedent after the will was signed and the name of each such child who is alive;

- that the executor named in the will is not disqualified from serving;

- whether the decedent was ever divorced, and if so, when and from whom; and,

- whether the state, governmental agency of the state, or charitable organization is named in the will as beneficiary.

For purposes of the discussion in this chapter, unless it is necessary to distinguish between an administrator or executor, the terms *executor* and *administrator* will be used interchangeably. Be careful, however, to make certain that in all filings or correspondence to the court or to third parties that you use the correct designation.

Regular Dependent Administration (RDA)

A regular dependent administration of a decedent's estate is called *regular* because there are no shortcuts. All of the formal procedures must be followed. It is a full-scale estate administration. It is referred to as *dependent* because the authority of the administrator is dependent upon the orders of the court. A regular dependent administration is used when a person dies without a will and there are debts that must be paid by the estate other than debts that are secured by liens on real estate.

Generally, any action that the administrator wants to take must first be approved by the probate court. This requires the administrator to file an application for permission with the court. The court will grant permission if it believes that such action is necessary and appropriate for the administration of the estate. This procedure can be very time consuming and often delays the distribution of the decedent's property to the family.

A regular dependent administration is started by filing an APPLICATION FOR LETTERS OF ADMINISTRATION (which will also be called simply the APPLICATION) with the probate court. (see form 5, p.111.) Texas Probate Code, Section 82, requires that the APPLICATION contain the following information:

- name and domicile (street, city, and county) of each applicant;
- relationship, if any, of applicant to decedent;
- a statement that the applicant is not disqualified to act as administrator;
- name, age if known, and domicile (street, city, and county) of the decedent, and a statement that he or she died without a will;
- the fact, time and place of decedent's death;
- facts showing that the court has jurisdiction and venue;
- whether decedent owned real or personal property and the estimated value of it;
- the name, age, relationship, marital status, and address of each heir of the decedent if known, including the name of the decedent's surviving spouse;
- whether children were born to, or adopted by, the decedent, and if so, their names and dates and places of birth;
- whether the decedent was ever divorced, and if so, when and from whom; and,
- statement that a necessity exists for the administration of the estate.

Filing the Application

The APPLICATION for any type of dependent administration should be filed with the Probate Court in the county in which the decedent was *domiciled* (had his or her primary residence) at the time of his or her death.

Appointment of Resident Agent

If the executor is not a resident of the State of Texas, he or she must appoint a *resident agent* (a person who is a resident of Texas and of the county in which the estate is probated) for the purpose of accepting any notice or service of summons. Often an attorney will act as the resident agent. However, any adult residing in Texas may act as resident agent. The APPOINTMENT OF RESIDENT AGENT must be signed in the presence of a notary public. (see form 26, p.159.)

Proof of Subscribing Witness

If the APPLICATION requests an Administration With Will Annexed (AWA) or Administration with Dependent Executor (ADE), the will must be presented to the court under the same procedure as required for an independent administration. (see Chapter 2.)

Self-proved wills, signed as required under Texas law, may be admitted to probate without additional documentation. *Self-proved* means that the testator (the person whose will it is) and witnesses took an oath at the time the will was signed, the statement being included with the will and notarized by a notary public.

If the will is not self-proved, the will may be admitted to probate only after one of the witnesses appears in court to give testimony regarding the signing of the will. The PROOF OF SUBSCRIBING WITNESS must be included in written form and signed in the presence of the judge or the judge's clerk. (see form 27, p.161.) This means that you must contact one of the witnesses and ask that they appear at the courthouse to give testimony to the judge and to sign the **Proof of Subscribing Witness**.

If the witnesses cannot appear in court to take the oath, one or more of the witnesses may give testimony in the form of a *deposition*. If this procedure must be used, you should talk to the judge's clerk for assistance. If none of the witnesses can be located, or if they are all dead, you will need to find someone who can come to court to testify that he or she is familiar with the decedent's handwriting, that the signature on the will is the decedent's signature, and that the decedent was of sound mind.

Filing Fees

The filing fee to probate the estate may vary somewhat from county to county. The filing fee must be paid at the time the **Application** is filed. This amount should be paid from the probate estate, or by the executor or applicant and reimbursed from the estate later. Be sure to check with the court clerk about the amount before filing.

Proof of Death and Other Facts

The court cannot have a hearing on the **Application** until after the first Monday following ten days from the date the **Application** is posted. When the **Application** is filed, the court will post a notice on the courthouse that the **Application** has been filed. When you file the **Application**, you can ask the clerk when you can have a hearing.

The applicant must appear before the court and prove the facts listed in the **Application** and also the following (Texas Probate Code, Section 88(a) and (d)):

- that the person is dead and four years have not elapsed since the date of death;

- that the court has jurisdiction and venue;
- that the executor is not disqualified from serving;
- that a necessity exists for an administration of the estate; and,
- that notice has been served or posted as required by the statute.

The applicant must sign the PROOF OF DEATH AND OTHER FACTS in the presence of the judge. Which PROOF OF DEATH AND OTHER FACTS form you use will depend upon the type of procedure you are following:

- Regular Dependent Administration (RDA) . . . . . .form 6, p.113
- Administration with Will Annexed (AWA) . . . . . . .form 10, p.121
- Administration with Dependent Executor (ADE) .form 14, p.129

ORDER ADMITTING WILL TO PROBATE AND AUTHORIZING LETTERS TESTAMENTARY OR LETTERS OF ADMINISTRATION

The judge will sign an ORDER ADMITTING WILL TO PROBATE AND AUTHORIZING LETTERS TESTAMENTARY or an ORDER ADMITTING WILL TO PROBATE AND AUTHORIZING LETTERS OF ADMINISTRATION. You will provide this form to the judge at the hearing. The order must include the name of the decedent, the name of the executor, the amount of bond, if any, the name of any appraisers appointed by the court to value estate property, if any, and that the clerk will issue letters when the executor qualifies. (Texas Probate Code, Section 181.) The executor qualifies when he or she takes the Oath and posts a bond with the court. Which of these forms you use will depend upon the type of procedure you follow:

- Regular Dependent Administration (RDA) . . . . . .form 7, p.115
- Administration with Will Annexed (AWA) . . . . . . .form 11, p.123
- Administration with Dependent Executor (ADE) .form 15, p.131

OATH OF ADMINISTRATOR OR EXECUTOR

After the probate court has signed the ORDER ADMITTING WILL TO PROBATE AND AUTHORIZING LETTERS TESTAMENTARY or the ORDER ADMITTING WILL TO PROBATE AND AUTHORIZING LETTERS OF ADMINISTRATION, the executor or administrator signs an OATH OF ADMINISTRATOR (for a Regular Dependent Administration see form 8, p.117), or an OATH (for Administration with Will Annexed or Administration with Dependent Executor see form 12, p.125 or form 16, p.133). The judge will then issue Letters Testamentary or Letters of Administration (a document authorizing the executor or administrator to act on behalf of the estate).

This OATH must be signed in the presence of a notary public and delivered to the court within twenty days after the judge signs the ORDER ADMITTING WILL TO PROBATE AND AUTHORIZING LETTERS TESTAMENTARY or the ORDER ADMITTING WILL TO PROBATE AND AUTHORIZING LETTERS OF ADMINISTRATION. In the OATH, the executor states that the decedent's will has been presented to probate and that the executor will perform all of the duties of an executor or administrator. Which Oath form you need will depend upon the type of procedure you follow:

- Regular Dependent Administration (RDA) . . . . . .form 8, p.117
- Administration with Will Annexed (AWA) . . . . . . .form 12, p.125
- Administration with Dependent Executor (ADE) .form 16, p.133

BOND

Even if bond is waived in the will, the court may still require the executor to obtain a bond in some circumstances. (Texas Probate Code, Section 194.) A *bond* is a guaranty by a bonding or insurance company that the executor will perform his or her required duties properly and will not misuse the estate funds. The clerk of the probate court may be able to find out what amount of bond the judge will require or whether the bond will be waived. Generally, if a bond is required, the probate court will require an amount sufficient to protect the estate and its creditors from the misdeeds of the executor. This amount is the value of the personal property, or liquid assets (cash, stocks, bonds, etc.) and the expected income to the estate for the next twelve months.

The amount of the bond may be increased or decreased by the court if the INVENTORY, APPRAISEMENT, AND LIST OF CLAIMS shows an increase or decrease in the amount of liquid assets. (see form 32, p.177.) Sometimes the administrator can reduce the amount of the bond by agreeing with the bonding company that the liquid assets will be deposited into an account with a bank or other financial institution and that the administrator cannot withdraw these assets without the bonding company's approval. These safekeeping agreements are a good idea even if the bond is not reduced, because they help protect the administrator from unintentionally misusing the estate's funds.

NOTICE TO CREDITORS

Creditors must be notified within one month after the executor has received Letters Testamentary (or after the administrator received Letters of Administration, if there was no will). However, if there is a secured creditor, notice is to be given within two months after receiving Letters Testamentary.

Notice should be given to:

- Comptroller of Public Accounts by certified mail if the decedent paid or owed taxes administered by the Comptroller (for example, if the decedent owned a business and was required to pay sales or franchise tax);

- unsecured creditors by publication in a newspaper printed in the county where the will has been probated. Use the NOTICE TO

CREDITORS form for this purpose. (see form 28, p.163.) There will be a fee for publishing this notice and this will vary from newspaper to newspaper;

- secured creditors by certified or registered mail (return receipt requested); and,

- all persons having an unpaid claim against the estate if the executor has knowledge of the claim. Although not legally required, this should be done by certified or registered mail (return receipt requested).

A copy of the notice to secured creditors together with the return receipt and PROOF OF SERVICE OF NOTICE UPON CLAIMANTS AGAINST ESTATE stating that notice was made by registered or certified mail must be filed with the court. (see form 29, p.165.) A copy of the published notice to unsecured creditors, together with the PUBLISHER'S AFFIDAVIT that notice was published (see form 30, p.167), must be filed with the court. The actual newspaper clipping should be attached to the PUBLISHER'S AFFIDAVIT. Sometimes the newspaper will prepare and file the PUBLISHER'S AFFIDAVIT directly with the court. You should check with the particular newspaper.

If the decedent left property to a charity, governmental agency, or the State of Texas, the executor must give written notice within thirty days after the will has been probated. The notice must state the county in which the will is probated and include a copy of the will. This notice must be given by registered or certified mail, return receipt requested. The executor must file proof with the court (an affidavit and the green return receipt cards) that notice was given.

ADMINISTERING THE ESTATE

Once the Letters Testamentary (or Letters of Administration) have been issued, the executor can begin administering the estate. This means that assets must be collected and legitimate claims against the estate must be paid.

One of the first things that you must do is open a checking account in the name of the estate with you as the executor authorized to sign on the account. For example, "Bob Smith as Independent Executor of the Estate of Jane Doe." You will need a taxpayer identification number to open the account. This is explained in the next section.

One of the duties of the executor is to convert the assets of the estate into cash so that it may be divided among the beneficiaries. If the beneficiaries of the estate prefer to receive certain items in the estate, such as personal items, real estate, or stocks and bonds, these items can be distributed to them. However, you should take certain precautions.

First, you must make certain that you are following the terms of the will. The will may give certain things to certain beneficiaries. Second, you should discuss the distribution with all of the beneficiaries. Ask them how they would like the assets distributed. Do they want the property sold and the cash proceeds divided? Do they want to receive some or all of the property instead?

If property is to be distributed instead of sold, be certain the beneficiaries are comfortable with the distribution plans. You do not want them fighting over such things as valuation and who should get what item of property.

Some of the things you may have to do in administering the estate are to close out bank accounts, sell or distribute personal belongings such as clothing and furniture, and sell stocks and bonds.

Texas Probate Code, Section 234(a), sets forth the powers that can be exercised by the executor only with the approval of the court. These powers include the power to:

- renew or extend any obligation owing by or to the estate;
- purchase or exchange property;
- accept claims or other property in payment of debts owed to the estate;
- resolve bad or doubtful debts due or owing to the estate;

- compromise or settle disputed claims owed to or by the estate; and,
- compromise secured claims allowed and approved against the estate.

Texas Probate Code, Section 234(b), permits the executor, without court approval, to:

- release liens upon payment of debts;
- vote stock by limited or general proxy;
- pay calls and assessments;
- insure the estate against liability, fire, theft, and other hazards; and,
- pay taxes, court costs (not attorney's fees), and bond premiums.

There are many other types of transactions for which court approval may be required. If you are about to do something and you are unsure of whether you need the court's approval, you should check with the probate court.

IRS Form SS-4

In the event a fiduciary tax return is required (explained below), the estate must obtain a federal taxpayer identification number. The APPLICATION FOR EMPLOYER IDENTIFICATION NUMBER (IRS FORM SS-4) must be completed and sent by the executor to the Internal Revenue Service Center in Austin, Texas. (see form 31, p.169.) The IRS will assign a taxpayer identification number to the estate and the executor will be notified by mail within approximately three to four weeks.

The executor may also obtain a taxpayer identification number by telephone by calling 512-462-7843. Have the completed form in front of you when you call because the IRS officer asks how the questions are completed on the form. The IRS officer will give you a number and you must mail in the form along with the assigned number written on the upper-right hand corner. You may also be permitted to fax the completed form. Just follow the instructions given by the IRS when you call.

Inventory, Appraisement, and List of Claims

An Inventory, Appraisement, and List of Claims (which will also be referred to as the Inventory) protects creditors and persons interested in the estate by identifying the estate assets that are available to pay debts and taxes. (see form 32, p.177.) An Inventory also assists in determining the proper amount of bond and affects the compensation of executors. (Texas Probate Code, Section 250.)

Within ninety days after the executor is appointed, an Inventory must be filed with the court. If necessary, the executor may ask the court for an extension of time to file in order to gather all of the necessary information to prepare an accurate and complete Inventory. The executor will usually be unable to get court approval for sales or payment of expenses, including attorney's fees, until the Inventory has been filed.

The Inventory should include a list of all of the decedent's probate property, including all real estate in Texas and all personal property wherever it is located. Real estate in other states and property passing to beneficiaries outside of the will (such as proceeds from life insurance, employee benefit plans, trust assets, and survivorship property) should not be included in the Inventory. The value of the assets on the date the decedent died should be listed on the Inventory.

Claims *owed to* the estate (*not* claims *against* the estate) should be listed. The description of the claims should include the name of the person who owes the estate money, the amount and type of the debt, interest rate, date the claim is due, and date the claim was originally made.

When listing the assets and claims, the executor must indicate whether the asset or claim is separate, community, or joint tenancy property. If the property is joint tenancy, the name of the co-owner must be included. If the executor later learns of additional property, the Inventory should be amended or supplemented.

The executor should sign the affidavit included as part of the INVENTORY, APPRAISEMENT AND LIST OF CLAIMS, stating that the INVENTORY is true, accurate and complete. (see form 32, p.177.) After reviewing the INVENTORY, the court will either approve or disapprove it. If disapproved, the executor must file a revised INVENTORY within the time specified by the court. If the INVENTORY is approved, the court will sign an ORDER APPROVING INVENTORY AND APPRAISEMENT, which you will supply to the court in advance. (see form 33, p.181.)

HOMESTEAD, EXEMPT PERSONAL PROPERTY, AND FAMILY ALLOWANCE

HOMESTEAD

The real estate used by the decedent as his or her primary residence is called the *homestead*. The homestead is either:

- one or more parcels totalling no more than 200 acres outside of a city, town or village or

- one or more lots in a city, town or village totalling no more than one acre, with improvements.

There is no dollar limit on the value of the property claimed as the homestead.

If there is a surviving spouse, minor children, or an unmarried adult child living in the homestead, the homestead passes to the spouse or children free of any creditor claims against the estate other than for taxes or mortgages on the property.

EXEMPT PERSONAL PROPERTY

Exempt personal property includes certain types of personal property such as household furnishings and vehicles totalling no more than $30,000 per decedent. This property is generally free from the claims of creditors. However, it can be used to pay claims for funeral expenses and expenses of the decedent's last illness. If the estate is *solvent* (assets are greater than debts), the exempt property is distributed when the executor distributes the other estate assets. If the estate is *insolvent* (debts are greater than assets), title to the exempt property passes to the spouse and children immediately. Use the APPLICATION TO SET ASIDE EXEMPT PROPERTY to request the exemption. (see form 34, p.183.)

FAMILY ALLOWANCE

The surviving spouse and minor children are entitled to a *family allowance* sufficient to support them for one year. (Texas Probate Code Sections 286 and 287.) The family allowance will not be paid if the surviving spouse has separate property adequate to support her during the year or the minor children have sufficient property to support themselves. The court will determine the amount of the family allowance after reviewing all of the facts, and may order that the allowance be paid in a lump sum or in installments. Use the APPLICATION FOR FAMILY ALLOWANCE and ORDER FOR FAMILY ALLOWANCE. (see form 36, p.187 and form 37, p.189.)

ANNUAL ACCOUNTINGS

The executor must file a sworn written account with the probate court within twelve months from the date he qualified and at the end of each twelve month period thereafter until the estate is closed. Use the ANNUAL ACCOUNT, and ORDER APPROVING ANNUAL ACCOUNT. (see form 39, p.193 and form 40, p.197.) When the estate is closed, the executor will file a final account. (Texas Probate Code, Section 399.) This is a very time consuming process and many problems are caused when an executor fails to file an ANNUAL ACCOUNT.

The ANNUAL ACCOUNT should include:

- a list of all claims presented to the executor during the period and an indication of which claims have been allowed, which have been paid, and which have been rejected;

- all property not listed on a previous account or the INVENTORY (form 32);

- any changes in the property of the estate;

- receipts and disbursements for the period;
- description of property still being administered;
- location and balance of cash accounts;
- description of other personal property such as bonds, stocks, and other securities; and,
- supporting vouchers from depository banks showing balances of cash on hand and securities held.

The ANNUAL ACCOUNT will remain with the clerk of the court for ten days before the court can consider it. If the account is satisfactory, the court will enter an order approving the account and may order an increase or decrease in bond. You will prepare the order in advance and present it to the clerk when you file the account.

After the ANNUAL ACCOUNT is approved, the court will order that the unpaid claims against the estate will be paid. If the ANNUAL ACCOUNT is not filed with the court, the court by its own motion or any other person who has an interest in the estate—may force the executor or administrator to appear before the court and present a good reason for failing to file the ANNUAL ACCOUNT. If the executor fails to comply, the court can revoke the Letters Testamentary or Letters of Administration and impose a fine of up to $1,000.

PAYMENT OF DEBTS AND EXPENSES

The executor must pay the decedent's debts and expenses as provided in Texas Probate Code, Section 322. The following is the order in which claims should be paid if the estate has sufficient funds:

1. funeral expenses and expenses of last illness up to $5,000, if the claims were presented to the executor within sixty days after the Letters Testamentary have been issued;

2. allowances to the surviving spouse and children;

3. expenses of administering the estate and expenses incurred to preserve, safekeep, and manage the estate;

4. secured claims up to the value of the property subject to the debt;

5. taxes, penalties, and interest due to the State of Texas;

6. claims for the costs of confinement in prison;

7. claims for the repayment of medical assistance made by the State of Texas;

8. claims made within six months after the Letters Testamentary have been issued; and,

9. claims made after six months after the Letters Testamentary have been issued.

If there is not sufficient money left in the estate after a certain priority of debts are paid, then the creditors in the next priority will be paid a pro rata share of their claim.

The executor must either approve or reject a claim presented by a creditor within thirty days of when it was presented, otherwise it will be deemed to be rejected. The executor must establish that the claim is valid and legal before the executor can approve it. (Texas Probate Code, Section 310.) If the claim is approved, the executor should notify the creditor. The executor must show good cause for failing to approve and pay any valid claims. If the executor does not pay a valid claim the executor may be required to pay the amount of the claim plus interest, costs and damages of 5% per month. (Texas Probate Code, Section 328.)

The executor is responsible for paying federal income taxes for the decedent and for the estate, and for paying federal estate taxes and Texas inheritance taxes.

TAX RETURNS

The executor is responsible for filing all tax returns that are required on behalf of the estate. These may include:

- decedent's last federal income tax return;
- annual federal income tax returns for the estate;
- federal gift tax return for the decedent;
- federal estate tax return; and/or,
- Texas inheritance tax return.

IRS FORM 1040 — If it is necessary to file a federal income tax return on behalf of a decedent who is single, the **U.S. INDIVIDUAL INCOME TAX RETURN (IRS FORM 1040)** will be signed by the executor as "[*executor's name*], Executor of the Estate of [*decedent's name*]." For example, "Jane Doe, Executor of the Estate of Jim Smith." (see form 48, p.215.).

The name of the decedent should be followed by the word "Deceased" and the date of death. For example, "Jim Smith, Deceased 10-31-94." "DECEASED" should be written across the top of the form.

If the decedent has a surviving spouse, the final joint return should be signed by the executor and the surviving spouse.

A copy of the current IRS publication explaining this subject can be obtained by going to the IRS local office or calling 800-829-1040. IRS publications can also be found on the Internet at:

http://www.irs.gov

IRS FORM 1041 — Income on the assets of the decedent is also taxable and must be shown on IRS Form 1041. The executor must report any income from the assets prior to distribution to the beneficiaries. This form can be obtained from the IRS.

FEDERAL ESTATE TAX RETURN IRS FORM 706 — The federal estate tax return must be filed within nine months of the decedent's death if the value of the gross estate exceeds $1,000,000. A tax return must be filed if the estate is above this amount, even if there is no tax due. If any tax is due, it must be paid when the return is filed.

TEXAS
INHERITANCE TAX
AND OTHER TAX
RETURNS

There may be other tax returns due, such as partnership returns, corporate returns, sales tax returns, etc. It is important to contact an accountant who is familiar with the decedent's financial affairs to assist with the preparation of these returns.

DISTRIBUTION OF THE ESTATE ASSETS

After the debts, expenses, and taxes have been paid, the executor must distribute the property remaining in the estate as provided in the decedent's will. If real estate is to be distributed, a deed of distribution should be prepared. To avoid problems, especially if homestead property is involved, an attorney familiar with real estate should be contacted to prepare this deed.

FINAL ACCOUNT AND APPLICATION FOR DISCHARGE

The executor must file a final account with the court when the estate is to be settled and closed. Use the ACCOUNT FOR FINAL SETTLEMENT, and the ORDER APPROVING ACCOUNT FOR FINAL SETTLEMENT AND AUTHORIZING DISTRIBUTION OF ESTATE. (see form 41, p.199 and form 42, p.203.) Texas Probate Code, Section 405, requires that the final account include a complete summary of all of the executor's acts, such as:

- all property that the executor acquired;
- all dispositions of property;
- all debts paid;
- all unpaid debts and expenses;
- all property still possessed by the executor;
- all persons entitled to receive the estate, if any; and,

- all advances or payments made.

Notice of the final account must be given to each heir and beneficiary of the estate by certified mail. A copy of the final account must be attached as well as the time and place that the court will have a hearing on it.

RECEIPTS The court will leave the account on file for ten days and then will examine, audit, and settle the account. The court will also hear any objections to the account. If the court approves of the account, it will order the executor to distribute the estate assets to the persons who are entitled to receive it. The executor should get receipts from everyone to whom the property is delivered. Use the RECEIPT AND RELEASE form in Appendix B. (see form 43, p.205.)

CLOSING THE ESTATE After all of the assets of the estate are distributed, the executor should file an APPLICATION TO CLOSE ESTATE AND TO DISCHARGE PERSONAL REPRESENTATIVE with the court. (see form 44, p.207.) The court will enter an order that releases the executor and the sureties on the bond. You will prepare this order for the judge in advance. Use the ORDER CLOSING ESTATE AND DISCHARGING PERSONAL REPRESENTATIVE. (see form 45, p.209.)

Texas Probate Checklist—Administration with Will Annexed (AWA)

- ❑ Gather information required for APPLICATION FOR PROBATE AND ADMINISTRATION OF ESTATE:
  - original will and any codicils
  - decedent's social security number
  - applicant's social security number
  - names and addresses of beneficiaries
  - names and addresses of witnesses to will
  - list of assets and approximate value
  - amount of bond, if any
- ❑ Prepare the following documents:
  - APPLICATION FOR PROBATE OF WILL AND ISSUANCE OF LETTERS TESTAMENTARY WITH WILL ANNEXED (form 9)
  - OATH (form 12)
  - ORDER ADMITTING WILL TO PROBATE AND AUTHORIZING LETTERS TESTAMENTARY WITH WILL ANNEXED (form 11)
- ❑ If will is not self-proved, prepare PROOF BY SUBSCRIBING WITNESS (form 27).
- ❑ If a bond is required, obtain forms from the probate court, bonding agency, or insurance company.
- ❑ If out-of-state executor, prepare APPOINTMENT OF RESIDENT AGENT (form 26).
- ❑ File APPLICATION FOR PROBATE along with original will, any codicils, and filing fee.
- ❑ Attend "Prove-up" hearing at probate court. Applicant must testify to facts contained in PROOF OF DEATH AND OTHER FACTS (form 10) and sign the PROOF OF DEATH AND OTHER FACTS in presence of court clerk or judge. Judge will sign ORDER ADMITTING WILL TO PROBATE AND AUTHORIZING LETTERS TESTAMENTARY WITH WILL ANNEXED (form 11).
- ❑ File OATH (form 12).
- ❑ Wait for Letters Testamentary to be issued by court (usually same day as hearing).
- ❑ Publish NOTICE TO CREDITORS (form 28).
- ❑ Prepare and file IRS forms: NOTICE CONCERNING FIDUCIARY RELATIONSHIP (IRS FORM 56) (form 46) and APPLICATION FOR TAXPAYER IDENTIFICATION NUMBER (IRS FORM SS-4) (form 31).
- ❑ Open checking account for estate.
- ❑ File change of address notice for the decedent at post office.
- ❑ Gather the assets and asset records of the estate. These include:
  - deeds
  - stocks and bonds
  - mutual funds
  - mortgages owned
  - bank books
  - contracts
  - savings bonds
  - car and boat titles
  - insurance policies
  - coins; stamps; antiques
  - promissory notes
  - personal property
- ❑ Prepare and file INVENTORY, APPRAISEMENT AND LIST OF CLAIMS (form 32).
- ❑ Provide the court with ORDER APPROVING INVENTORY AND APPRAISEMENT (form 33).
- ❑ Sell any assets necessary to settle the estate.
- ❑ Distribute assets to beneficiaries, leaving sufficient amount to pay taxes, if any.
- ❑ File federal and Texas estate tax returns, if necessary.
- ❑ File AFFIDAVIT REGARDING DEBTS AND TAXES (form 38).
- ❑ Close checking account.
- ❑ File final IRS Form 1041 (obtain form from IRS).
- ❑ Cancel bond.
- ❑ File NOTICE CONCERNING FIDUCIARY RELATIONSHIP (IRS FORM 56), with box for "termination" checked (form 46).

dependent administration

Texas Probate Checklist—Administration with Dependent Executor (ADE)

- ❑ Gather information required for APPLICATION FOR PROBATE AND ADMINISTRATION OF ESTATE:
  - •original will and any codicils
  - •decedent's social security number
  - •applicant's social security number
  - •names and addresses of beneficiaries
  - •names and addresses of witnesses to will
  - •list of assets and approximate value
  - •amount of bond, if any
- ❑ Prepare the following documents:
  - •APPLICATION FOR PROBATE OF WILL AND ISSUANCE OF LETTERS TESTAMENTARY (form 13)
  - •OATH (form 16)
  - •ORDER ADMITTING WILL TO PROBATE AND AUTHORIZING LETTERS TESTAMENTARY (form 15)
- ❑ If will is not self-proved, prepare PROOF BY SUBSCRIBING WITNESS (form 27).
- ❑ If a bond is required, obtain forms from the probate court, bonding agency, or insurance company.
- ❑ If out-of-state executor, prepare APPOINTMENT OF RESIDENT AGENT (form 26).
- ❑ File APPLICATION FOR PROBATE (form 13) along with original will, any codicils, and filing fee.
- ❑ Attend "Prove-up" hearing at probate court. Applicant must testify to facts contained in PROOF OF DEATH AND OTHER FACTS (form 14) and sign the PROOF OF DEATH AND OTHER FACTS in presence of court clerk or judge. Judge will sign ORDER ADMITTING WILL TO PROBATE AND AUTHORIZING LETTERS TESTAMENTARY (form 15).
- ❑ File OATH (form 16).
- ❑ Wait for Letters Testamentary to be issued by court (usually same day as hearing).
- ❑ Publish NOTICE TO CREDITORS (form 28).
- ❑ Prepare and file IRS forms: NOTICE CONCERNING FIDUCIARY RELATIONSHIP (IRS FORM 56) (form 46) and APPLICATION FOR TAXPAYER IDENTIFICATION NUMBER (IRS FORM SS-4) (form 31).
- ❑ Open checking account for estate.
- ❑ File change of address notice for the decedent at post office.
- ❑ Gather the assets and asset records of the estate. These include:
  - deeds
  - stocks and bonds
  - mutual funds
  - mortgages owned
  - bank books
  - contracts
  - savings bonds
  - car and boat titles
  - insurance policies
  - coins; stamps; antiques
  - promissory notes
  - personal property
- ❑ Prepare and file INVENTORY, APPRAISEMENT AND LIST OF CLAIMS (form 32).
- ❑ Provide the court with ORDER APPROVING INVENTORY AND APPRAISEMENT (form 33).
- ❑ Sell any assets necessary to settle the estate.
- ❑ Distribute assets to beneficiaries, leaving sufficient amount to pay taxes, if any.
- ❑ File federal and Texas estate tax returns, if necessary.
- ❑ Prepare and file AFFIDAVIT REGARDING DEBTS AND TAXES (form 38).
- ❑ Close checking account.
- ❑ File final IRS Form 1041 (obtain form from IRS).
- ❑ Cancel bond.
- ❑ File NOTICE CONCERNING FIDUCIARY RELATIONSHIP (IRS FORM 56), with box for "termination" checked (form 46).

Texas Probate Checklist—Regular Dependent Administration (RDA)

❑ Gather information required for APPLICATION FOR LETTERS OF ADMINISTRATION:
•decedent's social security number •list of assets and approximate value
•applicant's social security number •amount of bond, if any
•names and addresses of beneficiaries

❑ Prepare the following documents:
•APPLICATION FOR LETTERS OF ADMINISTRATION (form 5)
•OATH OF ADMINISTRATOR (form 8)
•ORDER AUTHORIZING LETTERS OF ADMINISTRATION (form 7)

❑ If a bond is required, obtain forms from the probate court, bonding agency, or insurance company.

❑ If out-of-state executor, prepare APPOINTMENT OF RESIDENT AGENT (form 26).

❑ File APPLICATION FOR LETTERS OF ADMINISTRATION (form 5) and pay filing fee.

❑ Attend "Prove-up" hearing at probate court. Applicant must testify to facts contained in PROOF OF DEATH AND OTHER FACTS (form 6) and sign the PROOF OF DEATH AND OTHER FACTS in presence of court clerk or judge. Judge will sign ORDER AUTHORIZING LETTERS OF ADMINISTRATION (form 7).

❑ File OATH OF ADMINISTRATOR (form 8).

❑ Wait for Letters of Administration to be issued by court (usually same day as hearing).

❑ Publish NOTICE TO CREDITORS (form 28).

❑ Prepare and file IRS forms: NOTICE CONCERNING FIDUCIARY RELATIONSHIP (IRS FORM 56) (form 46) and APPLICATION FOR TAXPAYER IDENTIFICATION NUMBER (IRS FORM SS-4) (form 31).

❑ Open checking account for estate.

❑ File change of address notice for the decedent at post office.

❑ Gather the assets and asset records of the estate. These include:

deeds	mortgages owned	savings bonds	coins; stamps; antiques
stocks and bonds	bank books	car and boat titles	promissory notes
mutual funds	contracts	insurance policies	personal property

❑ Prepare and file INVENTORY, APPRAISEMENT AND LIST OF CLAIMS (form 32).

❑ Provide the court with ORDER APPROVING INVENTORY AND APPRAISEMENT (form 33).

❑ Sell any assets necessary to settle the estate.

❑ Distribute assets to beneficiaries, leaving sufficient amount to pay taxes, if any.

❑ File federal and Texas estate tax returns, if necessary.

❑ File AFFIDAVIT REGARDING DEBTS AND TAXES (form 38).

❑ Close checking account.

❑ File final IRS Form 1041 (obtain form from IRS).

❑ Cancel bond.

❑ File NOTICE CONCERNING FIDUCIARY RELATIONSHIP (IRS FORM 56), with box for "termination" checked (form 46).

Procedures in Lieu of Administration 4

If the probate court does not believe that an administration of the estate is necessary, there are three separate procedures that are available to wind up the affairs of the decedent and distribute his or her property to his or her heirs or beneficiaries. These procedures are:

- Muniment of Title;
- Proceeding to Determine Heirship; and,
- Small Estate.

Each procedure has special qualifications and special forms that are used. The general qualification for each of these procedures is that there are no debts owed by the decedent, other than debts that are secured by a lien on real estate. The three procedures are discussed in detail below.

At the end of this chapter you will find a checklist for each of these procedures.

Muniment of Title

For decedent's dying after September 1, 1993, a proceeding called *Muniment of Title* is available, provided that the person had a will and there are no unpaid debts owed by the person's estate, except debts secured by a lien on real estate. (Texas Probate Code, Section 89A.) The Muniment of Title procedure is also utilized when:

- the will fails to name an executor;
- the will names an executor but the executor is dead, disqualified, or refuses to serve and there is no alternate executor designated in the will; or,

- an executor is named in the will but is not authorized to act as an independent executor.

By this procedure, the will is probated, but the court does not appoint an executor or administrator.

The advantage of this procedure is that very soon after the will is probated, the beneficiaries can receive property from the estate. Also, the expenses of a full scale administration are avoided.

The disadvantage to this procedure is that many banks, stock brokers, and companies are not familiar with the procedure. Therefore, it may be more difficult to close bank accounts, or to transfer stocks, bonds, and the like. Unlike an estate administration, there is not a specific person identified to act on behalf of the estate. Banks, stock brokers, etc., are uncertain of with whom they should be dealing.

Another disadvantage to a Muniment of Title is that unless an inventory or affidavit describing the property is filed with the court, there is nothing to identify the property belonging to the decedent. This can create problems for future title examiners.

An APPLICATION TO PROBATE THE WILL AS A MUNIMENT OF TITLE must be filed with the probate court. (see form 17, p.135.) The APPLICATION must specifically state that the decedent owed no debts other than liens on real estate and that there is no need for an administration of the estate. It must also request that the estate be probated as a Muniment of Title.

After the APPLICATION TO PROBATE THE WILL AS A MUNIMENT OF TITLE has been filed, you will have to return to the court for a hearing on the application. At the hearing you will be asked by the judge to give evidence supporting the facts in the APPLICATION TO PROBATE THE WILL AS A MUNIMENT OF TITLE.

The PROOF OF DEATH AND OTHER FACTS must also be given to the judge in written form. (see form 18, p.137.) In most cases, the applicant simply reads the written PROOF OF DEATH AND OTHER FACTS to the judge. You will sign the PROOF OF DEATH AND OTHER FACTS either at the hearing or shortly after in the presence of the judge or the judge's clerk. Be sure not to sign the PROOF OF DEATH AND OTHER FACTS before you arrive at court!

After the hearing, the judge will sign an ORDER ADMITTING THE WILL TO PROBATE AS A MUNIMENT OF TITLE. (see form 19, p.139.) You will prepare the ORDER ADMITTING THE WILL TO PROBATE AS A MUNIMENT OF TITLE in advance and give it to the judge to sign. Judges differ on whether they will sign it at the conclusion of the hearing or later that day. Because there is no executor appointed by the court, no Letters Testamentary are issued. However, the ORDER from the court is legally binding and anyone owing money to the estate or having property belonging to the estate must pay or transfer the property directly to the heirs or beneficiaries.

Some judges require that the person making the APPLICATION file with the court an inventory of the estate's assets and an affidavit stating that the terms of the will have been satisfied. The INVENTORY, APPRAISEMENT AND LIST OF CLAIMS and AFFIDAVIT REGARDING FULFILLMENT OF WILL must be filed within 181 days after the date of the order. (see form 32, p.177 and form 20, p.141.) Even if the judge does not require that an INVENTORY be filed with the probate court, it is a good idea to do so. By filing this INVENTORY, APPRAISEMENT AND LIST OF CLAIMS with the court, a permanent record is made identifying the property of the decedent. This is useful in the event there are title issues or creditor problems in the future.

PROCEEDINGS TO DETERMINE HEIRSHIP

Texas Probate Code, Sections 48 through 56, detail the procedures that can be used to distribute the estate of a person who died without a will or if there is property that is not disposed of by a will. An example of property that is not disposed of by a will is when the beneficiary named in the will is deceased and there is no alternate beneficiary named in the will. These procedures are commonly referred to as *heirship determination proceedings*.

The purpose of the heirship proceedings is to identify the persons who are entitled to receive the property of the decedent. Texas has a statute, as do all of the other states, that identifies the persons who will inherit the property of a decedent if there is no will or if there are no beneficiaries named in the will who are still living. (Texas Probate Code, Section 38.)

The process must be started within four years after the person died. There must be no will and there must be no need for administration of the estate. The proceedings must be started in the county where the decedent lived, or in a county in which any real property owned by the decedent is located. If the decedent did not own any real property, then the proceedings may be started in the county where the decedent had personal property.

The APPLICATION TO DETERMINE HEIRSHIP must be filed with the probate court. (see form 21, p.143.) All of the decedent's heirs and beneficiaries must be included in the proceedings. They can be included in one of several ways:

- being named parties to the APPLICATION TO DETERMINE HEIRSHIP filed with the court;

- being sent a formal citation (notice) of the proceeding either by certified mail or in person;

- signing papers waiving or giving up the right to be sent a formal notice; or,

- filing with the court a written response or answer to the APPLICATION TO DETERMINE HEIRSHIP.

Each applicant must also furnish the court with an AFFIDAVIT that states that, to the best of his or her knowledge, everything in the APPLICATION TO DETERMINE HEIRSHIP is true and no important facts or circumstances have been omitted from the APPLICATION TO DETERMINE HEIRSHIP. The AFFIDAVIT is included as part of the APPLICATION TO DETERMINE HEIRSHIP. (see form 21, p.143.)

You must include the full names, addresses, and relationship of the heirs and beneficiaries of the estate. If they are minors, you must indicate that on the form. You must also indicate the amount of the estate each heir or beneficiary will share. You must also give a complete description and approximate value of the decedent's assets and indicate if it is community or separate property.

Almost routinely the court will appoint an *attorney ad litem* to represent the interests of heirs whose names or whereabouts are not known. An attorney *ad litem* may also be appointed to represent an heir who is a minor or who is incompetent. It is the responsibility of the attorney *ad litem* to protect the legal rights of the heirs he or she represents. Often, if the attorney *ad litem* is representing the interests of the unknown heirs, he or she will investigate the family history to make certain that there are no heirs of the decedent who have not been identified. The attorney *ad litem* will often obtain written affidavits from two people who can testify that they are familiar with the family history of the decedent and that all of the decedent's heirs have been included in the heirship proceeding.

The probate court will likely ask that the applicant appear in court to give testimony regarding the family history of the decedent and identify the heirs of the decedent. You should prepare a written STATEMENT OF FACTS and give it to the judge at the hearing. (see form 22, p.147.) The STATEMENT OF FACTS covers all of the information contained in the APPLICATION TO DETERMINE HEIRSHIP. (see form 21, p.143.) The judge may simply ask that you read the STATEMENT OF FACTS aloud in court instead of giving other testimony.

Sometimes the court will require that two persons who have no financial or personal interest in the estate appear in court to testify in support of the facts in the APPLICATION TO DETERMINE HEIRSHIP. The preferences of the judges will differ in this regard and it is best to contact the judge's clerk to determine what the judge will require. Many times if the attorney *ad litem* provides the court with affidavits, the judge will only require the testimony of the applicant.

After the judge has heard the evidence to support the APPLICATION TO DETERMINE HEIRSHIP, the judge will enter a JUDGMENT DECLARING HEIRSHIP. (see form 23, p.149.) The JUDGMENT DECLARING HEIRSHIP serves as the authority for the applicant to transfer the decedent's assets to the heirs, collect money from persons owing to the estate, and collect property from persons having custody of the estate.

The JUDGMENT DECLARING HEIRSHIP must include a complete list of the heirs and beneficiaries, their addresses, their shares of the estate, including a description of the real and personal property to which they are entitled, and a designation of which property is community or separate.

SMALL ESTATES

Sections 137 and 138 of the Texas Probate Code contain procedures that permit the estate of a decedent to be handled without an administration by filing an affidavit with the court. Most lawyers use the Muniment of Title procedure or an independent administration if the decedent died with a will. The banks and financial institutions are more familiar with those proceedings and the orders that courts issue in those proceedings.

The Small Estates procedure is not available if the decedent owned real estate, unless the real estate was used as the decedent's homestead. (A homestead is the primary residence of the decedent, and for property tax purposes has been elected to be treated as a homestead.) Two requirements must be met in order for an estate to qualify as a small estate:

1. the decedent's property (other than the homestead and exempt property) must exceed the decedent's liabilities and

2. the gross value of the property (not subtracting the liabilities) must be less than $50,000.

Exempt property means personal property worth no more than $30,000, and includes such things as home furnishings, clothes, automobiles, and other personal items. Therefore, the value of the decedent's separate property and his or her one-half interest in the community property must not exceed $50,000. If the value of the decedents' estate exceeds $50,000, or the liabilities are greater than the value of the assets, the Small Estate procedure is not available.

These proceedings cannot be started until at least thirty days after the decedent's death. If a petition has been filed with the court to appoint a personal representative for the estate, or if a personal representative has previously been appointed, the Small Estate procedure cannot be used.

To begin a Small Estate procedure a SMALL ESTATE AFFIDAVIT AND ORDER must be filed with the court. (see form 24, p.151.) The SMALL ESTATE AFFIDAVIT AND ORDER must contain:

- a complete list of the decedent's assets and liabilities;

- the names and addresses of all of the *distributees* (the persons who will receive property from the estate);

- a statement showing the relevant family history facts concerning heirship that show the distributees' rights to receive the property; and,

- a description of the decedent's property, an approximate value of the property, and any liens against the property. If the decedent's homestead is included, this must be noted.

The SMALL ESTATE AFFIDAVIT AND ORDER must be:

- sworn to and signed by all of the distributees. If a distributee is a minor or incompetent, the natural guardian or next of kin must sign for the minor or incompetent and

- signed by two witnesses who are not distributees and who are not related by blood or marriage to the decedent or a distributee.

Generally, the judge will approve the SMALL ESTATE AFFIDAVIT AND ORDER without holding a hearing. However, if the judge has any doubt about any of the matters in the SMALL ESTATE AFFIDAVIT AND ORDER, or if the judge wants to ensure that all of the decedent's debts will be paid, the judge may hold a hearing and question the distributees about these issues.

After the SMALL ESTATE AFFIDAVIT AND ORDER has been approved by the judge, the judge will sign the ORDER portion of the form. The SMALL ESTATE AFFIDAVIT AND ORDER will be recorded by the court in the Small Estates Records. One or more certified copies of the SMALL ESTATE AFFIDAVIT AND ORDER can be obtained from the court clerk and can be given to those persons or financial institutions who have possession of the decedent's property. Based on these documents, the property can be transferred to the distributees listed in the SMALL ESTATE AFFIDAVIT AND ORDER. The SMALL ESTATE AFFIDAVIT AND ORDER will not affect the disposition of the property under the terms of the will.

AFFIDAVIT OF HEIRSHIP

The Texas Legislature has enacted Section 52A of the Probate Code, which sets forth a statutory form that can be used to identify the heirs of a deceased person. The AFFIDAVIT OF HEIRSHIP may be appropriate to use when there was only a limited amount of personal property and/or real estate owned by the deceased person. (see form 47, p.213.) The form can be filed with the deed records of the county in which the decedent died and in the county in which the decedent owned real property.

It is more economical and time efficient to use the AFFIDAVIT OF HEIRSHIP. However, there is a lot of information that is required by the form, and the person signing the form must swear under oath to the correctness of all of the information provided on the form. Additionally, this form is not valid against any claims of any creditors or against any heirs that have been omitted from the AFFIDAVIT OF HEIRSHIP. If the assets of the decedent's estate and the identity of the heirs and creditors are not in doubt, then it would be wise to use this AFFIDAVIT OF HEIRSHIP.

Texas Probate Checklist—Muniment of Title

❑ Gather information required for the APPLICATION FOR PROBATE AND ADMINISTRATION OF ESTATE:
- original will and any codicils
- decedent's social security number
- applicant's social security number
- names and addresses of beneficiaries
- names and addresses of witnesses to will
- list of assets and approximate value
- amount of bond, if any

❑ Prepare the following documents:
- APPLICATION FOR PROBATE OF WILL AS A MUNIMENT OF TITLE (form 17)
- PROOF OF DEATH AND OTHER FACTS (form 18)
- ORDER ADMITTING WILL TO PROBATE AS A MUNIMENT OF TITLE (form 19)
- AFFIDAVIT REGARDING FULFILLMENT OF WILL ADMITTED TO PROBATE AS A MUNIMENT OF TITLE (form 20)

❑ Prepare and file IRS forms: NOTICE CONCERNING FIDUCIARY RELATIONSHIP (IRS FORM 56) (form 46); and APPLICATION FOR TAXPAYER IDENTIFICATION NUMBER (IRS FORM SS-4) (form 31).

❑ File change of address notice for the decedent at the post office.

❑ Gather the assets and asset records of the estate. These include:

deeds	mortgages owned	savings bonds	coins; stamps; antiques
stocks and bonds	bank books	car and boat titles	promissory notes
mutual funds	contracts	insurance policies	personal property

❑ Sell any assets necessary to settle the estate.

❑ Distribute remaining assets to beneficiaries, leaving sufficient amount to pay taxes, if any.

❑ File federal and Texas estate tax returns, if necessary.

❑ File final IRS Form 1041 (obtain form from IRS).

❑ File NOTICE CONCERNING FIDUCIARY RELATIONSHIP (IRS FORM 56), with box for "termination" checked (form 46).

procedures in lieu of administration

Texas Probate Checklist—Heirship Determination

❑ Gather information required for the APPLICATION TO DETERMINE HEIRSHIP AND ADMINISTRATION OF ESTATE:
- original will and any codicils
- decedent's social security number
- applicant's social security number
- names and addresses of beneficiaries
- names and addresses of witnesses to will
- list of assets and approximate value
- amount of bond, if any

❑ Prepare the following documents:
- APPLICATION TO DETERMINE HEIRSHIP (form 21)
- STATEMENT OF FACTS (form 22)
- JUDGMENT DECLARING HEIRSHIP (form 23)

(Continued on next page)

❑ Prepare and file IRS forms: NOTICE CONCERNING FIDUCIARY RELATIONSHIP (IRS FORM 56) (form 46); and APPLICATION FOR TAXPAYER IDENTIFICATION NUMBER (IRS FORM SS-4) (form 31).

❑ File change of address notice for the decedent at the post office.

❑ Gather the assets and asset records of the estate. These include:

deeds	mortgages owned	savings bonds	coins; stamps; antiques
stocks and bonds	bank books	car and boat titles	promissory notes
mutual funds	contracts	insurance policies	personal property

❑ Sell any assets necessary to settle the estate.

❑ Distribute remaining assets to beneficiaries, leaving sufficient amount to pay taxes, if any.

❑ File federal and Texas estate tax returns, if necessary.

❑ File final IRS Form 1041 (obtain form from IRS).

❑ File NOTICE CONCERNING FIDUCIARY RELATIONSHIP (IRS FORM 56), with box for "termination" checked (form 46).

Texas Probate Checklist—Small Estates

- ❏ Gather information required for the SMALL ESTATE AFFIDAVIT AND ORDER AND ADMINISTRATION OF ESTATE:
  - •original will and any codicils
  - •decedent's social security number
  - •applicant's social security number
  - •names and addresses of beneficiaries
  - •names and addresses of witnesses to will
  - •list of assets and approximate value
  - •amount of bond, if any
- ❏ Prepare the following document:
  - •SMALL ESTATE AFFIDAVIT AND ORDER (form 24)
- ❏ Prepare and file IRS forms: NOTICE CONCERNING FIDUCIARY RELATIONSHIP (IRS FORM 56) (form 46); and APPLICATION FOR TAXPAYER IDENTIFICATION NUMBER (IRS FORM SS-4) (form 31).
- ❏ File change of address notice for the decedent at the post office.
- ❏ Gather the assets and asset records of the estate. These include:

deeds	mortgages owned	savings bonds	coins; stamps; antiques
stocks and bonds	bank books	car and boat titles	promissory notes
mutual funds	contracts	insurance policies	personal property

- ❏ Sell any assets necessary to settle the estate.
- ❏ Distribute remaining assets to beneficiaries, leaving sufficient amount to pay taxes, if any.
- ❏ File federal and Texas estate tax returns, if necessary.
- ❏ File final IRS Form 1041 (obtain form from IRS).
- ❏ File NOTICE CONCERNING FIDUCIARY RELATIONSHIP (IRS FORM 56), with box for "termination" checked (form 46).

Glossary

A

Administration with Dependent Executor (ADE). This procedure is used when an administration is necessary for the estate of a decedent who has a will, but the will does not name an independent executor, or does not provide for an independent administration.

Administration with Will Annexed (AWA). This procedure is used when administration is necessary for the estate of a decedent who has a will, but the will does not name an executor, or names an executor who is dead or unable to act, and does not name an alternate executor.

administrator. *See* executor.

affidavit. A written declaration of facts voluntarily made and confirmed under oath before someone authorized to administer an oath (notary public).

ancillary administration. If the decedent was not a resident of Texas but left Texas property, the property may be probated through this process. Typically, this means the primary probate proceeding is handled in the state where the decedent had his or her primary residence. A second proceeding is then handled in the Texas county where the property is located in order to pass title to the property to the heirs or beneficiaries.

B

beneficiary. Persons named in the will to receive the decedent's property.

bond. A guaranty by a bonding or insurance company that the executor will perform his or her required duties properly and will not misuse the estate funds.

C

community property. All other property of the spouses that is not determined to be separate property.

contesting the will. This occurs if a person challenges the validity of a will. The probate court then will determine whether the will is valid and who legally is entitled to the decedent's property.

D

decedent. The person who has died.

dependent administration. Type of estate administration that holds the probate judge responsible for making sure that the executor or administrator of the estate performs his or her duties in strict compliance with the court's orders.

devisee. Person who inherits real estate under the terms of a will.

E

executor. The person designated in the will to be responsible for probating the estate of the decedent.

exempt property. Estate property that is not subject to probate proceedings.

F

family allowance. A cash allowance given by the court to a surviving spouse and/or minor children from the probate estate of the decedent.

H

heir. Persons entitled by law to receive a decedent's property if the decedent died without a will.

heirship determination proceedings. Procedure that can be used under Texas Probate Code to distribute the estate of a person who died without a will or if there is property that is not disposed of by the will.

homestead. Real estate used by the decedent as his or her primary residence.

I

independent administration. This is the administration of an estate without the supervision of the probate court.

insolvent estate. An estate where the debts are greater than the assets.

intestate. Decedent died without a will.

inventory. List of estate assets and liabilities.

J

joint tenancy with rights of survivorship. When two or more persons own property, the survivor will automatically own all of the property upon the death of the other co-owner. This property does not go through probate.

L

legatee. Person who inherits personal property under a will.

M

Muniment of Title. A procedure by which the will of a decedent is accepted as valid by the probate court and the distribution of assets set forth in the will is authorized by the Court. No executor or administrator is appointed by the Court. This procedure is available only if thedecedent died with a will and there are no debts of the decedent other than those secured by real estate.

P

personal representative. In some states, not including Texas, this is the title of the person designated in the will or appointed by the court to act on behalf of the estate during probate proceedings.

probate property. Property that is subject to the probate process. This includes sole property and tenancy in common property.

probate. A legal process to transfer property of a deceased person to the heirs or beneficiaries.

R

Regular Dependent Administration (RDA). This is a full-scale estate administration with no shortcuts and with all formal procedures being followed.

resident agent. A person or corporation (namely a bank or trust company) which can accept service of process in all actions or proceedings involving the estate. A resident agent is necessary if the executor of the will is not a Texas resident.

S

secured creditor. A creditor who may take certain property to satisfy the decedent's debt; most commonly this is a mortgage on a home or a car loan.

self-proved will. A will where both the testator and witnesses took an oath at the time the will was signed. The notarized statement is included with the will.

separate property. Property owned by a spouse before marriage, property acquired during marriage by gift or inheritance, and funds recovered by the spouse for personal injuries.

small estate. A procedure by which the estate of an individual who dies without a will can be distributed to the heirs without the necessity of a lengthy dependent administration. The value of the estate cannot exceed $50,000.00 and there must be no debts of the decedent other than those secured by real estate.

sole ownership. One person owns the entire property in his or her name alone.

solvent estate. An estate where the assets are greater than the debts.

T

tenancy by the entireties. A special type of joint tenancy that can exist only between a husband and wife. If one spouse dies, the survivor gets the property without going through probate.

tenancy in common. When two or more persons own property and each co-owner owns his or her share of the property independently. Upon the death of the co-owner, his or her share goes to the beneficiaries—not to the co-owner.

testate. Decedent dies with a will.

W

will. A document, which at someone's death, directs the distribution of the decedent's assets.

witness. Individual who observed a person signing his or her will, and who also signed the will as an observer.

Appendix A
Texas Probate Code

Sec. 38. Persons Who Take Upon Intestacy.

(a) *Intestate Leaving No Husband or Wife.* Where any person, having title to any estate, real, personal or mixed, shall die intestate, leaving no husband or wife, it shall descend and pass in parcenary to his kindred, male and female, in the following course:

1. To his children and their descendants.
2. If there be no children nor their descendants, then to his father and mother, in equal portions. But if only the father or mother survive the intestate, then his estate shall be divided into two equal portions, one of which shall pass to such survivor, and the other half shall pass to the brothers and sisters of the deceased, and to their descendants; but if there be none such, then the whole estate shall be inherited by the surviving father or mother.
3. If there be neither father nor mother, then the whole of such estate shall pass to the brothers and sisters of the intestate, and to their descendants.
4. If there be none of the kindred aforesaid, then the inheritance shall be divided into two moieties, one of which shall go to the paternal and the other to the maternal kindred, in the following course: To the grandfather and grandmother in equal portions, but if only one of these be living, then the estate shall be divided into two equal parts, one of which shall go to such survivor, and the other shall go to the descendant or descendants of such deceased grandfather or grandmother. If there be no such descendants, then the whole estate shall be inherited by the surviving grandfather or grandmother. If there be no surviving grandfather or grandmother, then the whole of such estate shall go to their descendants, and so on without end, passing in like manner to the nearest lineal ancestors and their descendants.

(b) *Intestate Leaving Husband or Wife.* Where any person having title to any estate, real, personal or mixed, other than a community estate, shall die intestate as to such estate, and shall leave a surviving husband or wife, such estate of such intestate shall descend and pass as follows:

1. If the deceased have a child or children, or their descendants, the surviving husband or wife shall take one-third of the personal estate, and the balance of such personal estate shall go to the child or children of the deceased and their descendants. The surviving husband or wife shall also be entitled to an estate for life, in one-third of the land of the intestate, with remainder to the child or children of the intestate and their descendants.
2. If the deceased have no child or children, or their descendants, then the surviving husband or wife shall be entitled to all the personal estate, and to one-half of the lands of the intestate, without remainder to any person, and the other half shall pass and be inherited according to the rules of descent and distribution; provided, however, that if the deceased has neither surviving father nor mother nor surviving brothers or sisters, or their descendants, then the surviving husband or wife shall be entitled to the whole of the estate of such intestate.

Sec. 45. Community Estate.

(a) On the intestate death of one of the spouses to a marriage, the community property estate of the deceased spouse passes to the surviving spouse if:

(1) no child or other descendant of the deceased spouse survives the deceased spouse; or
(2) all surviving children and descendants of the deceased spouse are also children or descendants of the surviving spouse.

(b) On the intestate death of one of the spouses to a marriage, if a child or other descendant of the deceased spouse survives the deceased spouse and the child or descendant is not a child or descendant of the surviving spouse, one-half of the community estate is retained by the surviving spouse and the other one-half passes to the children or descendants of the deceased spouse. The descendants shall inherit only such portion of said property to which they would be entitled under Section 43 of this code. In every case, the community estate passes charged with the debts against it.

Sec. 47. Requirement of Survival by 120 Hours.

(a) Survival of Heirs. A person who fails to survive the decedent by 120 hours is deemed to have predeceased the decedent for purposes of homestead allowance, exempt property, and intestate succession, and the decedent's heirs are determined accordingly, except as otherwise provided in this section. If the time of death of the decedent or of the person who would otherwise be an heir, or the times of death of both, cannot be determined, and it cannot be established that the person who would otherwise be an heir has survived the decedent by 120 hours, it is deemed that the person failed to survive for the required period. This subsection does not apply where its application would result in the escheat of an intestate estate.

(b) Disposal of Community Property. When a husband and wife have died, leaving community property, and neither the husband nor wife survived the other by 120 hours, one-half of all community property shall be distributed as if the husband had survived, and the other one-half thereof shall be distributed as if the wife had survived. The provisions of this subsection apply to proceeds of life or accident insurance which are community property and become payable to the estate of either the husband or the wife, as well as to other kinds of community property.

(c) Survival of Devisees or Beneficiaries. A devisee who does not survive the testator by 120 hours is treated as if he predeceased the testator, unless the will of the decedent contains some language dealing explicitly with simultaneous death or deaths in a common disaster, or requiring that the devisee survive the testator or survive the testator for a stated period in order to take under the will. If property is so disposed of that the right of a beneficiary to succeed to any interest therein is conditional upon his surviving another person, the beneficiary shall be deemed not to have survived unless he or she survives the person by 120 hours. However, if any interest in property is given alternatively to one of two or more beneficiaries, with the right of each to take being dependent upon his surviving the other or others, and all shall die within a period of less than 120 hours, the property shall be divided into as many equal portions as there are beneficiaries, and those portions shall be distributed respectively to those who would have taken in the event that each beneficiary had survived.

(d) Joint Owners. If any real or personal property, including community property with a right of survivorship, shall be so owned that one of two joint owners is entitled to the whole on the death of the other, and neither survives the other by 120 hours, these assets shall be distributed one-half as if one joint owner had survived and the other one-half as if the other joint owner had survived. If there are more than two joint owners and all have died within a period of less than 120 hours, these assets shall be divided into as many equal portions as there are joint owners and these portions shall be distributed respectively to those who would have taken in the event that each joint owner survived.

(e) Insured and Beneficiary. When the insured and a beneficiary in a policy of life or accident insurance have died within a period of less than 120 hours, the insured shall be deemed to have survived the beneficiary for the purpose of determining the rights under the policy of the beneficiary or beneficiaries as such. The provisions of this subsection shall not prevent the application of subsection (b) above to the proceeds of life or accident insurance which are community property.

(f) Instruments Providing Different Disposition. When provision has been made in the case of wills, living trusts, deeds, or contracts of insurance, or any other situation, for disposition of property different from the provisions of this Section, this Section shall not apply.

Proceedings to Declare Heirship

Sec. 48. Proceedings to Declare Heirship. When and Where Instituted.

(a) When a person dies intestate owning or entitled to real or personal property in Texas, and there shall have been no administration in this State upon his estate; or when there has been a will probated in this State or elsewhere, or an administration in this State upon the estate of such decedent, and any real or personal property in this State has been omitted from such will or from such administration, or no final disposition thereof has been made in such administration, the court of the county in which such proceedings were last pending, or in the event no will of such decedent has been admitted to probate in this State, and no administration has been granted in this State upon the estate of such decedent, then the court of the county in which any of the real property belonging to such estate is situated, or if there is no such real estate, then of the county in which any personal property belonging to such estate is found, may determine and declare in the manner hereinafter provided who are the heirs and only heirs of such decedent, and their respective shares and interests, under the laws of this State, in the estate of such decedent, and proceedings therefor shall be known as proceedings to declare heirship.

(b) If an application for determination of heirship is filed within four (4) years from the date of the death of the decedent, the applicant may request that the court determine whether a necessity for administration exists. The court shall hear evidence upon the issue and make a determination thereof in its judgment.

(c) Notwithstanding any other provision of this section, a probate court in which the proceedings for the guardianship of the estate of a ward who dies intestate were pending at the time of the death of the ward may, if there is no administration pending in the estate, determine and declare who are the heirs and only heirs of the ward, and their respective shares and interests, under the laws of this State, in the estate of the ward.

Sec. 49. Who May Institute Proceedings to Declare Heirship.

(a) Such proceedings may be instituted and maintained in any of the instances enumerated above by the qualified personal representative of the estate of such decedent, by any person or persons claiming to be a secured creditor or the owner of the whole or a part of the estate of such decedent, or by the guardian of the estate of a ward, if the proceedings are instituted and maintained in the probate court in which the proceedings for the guardianship of the estate were pending at the time of the death of the ward. In such a case an application shall be filed in a proper court stating the following information:

(1) the name of the decedent and the time and place of death;

(2) the names and residences of the decedent's heirs, the relationship of each heir to the decedent, and the true interest of the applicant and each of the heirs in the estate of the decedent;

(3) all the material facts and circumstances within the knowledge and information of the applicant that might reasonably tend to show the time or place of death or the names or residences of all heirs, if the time or place of death or the names or residences of all the heirs are not definitely known to the applicant;

(4) a statement that all children born to or adopted by the decedent have been listed;

(5) a statement that each marriage of the decedent has been listed with the date of the marriage, the name of the spouse, and if the marriage was terminated, the date and place of termination, and other facts to show whether a spouse has had an interest in the property of the decedent;

(6) whether the decedent died testate and if so, what disposition has been made of the will;

(7) a general description of all the real and personal property belonging to the estate of the decedent; and

(8) an explanation for the omission of any of the foregoing information that is omitted from the application.

(b) Such application shall be supported by the affidavit of each applicant to the effect that, insofar as is known to such applicant, all the allegations of such application are true in substance and in fact and that no such material fact or circumstance has, within the affiant's knowledge, been omitted from such application. The unknown heirs of such decedent, all persons who are named in the application as heirs of such decedent, and all persons who are, at the date of the filing of the application, shown by the deed records of the county in which any of the real property described in such application is situated to own any share or interest in any such real property, shall be made parties in such proceeding.

Sec. 50. Notice.

(a) Citation shall be served by registered or certified mail upon all distributees whose names and addresses are known, or whose names and addresses can be learned through the exercise of reasonable diligence, provided that the court may in its discretion require that service of citation shall be made by personal service upon some or all of those named as distributees in the application.

(b) Unknown heirs, and known heirs whose addresses cannot be ascertained, shall be served by publication in the county in which the proceedings are commenced, and if the decedent resided in another county, then a citation shall also be published in the county of his last residence.

(c) Except in proceedings in which there is service of citation by publication as provided by Subsection (b) of this section, citation shall also be posted in the county in which the proceedings are commenced and in the county of the decedent's last residence.

(d) A party to the proceedings who has executed the application need not be served by any method.

Sec. 52. Recorded Instruments as Prima Facie Evidence.

Any statement of facts concerning the family history, genealogy, marital status, or the identity of the heirs of a decedent shall be received in a proceeding to declare heirship, or in any suit involving title to real or personal property, as prima facie evidence of the facts therein stated, when such statement is contained in either an affidavit or any other instrument legally executed and acknowledged or sworn to before, and certified by, an officer authorized to take acknowledgments or oaths as applicable, or any judgment of a court of record, if such affidavit or instrument has been of record for five years or more in the deed records of any county in this state in which such real or personal property is located at the time the suit is instituted, or in the deed records of any county of this state in which the decedent had his domicile or fixed place of residence at the time of his death. If there is any error in the statement of facts in such recorded affidavit or instrument, the true facts may be proved by anyone interested in the proceeding in which said affidavit or instrument is offered in evidence. This statute shall be cumulative of all other statutes on the same subject, and shall not be construed as abrogating any right to present evidence conferred by any other statute or rule of law.

Sec. 53.   Evidence; Unknown Parties.

(a) The court in its discretion may require all or any part of the evidence admitted in a proceeding to declare heirship to be reduced to writing, and subscribed and sworn to by the witnesses, respectively, and filed in the cause, and recorded in the minutes of the court.

(b) If it appears to the court that there are or may be living heirs whose names or whereabouts are unknown, or that any defendant is an incapacitated person, the court may, in its discretion, appoint an attorney ad litem or guardian ad litem to represent the interests of any such persons. The court may not appoint an attorney ad litem or guardian ad litem unless the court finds that the appointment is necessary to protect the interests of the living heir or incapacitated person.

Sec. 54.   Judgment.

The judgment of the court in a proceeding to declare heirship shall declare the names and places of residence of the heirs of the decedent, and their respective shares and interests in the real and personal property of such decedent. If the proof is in any respect deficient, the judgment shall so state.

Sec. 55.   Effect of Judgment.

(a) Such judgment shall be a final judgment, and may be appealed or reviewed within the same time limits and in the same manner as may other judgments in probate matters at the instance of any interested person. If any person who is an heir of the decedent is not served with citation by registered or certified mail, or by personal service, he may at any time within four years from the date of such judgment have the same corrected by bill of review, or upon proof of actual fraud, after the passage of any length of time, and may recover from the heirs named in the judgment, and those claiming under them who are not bona fide purchasers for value, his just share of the property or its value.

(b) Although such judgment may later be modified, set aside, or nullified, it shall nevertheless be conclusive in any suit between any heir omitted from the judgment and a bona fide purchaser for value who has purchased real or personal property after entry of the judgment without actual notice of the claim of the omitted heir. Similarly, any person who has delivered funds or property of the decedent to the persons declared to be heirs in the judgment, or has engaged in any other transaction with them, in good faith, after entry of such judgment, shall not be liable therefor to any person.

(c) If the court states in its judgment that there is no necessity for administration on the estate, such recital shall constitute authorization to all persons owing any money to the estate of the decedent, or having custody of any property of such estate, or acting as registrar or transfer agent of any evidence of interest, indebtedness, property, or right belonging to the estate, and to persons purchasing from or otherwise dealing with the heirs as determined in the judgment, to pay, deliver, or transfer such property or evidence of property rights to such heirs, or to purchase property from such heirs, without liability to any creditor of the estate or other person. Such heirs shall be entitled to enforce their right to payment, delivery, or transfer by suit. Nothing in this chapter shall affect the rights or remedies of the creditors of the decedent except as provided in this subsection.

Sec. 56.   Filing of Certified Copy of Judgment.

A certified copy of such judgment may be filed for record in the office of the county clerk of the county in which any of the real property described in such judgment is situated, and recorded in the deed records of such county, and indexed in the name of such decedent as grantor and of the heirs named in such judgment as grantees; and, from and after such filing, such judgment shall constitute constructive notice of the facts set forth therein.

CHAPTER V. PROBATE AND GRANT OF ADMINISTRATION
PART 1. ESTATES OF DECEDENTS

Sec. 74.   Time to File Application for Letters Testamentary or Administration.

All applications for the grant of letters testamentary or of administration upon an estate must be filed within four years after the death of the testator or intestate; provided, that this section shall not apply in any case where administration is necessary in order to receive or recover funds or other property due to the estate of the decedent.

Sec. 76.   Persons Who May Make Application.

An executor named in a will or any interested person may make application to the court of a proper county:

(a) For an order admitting a will to probate, whether the same is written or unwritten, in his possession or not, is lost, is destroyed, or is out of the State.

(b) For the appointment of the executor named in the will.

(c) For the appointment of an administrator, if no executor is designated in the will, or if the person so named is disqualified, or refuses to serve, or is dead, or resigns, or if there is no will. An application for probate may be combined with an application for the appointment of an executor or administrator; and a person interested in either the probate of the will or the appointment of a personal representative may apply for both.

Sec. 77. Order of Persons Qualified to Serve.

Letters testamentary or of administration shall be granted to persons who are qualified to act, in the following order:

(a) To the person named as executor in the will of the deceased.

(b) To the surviving husband or wife.

(c) To the principal devisee or legatee of the testator.

(d) To any devisee or legatee of the testator.

(e) To the next of kin of the deceased, the nearest in order of descent first, and so on, and next of kin includes a person and his descendants who legally adopted the deceased or who have been legally adopted by the deceased.

(f) To a creditor of the deceased.

(g) To any person of good character residing in the county who applies therefor.

(h) To any other person not disqualified under the following Section. When applicants are equally entitled, letters shall be granted to the applicant who, in the judgment of the court, is most likely to administer the estate advantageously, or they may be granted to any two or more of such applicants.

Sec. 78. Persons Disqualified to Serve as Executor or Administrator.

No person is qualified to serve as an executor or administrator who is:

(a) An incapacitated person;

(b) A convicted felon, under the laws either of the United States or of any state or territory of the United States, or of the District of Columbia, unless such person has been duly pardoned, or his civil rights restored, in accordance with law;

(c) A non-resident (natural person or corporation) of this State who has not appointed a resident agent to accept service of process in all actions or proceedings with respect to the estate, and caused such appointment to be filed with the court;

(d) A corporation not authorized to act as a fiduciary in this State; or

(e) A person whom the court finds unsuitable.

Sec. 84. Proof of Written Will Produced in Court.

(a) Self-Proved Will. If a will is self-proved as provided in this Code, no further proof of its execution with the formalities and solemnities and under the circumstances required to make it a valid will shall be necessary.

(b) Attested Written Will. If not self-proved as provided in this Code, an attested written will produced in court may be proved:

(1) By the sworn testimony or affidavit of one or more of the subscribing witnesses thereto, taken in open court.

(2) If all the witnesses are non-residents of the county, or those who are residents are unable to attend court, by the sworn testimony of any one or more of them by deposition, either written or oral, taken in the same manner and under the same rules as depositions taken in other civil actions; or, if no opposition in writing to such will is filed on or before the date set for hearing thereon, then by the sworn testimony or affidavit of two witnesses taken in open court, or by deposition in the manner provided herein, to the signature or the handwriting evidenced thereby of one or more of the attesting witnesses, or of the testator, if he signed the will; or, if it be shown under oath to the satisfaction of the court that, diligent search having been made, only one witness can be found who can make the required proof, then by the sworn testimony or affidavit of such one taken in open court, or by deposition in the manner provided herein, to such signatures or handwriting.

(3) If none of the witnesses is living, or if all of such witnesses are members of the armed forces of the United States of America or of any auxiliary thereof, or of the armed forces reserve of the United States of America or of any auxiliary thereof, or of the Maritime Service, and are beyond the jurisdiction of the court, by two witnesses to the handwriting of one or both of the subscribing witnesses thereto, or of the testator, if signed by him, and such proof may be either by sworn testimony or affidavit taken in open court, or by deposition, either written or oral, taken in the same manner and under the same rules as depositions taken in other civil actions; or, if it be shown under oath to the satisfaction of the court that, diligent search having been made, only one witness can be found who can make the required proof, then by the sworn testimony or affidavit of such one taken in open court, or by deposition in the manner provided herein, to such signatures or handwriting.

(c) Holographic Will. If not self-proved as provided in this Code, a will wholly in the handwriting of the testator may be proved by two witnesses to his handwriting, which evidence may be by sworn testimony or affidavit taken in open court, or, if such witnesses are non-residents of the county or are residents who are unable to attend court, by deposition, either written or oral, taken in the same manner and under the same rules as depositions taken in other civil actions.

(d) Depositions if No Contest Filed. If no contest has been filed, depositions for the purpose of establishing a will may be taken in the same manner as provided in this Code for the taking of depositions where there is no opposing party or attorney of record upon whom notice and copies of interrogatories may be served; and, in such event, this Subsection, rather than the preceding portions of this Section which provide for the taking of depositions under the same rules as depositions in other civil actions, shall be applicable.

Sec. 85.   Proof of Written Will Not Produced in Court.

A written will which cannot be produced in court shall be proved in the same manner as provided in the preceding Section for an attested written will or an holographic will, as the case may be, and the same amount and character of testimony shall be required to prove such will as is required to prove a written will produced in court; but, in addition thereto, the cause of its non-production must be proved, and such cause must be sufficient to satisfy the court that it cannot by any reasonable diligence be produced, and the contents of such will must be substantially proved by the testimony of a credible witness who has read it or heard it read.

Sec. 88.   Proof Required for Probate and Issuance of Letters Testamentary or of Administration.

(a) General Proof. Whenever an applicant seeks to probate a will or to obtain issuance of letters testamentary or of administration, he must first prove to the satisfaction of the court:

(1) That the person is dead, and that four years have not elapsed since his decease and prior to the application; and

(2) That the court has jurisdiction and venue over the estate; and

(3) That citation has been served and returned in the manner and for the length of time required by this Code; and

(4) That the person for whom letters testamentary or of administration are sought is entitled thereto by law and is not disqualified.

(b) Additional Proof for Probate of Will. To obtain probate of a will, the applicant must also prove to the satisfaction of the court:

(1) If the will is not self-proved as provided by this Code, that the testator, at the time of executing the will, was at least eighteen years of age, or was or had been lawfully married, or was a member of the armed forces of the United States or of the auxiliaries thereof, or of the Maritime Service of the United States, and was of sound mind; and

(2) If the will is not self-proved as provided by this Code, that the testator executed the will with the formalities and solemnities and under the circumstances required by law to make it a valid will; and

(3) That such will was not revoked by the testator.

(c) Additional Proof for Issuance of Letters Testamentary. If letters testamentary are to be granted, it must appear to the court that proof required for the probate of the will has been made, and, in addition, that the person to whom the letters are to be granted is named as executor in the will.

(d) Additional Proof for Issuance of Letters of Administration. If letters of administration are to be granted, the applicant must also prove to the satisfaction of the court that there exists a necessity for an administration upon such estate.

(e) Proof Required Where Prior Letters Have Been Granted. If letters testamentary or of administration have previously been granted upon the estate, the applicant need show only that the person for whom letters are sought is entitled thereto by law and is not disqualified.

Muniments of Title

Sec. 89A.   Probate of Wills as Muniments of Title.

(a) In each instance where the court is satisfied that a will should be admitted to probate, and where the court is further satisfied that there are no unpaid debts owing by the estate of the testator, excluding debts secured by liens on real estate, or for other reason finds that there is no necessity for administration upon such estate, the court may admit such will to probate as a muniment of title.

(b) If a person who is entitled to property under the provisions of the will cannot be ascertained solely by reference to the will or if a question of construction of the will exists, on proper application and notice as provided by Chapter 37, Civil Practice and Remedies Code, the court may hear evidence and include in the order probating the will as a muniment of title a declaratory judgment construing the will or determining those persons who are entitled to receive property under the will and the persons' shares or interests in the estate. The judgment is conclusive in any suit between any person omitted from the judgment and a bona fide purchaser for value who has purchased real or personal property after entry of the judgment without actual notice of the claim of the omitted person to an interest in the estate. Any person who has delivered property of the decedent to a person declared to be entitled to the property under the judgment or has engaged in any other transaction with the person in good faith after entry of the judgment is not liable to any person for actions taken in reliance on the judgment.

(c) The order admitting a will to probate as a muniment of title shall constitute sufficient legal authority to all persons owing any money to the estate of the decedent, having custody of any property, or acting as registrar or transfer agent of any evidence of interest, indebtedness, property, or right belonging to the estate, and to persons purchasing from or otherwise dealing with the estate, for payment or transfer, without liability, to the persons described in such will as entitled to receive the particular asset without administration. The person or persons entitled to property under the provisions of such wills shall be entitled to deal with and treat the properties to which they are so entitled in the same manner as if the record of title thereof were vested in their names.

(d) Unless waived by the court, before the 181st day, or such later day as may be extended by the court, after the date a will is admitted to probate as a muniment of title, the applicant for probate of the will shall file with the clerk of the court a sworn affidavit stating specifically the terms of the will that have been fulfilled and the terms of the will that have been unfulfilled. Failure of the applicant for probate of the will to file such affidavit shall not otherwise affect title to property passing under the terms of the will.

CHAPTER VI. SPECIAL TYPES OF ADMINISTRATION
PART 3. SMALL ESTATES

Sec. 137.   Collection of Small Estates Upon Affidavit.

(a) The distributees of the estate of a decedent who dies intestate shall be entitled thereto, to the extent that the assets, exclusive of homestead and exempt property, exceed the known liabilities of said estate, exclusive of liabilities secured by homestead and exempt property, without awaiting the appointment of a personal representative when:

(1) No petition for the appointment of a personal representative is pending or has been granted; and

(2) Thirty days have elapsed since the death of the decedent; and

(3) The value of the entire assets of the estate, not including homestead and exempt property, does not exceed $50,000; and

(4) There is filed with the clerk of the court having jurisdiction and venue an affidavit sworn to by two disinterested witnesses, by all such distributees that have legal capacity, and, if the facts warrant, by the natural guardian or next of kin of any minor or the guardian of any other incapacitated person who is also a distributee, which affidavit shall be examined by the judge of the court having jurisdiction and venue; and

(5) The affidavit shows the existence of the foregoing conditions and includes a list of all of the known assets and liabilities of the estate, the names and addresses of the distributees, and the distributees' rights to receive the money or property of the estate or to have such evidences of money, property, or other rights of the estate as are found to exist transferred to them as heirs or assignees; and

(6) The judge, in the judge's discretion, finds that the affidavit conforms to the terms of this section and approves the affidavit; and

(7) A copy of the affidavit, certified to by said clerk, is furnished by the distributees of the estate to the person or persons owing money to the estate, having custody or possession of property of the estate, or acting as registrar, fiduciary or transfer agent of or for evidences of interest, indebtedness, property, or other right belonging to the estate.

(b) This section does not affect the disposition of property under the terms of a will or other testamentary document nor, except as provided by Subsection (c) of this section, does it transfer title to real property.

(c) Title to a decedent's homestead that is the only real property in a decedent's estate may be transferred on an affidavit that meets the requirements of this section. An affidavit that is used to transfer title to a homestead under this section must be recorded in the deed records of a county in which the homestead is located. A bona fide purchaser for value may rely on a recorded affidavit under this section. A bona fide purchaser for value without actual or constructive notice of an heir who is not disclosed in a recorded affidavit under this section acquires title to a homestead free of the interests of the undisclosed heir, but the bona fide purchaser remains subject to any claim a creditor of the decedent has by law. A purchaser has constructive notice of an heir who is not disclosed in a recorded affidavit under this section if an affidavit, judgment of heirship, or title transaction in the chain of title in the deed records identifies the heir of the decedent who is not disclosed in the affidavit as an heir of the decedent. An heir who is not disclosed in a recorded affidavit under this section may recover from an heir who receives consideration from a purchaser in a transfer for value of title to a homestead passing under the affidavit.

(d) If the judge approves the affidavit under this section, the affidavit is to be recorded as an official public record under Chapter 194, Local Government Code. If the county has not adopted a microfilm or microphotographic process under Chapter 194, Local Government Code, the county clerk shall provide and keep in his office an appropriate book labeled "Small Estates," with an accurate index showing the name of the decedent and reference to land, if any, involved, in which he shall record every such affidavit so filed, upon being paid his legal recording fee.

Sec. 138.   Effect of Affidavit.

The person making payment, delivery, transfer or issuance pursuant to the affidavit described in the preceding Section shall be released to the same extent as if made to a personal representative of the decedent, and shall not be required to see to the application thereof or to inquire into the truth of any statement in the affidavit, but the distributees to whom payment, delivery, transfer, or issuance is made shall be answerable therefor to any person having a prior right and be accountable to any personal representative thereafter appointed. In addition, the person or persons who execute the affidavit shall be liable for any damage or loss to any person which arises from any payment, delivery, transfer, or issuance made in reliance on such affidavit. If the person to whom such affidavit is delivered refuses to pay, deliver, transfer, or issue the property as above provided, such property may be recovered in an action brought for such purpose by or on behalf of the distributees entitled thereto, upon proof of the facts required to be stated in the affidavit.

Sec. 139. Application for Order of No Administration.

If the value of the entire assets of an estate, not including homestead and exempt property, does not exceed the amount to which the surviving spouse and minor children of the decedent are entitled as a family allowance, there may be filed by or on behalf of the surviving spouse or minor children an application in any court of proper venue for administration, or, if an application for the appointment of a personal representative has been filed but not yet granted, then in the court where such application has been filed, requesting the court to make a family allowance and to enter an order that no administration shall be necessary. The application shall state the names of the heirs or devisees, a list of creditors of the estate together with the amounts of the claims so far as the same are known, and a description of all real and personal property belonging to the estate, together with the estimated value thereof according to the best knowledge and information of the applicant, and the liens and encumbrances thereon, with a prayer that the court make a family allowance and that, if the entire assets of the estate, not including homestead and exempt property, are thereby exhausted, the same be set aside to the surviving spouse and minor children, as in the case of other family allowances provided for by this Code.

Sec. 140. Hearing and Order Upon the Application.

Upon the filing of an application for no administration such as that provided for in the preceding Section, the court may hear the same forthwith without notice, or at such time and upon such notice as the court requires. Upon the hearing of the application, if the court finds that the facts contained therein are true and that the expenses of last illness, funeral charges, and expenses of the proceeding have been paid or secured, the court shall make a family allowance and, if the entire assets of the estate, not including homestead and exempt property, are thereby exhausted, shall order that no administration be had of the estate and shall assign to the surviving spouse and minor children the whole of the estate, in the same manner and with the same effect as provided in this Code for the making of family allowances to the surviving spouse and minor children.

Sec. 141. Effect of Order.

The order that no administration be had on the estate shall constitute sufficient legal authority to all persons owing any money, having custody of any property, or acting as registrar or transfer agent of any evidence of interest, indebtedness, property, or right, belonging to the estate, and to persons purchasing from or otherwise dealing with the estate, for payment or transfer to the persons described in the order as entitled to receive the estate without administration, and the persons so described in the order shall be entitled to enforce their right to such payment or transfer by suit.

Sec. 142. Proceeding to Revoke Order.

At any time within one year after the entry of an order of no administration, and not thereafter, any interested person may file an application to revoke the same, alleging that other property has been discovered, or that property belonging to the estate was not included in the application for no administration, or that the property described in the application was incorrectly valued, and that if said property were added, included, or correctly valued, as the case may be, the total value of the property would exceed that necessary to justify the court in ordering no administration. Upon proof of any of such grounds, the court shall revoke the order of no administration. In case of any contest as to the value of any property, the court may appoint two appraisers to appraise the same in accordance with the procedure hereinafter provided for inventories and appraisements, and the appraisement of such appraisers shall be received in evidence but shall not be conclusive.

Sec. 143. Summary Proceedings for Small Estates After Personal Representative Appointed.

Whenever, after the inventory, appraisement, and list of claims has been filed by a personal representative, it is established that the estate of a decedent, exclusive of the homestead and exempt property and family allowance to the surviving spouse and minor children, does not exceed the amount sufficient to pay the claims of Classes One to Four, inclusive, as claims are hereinafter classified, the personal representative shall, upon order of the court, pay the claims in the order provided and to the extent permitted by the assets of the estate subject to the payment of such claims, and thereafter present his account with an application for the settlement and allowance thereof. Thereupon the court, with or without notice, may adjust, correct, settle, allow or disallow such account, and, if the account is settled and allowed, may decree final distribution, discharge the personal representative, and close the administration.

PART 4. INDEPENDENT ADMINISTRATION

Sec. 145. Independent Administration.

(a) Independent administration of an estate may be created as provided in Subsections (b) through (e) of this section.

(b) Any person capable of making a will may provide in his will that no other action shall be had in the county court in relation to the settlement of his estate than the probating and recording of his will, and the return of an inventory, appraisement, and list of claims of his estate.

(c) In situations where an executor is named in a decedent's will, but the will does not provide for independent administration of the decedent's estate as provided in Subsection (b) of this section, all of the distributees of the decedent may agree on the advisability of having an independent administration and collectively designate in the application for probate of the decedent's will the executor named in the will to serve as independent executor and request in the application that no other action shall be had in the county court in relation to the settlement of the decedent's estate other than the probating and recording of the decedent's will, and the return of an inventory, appraisement, and list of claims of the decedent's estate. In such case the county court shall enter an order granting independent administration and appointing the person, firm, or corporation designated in the application as independent executor, unless the county court finds that it would not be in the best interest of the estate to do so.

(d) In situations where no executor is named in the decedent's will, or in situations where each executor named in the will is deceased or is disqualified to serve as executor or indicates by affidavit filed with the application for administration of the decedent's estate his inability or unwillingness to serve as executor, all of the distributees of the decedent may agree on the advisability of having an independent administration and collectively designate in the application for probate of the decedent's will a qualified person, firm, or corporation to serve as independent administrator and request in the application that no other action shall be had in the county court in relation to the settlement of the decedent's estate other than the probating and recording of the decedent's will, and the return of an inventory, appraisement, and list of claims of the decedent's estate. In such case the county court shall enter an order granting independent administration and appointing the person, firm, or corporation designated in the application as independent administrator, unless the county court finds that it would not be in the best interest of the estate to do so.

(e) All of the distributees of a decedent dying intestate may agree on the advisability of having an independent administration and collectively designate in the application for administration of the decedent's estate a qualified person, firm, or corporation to serve as independent administrator and request in the application that no other action shall be had in the county court in relation to the settlement of the decedent's estate other than the return of an inventory, appraisement, and list of claims of the decedent's estate. In such case the county court shall enter an order granting independent administration and appointing the person, firm, or corporation designated in the application as independent administrator, unless the county court finds that it would not be in the best interest of the estate to do so.

(f) In those cases where an independent administration is sought under the provisions of Subsections (c) through (e) above, all distributees shall be served with citation and notice of the application for independent administration unless the distributee waives the issuance or service of citation or enters an appearance in court.

(g) In no case shall any independent administrator be appointed by any court to serve in any intestate administration until those parties seeking the appointment of said independent administrator offer clear and convincing evidence to the court that they constitute all of the said decedent's heirs.

(h) When an independent administration has been created, and the order appointing an independent executor has been entered by the county court, and the inventory, appraisement, and list aforesaid has been filed by the executor and approved by the county court, as long as the estate is represented by an independent executor, further action of any nature shall not be had in the county court except where this Code specifically and explicitly provides for some action in the county court.

(i) If a distributee described in Subsections (c) through (e) of this section is an incapacitated person, the guardian of the person of the distributee may sign the application on behalf of the distributee. If the county court finds that either the granting of independent administration or the appointment of the person, firm, or corporation designated in the application as independent executor would not be in the best interests of the incapacitated person, then, notwithstanding anything to the contrary in Subsections (c) through (e) of this section, the county court shall not enter an order granting independent administration of the estate. If such distributee who is an incapacitated person has no guardian of the person, the county court may appoint a guardian ad litem to make application on behalf of the incapacitated person if the county court considers such an appointment necessary to protect the interest of the distributees.

(j) If a trust is created in the decedent's will, the person or class of persons first eligible to receive the income from the trust, when determined as if the trust were to be in existence on the date of the decedent's death, shall, for the purposes of Subsections (c) and (d) of this section, be deemed to be the distributee or distributees on behalf of such trust, and any other trust or trusts coming into existence upon the termination of such trust, and are authorized to apply for independent administration on behalf of the trusts without the consent or agreement of the trustee or any other beneficiary of the trust, or the trustee or any beneficiary of any other trust which may come into existence upon the termination of such trust.

(k) If a life estate is created either in the decedent's will or by law, the life tenant or life tenants, when determined as if the life estate were to commence on the date of the decedent's death, shall, for the purposes of Subsections (c) through (e) of this section, be deemed to be the distributee or distributees on behalf of the entire estate created, and are authorized to apply for independent administration on behalf of the estate without the consent or approval of any remainderman.

(l) If a decedent's will contains a provision that a distributee must survive the decedent by a prescribed period of time in order to take under the decedent's will, then, for the purposes of determining who shall be the distributee under Subsections (c), (d), (h), and (i) of this section, it shall be presumed that the distributees living at the time of the filing of the application for probate of the decedent's will survived the decedent by the prescribed period.

(m) In the case of all decedents, whether dying testate or intestate, for the purposes of determining who shall be the distributees under Subsections (c), (d), (e), (h), and (i) of this section, it shall be presumed that no distributee living at the time the application for independent administration is filed shall subsequently disclaim any portion of such distributee's interest in the decedent's estate.

(n) If a distributee of a decedent's estate should die and if by virtue of such distributee's death such distributee's share of the decedent's estate shall become payable to such distributee's estate, then the deceased distributee's personal representative may sign the application for independent administration of the decedent's estate under Subsections (c), (d), (e), (h), and (i) of this section.

(o) Notwithstanding anything to the contrary in this section, a person capable of making a will may provide in his will that no independent administration of his estate may be allowed. In such case, his estate, if administered, shall be administered and settled under the direction of the county court as other estates are required to be settled.

(p) If an independent administration of a decedent's estate is created pursuant to Subsections (c), (d), or (e) of this section, then, unless the county court shall waive bond on application for waiver, the independent executor shall be required to enter into bond payable to and to be approved by the judge and his or her successors in a sum that is found by the judge to be adequate under all circumstances, or a bond with one surety in a sum that is found by the judge to be adequate under all circumstances, if the surety is an authorized corporate surety. This subsection does not repeal any other section of this Code.

(q) Absent proof of fraud or collusion on the part of a judge, no judge may be held civilly liable for the commission of misdeeds or the omission of any required act of any person, firm, or corporation designated as an independent executor or independent administrator under Subsections (c), (d), and (e) of the section. Section 36 of this code does not apply to the appointment of an independent executor or administrator under Subsection (c), (d), or (e) of this section.

(r) A person who declines to serve or resigns as independent executor or administrator of a decedent's estate may be appointed an executor or administrator of the estate if the estate will be administered and settled under the direction of the court.

Sec. 146. Payment of Claims and Delivery of Exemptions and Allowances.

(a) Duty of the Independent Executor. An independent executor, in the administration of an estate, independently of and without application to, or any action in or by the court:

(1) shall give the notices required under Sections 294 and 295;

(2) may give the notice permitted under Section 294(d) and bar a claim under that subsection;

(3) shall approve, classify, and pay, or reject, claims against the estate in the same order of priority, classification, and proration prescribed in this Code; and

(4) shall set aside and deliver to those entitled thereto exempt property and allowances for support, and allowances in lieu of exempt property, as prescribed in this Code, to the same extent and result as if the independent executor's actions had been accomplished in, and under orders of, the court.

(b) Secured Claims for Money. Within six months after the date letters are granted or within four months after the date notice is received under Section 295, whichever is later, a creditor with a claim for money secured by real or personal property of the estate must notify the independent executor by certified or registered mail of the creditor's election to have the creditor's claim approved as a matured secured claim to be paid in due course of administration. If the election is not made, the claim is a preferred debt and lien against the specific property securing the indebtedness and shall be paid according to the terms of the contract that secured the lien, and the claim may not be asserted against other assets of the estate. The independent executor may pay the claim before the claim matures if paying the claim before maturity is in the best interest of the estate.

(c) Liability of Independent Executor. An independent executor, in the administration of an estate, may pay at any time and without personal liability a claim for money against the estate to the extent approved and classified by the personal representative if:

(1) the claim is not barred by limitations; and

(2) at the time of payment, the independent executor reasonably believes the estate will have sufficient assets to pay all claims against the estate.

Sec. 149A. Accounting.

(a) Interested Person May Demand Accounting. At any time after the expiration of fifteen months from the date that an independent administration was created and the order appointing an independent executor was entered by the county court, any person interested in the estate may demand an accounting from the independent executor. The independent executor shall thereupon furnish to the person or persons making the demand an exhibit in writing, sworn and subscribed by the independent executor, setting forth in detail:

1. The property belonging to the estate which has come into his hands as executor.
2. The disposition that has been made of such property.
3. The debts that have been paid.
4. The debts and expenses, if any, still owing by the estate.
5. The property of the estate, if any, still remaining in his hands.
6. Such other facts as may be necessary to a full and definite understanding of the exact condition of the estate.
7. Such facts, if any, that show why the administration should not be closed and the estate distributed.

Any other interested person shall, upon demand, be entitled to a copy of any exhibit or accounting that has been made by an independent executor in compliance with this section.

(b) Enforcement of Demand. Should the independent executor not comply with a demand for an accounting authorized by this section within sixty days after receipt of the demand, the person making the demand may compel compliance by an action in the county court or by a suit in the district court. After a hearing, the court shall enter an order requiring the accounting to be made at such time as it deems proper under the circumstances.

(c) Subsequent Demands. After an initial accounting has been given by an independent executor, any person interested in an estate may demand subsequent periodic accountings at intervals of not less than twelve months, and such subsequent demands may be enforced in the same manner as an initial demand.

(d) Remedies Cumulative. The right to an accounting accorded by this section is cumulative of any other remedies which persons interested in an estate may have against the independent executor thereof.

Sec. 149B. Accounting and Distribution.

(a) In addition to or in lieu of the right to an accounting provided by Section 149A of this code, at any time after the expiration of two years from the date that an independent administration was created and the order appointing an independent executor was entered, a person interested in the estate may petition the court for an accounting and distribution. The proceeding for an accounting and distribution may be brought in the county court if the county judge is licensed to practice law in the State of Texas or may be brought in a statutory probate court, a county court at law with probate jurisdiction, or a district court of the county. The court may order an accounting to be made with the court by the independent executor at such time as the court deems proper. The accounting shall include the information that the court deems necessary to determine whether any part of the estate should be distributed.

(b) On receipt of the accounting and, after notice to the independent executor and a hearing, unless the court finds a continued necessity for administration of the estate, the court shall order its distribution by the independent executor to the persons entitled to the property. If the court finds there is a continued necessity for administration of the estate, the court shall order the distribution of any portion of the estate that the court finds should not be subject to further administration by the independent executor. If any portion of the estate that is ordered to be distributed is incapable of distribution without prior partition or sale, the court shall order partition and distribution, or sale, in the manner provided for the partition and distribution of property incapable of division in estates administered under the direction of the county court.

(c) If all the property in the estate is ordered distributed by the executor and the estate is fully administered, the court also may order the independent executor to file a final account with the court and may enter an order closing the administration and terminating the power of the independent executor to act as executor.

Sec. 151. Closing Independent Administration by Affidavit.

(a) Filing of Affidavit. When all of the debts known to exist against the estate have been paid, or when they have been paid so far as the assets in the hands of the independent executor will permit, when there is no pending litigation, and when the independent executor has distributed to the persons entitled thereto all assets of the estate, if any, remaining after payment of debts, the independent executor may file with the court:

(1) a closing report verified by affidavit that shows:

(i) The property of the estate which came into the hands of the independent executor;

(ii) The debts that have been paid;

(iii) The debts, if any, still owing by the estate;

(iv) The property of the estate, if any, remaining on hand after payment of debts; and

(v) The names and residences of the persons to whom the property of the estate, if any, remaining on hand after payment of debts has been distributed; and

(2) signed receipts or other proof of delivery of property to the distributees named in the closing report if the closing report reflects that there was property remaining on hand after payment of debts.

(b) Effect of Filing the Affidavit.

(1) The filing of such an affidavit and proof of delivery, if required, shall terminate the independent administration and the power and authority of the independent executor, but shall not relieve the independent executor from liability for any mismanagement of the estate or from liability for any false statements contained in the affidavit. When such an affidavit has been filed, persons dealing with properties of the estate, or with claims against the estate, shall deal directly with the distributees of the estate; and the acts of such distributees with respect to such properties or claims shall in all ways be valid and binding as regards the persons with whom they deal, notwithstanding any false statements made by the independent executor in such affidavit.

(2) If the independent executor is required to give bond, the independent executor's filing of the affidavit and proof of delivery, if required, automatically releases the sureties on the bond from all liability for the future acts of the principal.

(c) Authority to Transfer Property of a Decedent After Filing the Affidavit. An independent executor's affidavit closing the independent administration shall constitute sufficient legal authority to all persons owing any money, having custody of any property, or acting as registrar or transfer agent or trustee of any evidence of interest, indebtedness, property, or right that belongs to the estate, for payment or transfer without additional administration to the persons described in the will as entitled to receive the particular asset or who as heirs at law are entitled to receive the asset. The persons described in the will as entitled to receive the particular asset or the heirs at law entitled to receive the asset may enforce their right to the payment or transfer by suit.

(d) Delivery Subject to Receipt or Proof of Delivery. An independent executor may not be required to deliver tangible or intangible personal property to a distributee unless the independent executor shall receive, at or before the time of delivery of the property, a signed receipt or other proof of delivery of the property to the distributee. An independent executor shall not require a waiver or release from the distributee as a condition of delivery of property to a distributee.

(e) Community Administration. A community administrator may use the procedures in this section to terminate community administration under Section 175 of this code. The independent executor's filing of the affidavit releases the sureties on the community administrator's bond from all liability for the future acts of the principal.

PART 5. ADMINISTRATION OF COMMUNITY PROPERTY

Sec. 155. Administration of Community Property.

When a husband or wife dies intestate and the community property passes to the survivor, no administration thereon, community or otherwise, shall be necessary.

Sec. 156. Liability of Community Property for Debts.

The community property subject to the sole or joint management, control, and disposition of a spouse during marriage continues to be subject to the liabilities of that spouse upon death. In addition, the interest that the deceased spouse owned in any other nonexempt community property passes to his or her heirs or devisees charged with the debts which were enforceable against such deceased spouse prior to his or her death. In the administration of community estates, the survivor or personal representative shall keep a separate, distinct account of all community debts allowed or paid in the administration and settlement of such estate.

Sec. 160. Powers of Surviving Spouse When No Administration is Pending.

(a) When no one has qualified as executor or administrator of the estate of a deceased spouse, the surviving spouse, whether the husband or wife, as the surviving partner of the marital partnership, without qualifying as community administrator as hereinafter provided, has power to sue and be sued for the recovery of community property; to sell, mortgage, lease, and otherwise dispose of community property for the purpose of paying community debts; to collect claims due to the community estate; and has such other powers as shall be necessary to preserve the community property, discharge community obligations, and wind up community affairs.

(b) If an affidavit stating that the affiant is the surviving spouse and that no one has qualified as executor or administrator of the estate of the deceased spouse is furnished to a person owing money to the community estate for current wages at the time of the death of the deceased spouse, the person making payment or delivering to the affiant the deceased spouse's final paycheck for wages, including unpaid sick pay or vacation pay, if any, is released from liability to the same extent as if the payment or delivery was made to a personal representative of the deceased spouse. The person is not required to inquire into the truth of the affidavit. The affiant to whom the payment or delivery is made is answerable to any person having a prior right and is accountable to any personal representative who is appointed. The affiant is liable for any damage or loss to any person that arises from a payment or delivery made in reliance on the affidavit.

(c) This section does not affect the disposition of the property of the deceased spouse.

Sec. 161. Community Administration.

Whenever an interest in community property passes to someone other than the surviving spouse, the surviving spouse may qualify as community administrator in the manner hereinafter provided if

(a) The deceased spouse failed to name an executor in his will, or

(b) If the executor named in the will of the deceased spouse is for any reason unable or unwilling to qualify as such, or

(c) If the deceased spouse died intestate.

Sec. 162. Application for Community Administration.

A surviving spouse who desires to qualify as a community administrator shall, within four years after the death of the other spouse, file a written application in the court having venue over the estate of the deceased spouse, stating:

(a) That the other spouse is dead, setting forth the time and place of such death; and

(b) The name and residence of each person to whom an interest in community property has passed by the will of the decedent or by intestacy; and

(c) That there is a community estate between the deceased spouse and the applicant, and the facts that authorize the applicant to be appointed as community administrator; and

(d) That, by virtue of facts set forth in the application, the court has venue over the estate of the deceased spouse; and

(e) If the applicant desires that appraisers be appointed, that not less than one nor more than three appraisers should be appointed to appraise such estate.

Sec. 164. Inventory, Appraisement, and List of Claims.

The surviving spouse, with the assistance of the appraisers, if any be appointed, shall make out a full, fair, and complete inventory, appraisement, and list of claims of the community estate as in other administrations, shall attach thereto a list of all indebtedness owing by said community estate to other parties, giving the amount of each debt and the name of the party or parties to whom it is owing, and his or their postoffice address, and shall return same to the court within ninety (90) days after the date of the order appointing appraisers, if any be appointed, unless a longer time shall be granted by the court. If no appraisers be appointed, such return shall be made within ninety (90) days after the date of the application for community administration, unless a longer time shall be granted by the court. In either event, the court may, for good cause shown, require the filing of the inventory and appraisement within a shorter period of time. Such inventory, list of claims, and list of indebtedness of such community estate shall be sworn to by said surviving spouse, and said inventory, appraisement, and list of claims owing said community estate shall be sworn to by said appraisers, if any appraisers have been appointed.

Sec. 165. Bond of Community Administrator.

The community administrator shall at the time the inventory, appraisement, and list of claims are returned, present to the court a bond with two or more good and sufficient sureties, payable to and to be approved by the judge and his successors in a sum as is found by the judge to be adequate under all the circumstances, or a bond with one surety in a sum as is found by the judge to be adequate under all the circumstances, if the surety is an authorized corporate surety. The condition of the bond shall be that such surviving spouse will faithfully administer such community estate and will, after the payment of debts with which such property is properly chargeable, deliver to such person or persons as shall be entitled to receive the same the portion of the community estate devised or bequeathed to them under the terms of the will of the deceased spouse, or which passes to them under the laws of descent and distribution. Either spouse may by will apportion community indebtedness as between the devisees and legatees of such testator and the surviving spouse, but this shall not include the power to charge the community share of the surviving spouse with more than the portion of the community debts for which it would otherwise be liable.

Sec. 167. Powers of Community Administrator.

When the order mentioned in the preceding section has been entered, the survivor, without any further action in the court, shall have the power to control, manage, and dispose of the community property, as provided in this Code, as fully and completely as if he or she were the sole owner thereof, and to sue and be sued with regard to the same; and a certified copy of the order of the court shall be evidence of the qualification and right of such survivor. After paying community debts outstanding at the death of the deceased spouse, the qualified community administrator may carry on as statutory trustee for the owners of the community estate, investing and reinvesting the funds of the estate and continuing the operation of community enterprises until the termination of the trust as provided in this Code. The qualified community administrator is not entitled to mortgage community property to secure debts incurred for his individual benefit, or otherwise to appropriate the community estate to his individual benefit; but he may transfer or encumber his individual interest in the community estate.

Sec. 168. Accounting by Survivor.

The survivor, whether qualified as community administrator or not, shall keep a fair and full account and statement of all community debts and expenses paid by him, and of the disposition made of the community property; and, upon final partition of such estate, shall deliver to the heirs, devisees or legatees of the deceased spouse their interest in such estate, and the increase and profits of the same, after deducting therefrom the proportion of the community debts chargeable thereto, unavoidable losses, necessary and reasonable expenses, and a reasonable commission for the management of the same. Neither the survivor nor his bondsmen shall be liable for losses sustained by the estate, except when the survivor has been guilty of gross negligence or bad faith.

Sec. 169. Payment of Debts.

The community administrator shall pay all just and legal community debts within the time, and according to the classification, and in the order prescribed for the payment of debts in other administrations. Where there is a deficiency of assets to pay all claims of the same class, such claims shall be paid pro rata.

Sec. 175. Termination of Community Administration.

After the lapse of twelve months from the filing of the bond of the survivor, the community administration may be terminated whenever termination is desired by either the survivor or the persons entitled to the share of the deceased spouse, or to any portion thereof. Partition and distribution of the community estate may be had and the administration closed either by proceedings as in other independent administration or by proceedings in the appropriate District Court. When the community administration is closed, the community administrator shall be discharged and his bondsmen released from further liability.

Sec. 177. Distribution of Powers Among Personal Representatives and Surviving Spouse.

(a) When Community Administrator Has Qualified. The qualified community administrator is entitled to administer the entire community estate, including the part which was by law under the management of the deceased spouse during the continuance of the marriage.

(b) When No Community Administrator Has Qualified. When an executor of the estate of a deceased spouse has duly qualified, such executor is authorized to administer, not only the separate property of the deceased spouse, but also the community property which was by law under the management of the deceased spouse during the continuance of the marriage and all of the community property that was by law under the joint control of the spouses during the continuance of the marriage. The surviving spouse, as surviving partner of the marital partnership, is entitled to retain possession and control of all community property which was legally under the sole management of the surviving spouse during the continuance of the marriage and to exercise over that property all the powers elsewhere in this part of this Code authorized to be exercised by the surviving spouse when there is no administration pending on the estate of the deceased spouse. The surviving spouse may by written instrument filed with the clerk waive any right to exercise powers as community survivor, and in such event the executor or administrator of the deceased spouse shall be authorized to administer upon the entire community estate.

CHAPTER VII. EXECUTORS AND ADMINISTRATORS

PART 1. APPOINTMENT AND ISSUANCE OF LETTERS

Sec. 178. When Letters Testamentary or of Administration Shall Be Granted.

(a) Letters Testamentary. When a will has been probated, the court shall, within twenty days thereafter, grant letters testamentary, if permitted by law, to the executor or executors appointed by such will, if any there be, or to such of them as are not disqualified, and are willing to accept the trust and qualify according to law.

(b) Letters of Administration. When a person shall die intestate, or where no executor is named in a will, or where the executor is dead or shall fail or neglect to accept and qualify within twenty days after the probate of the will, or shall neglect for a period of thirty days after the death of the testator to present the will for probate, then administration of the estate of such intestate, or administration with the will annexed of the estate of such testator, shall be granted, should administration appear to be necessary. No administration of any estate shall be granted unless there exists a necessity therefor, such necessity to be determined by the court hearing the application. Such necessity shall be deemed to exist if two or more debts exist against the estate, or if or when it is desired to have the county court partition the estate among the distributees, but mention of these two instances of necessity for administration shall not prevent the court from finding other instances of necessity upon proof before it.

(c) Failure to Issue Letters Within Prescribed Time. Failure of a court to issue letters testamentary within the twenty day period prescribed by this Section shall not affect the validity of any letters testamentary which are issued subsequent to such period, in accordance with law.

PART 5. GENERAL POWERS OF PERSONAL REPRESENTATIVES

Sec. 230. Care of Property of Estates.

The executor or administrator shall take care of the property of the estate of his testator or intestate as a prudent man would take of his own property, and if there be any buildings belonging to the estate, he shall keep the same in good repair, extraordinary casualties excepted, unless directed not to do so by an order of the court.

Sec. 232. Representative of Estate Shall Take Possession of Personal Property and Records.

The personal representative of an estate, immediately after receiving letters, shall collect and take into possession the personal property, record books, title papers, and other business papers of the estate, and all such in his possession shall be delivered to the person or persons legally entitled thereto when the administration has been closed or a successor has received letters.

Sec. 233. Collection of Claims and Recovery of Property.

(a) Every personal representative of an estate shall use ordinary diligence to collect all claims and debts due the estate and to recover possession of all property of the estate to which its owners have claim or title, provided there is a reasonable prospect of collecting such claims or of recovering such property. If he wilfully neglects to use such diligence, he and the sureties on his bond shall be liable, at the suit of any person interested in the estate, for the use of the estate, for the amount of such claims or the value of such property as has been lost by such neglect.

(b) Except as provided by Subsection (c) of this section, a personal representative may enter into a contract to convey, or may convey, a contingent interest in any property sought to be recovered, not exceeding one-third thereof, for services of attorneys, subject only to approval of the court in which the estate is being administered.

(c) A personal representative, including an independent executor or independent administrator, may convey or contract to convey for services of an attorney a contingent interest that exceeds one-third of the property sought to be recovered under this section only on the approval of the court in which the estate is being administered. The court must approve a contract entered into or conveyance made under this section before an attorney performs any legal services. A contract entered into or conveyance made in violation of this section is void, unless the court ratifies or reforms the contract or documents relating to the conveyance to the extent necessary to cause the contract or conveyance to meet the requirements of this section.

(d) In approving a contract or conveyance under Subsection (b) or (c) of this section for services of an attorney, the court shall consider:

(1) the time and labor that will be required, the novelty and difficulty of the questions to be involved, and the skill that will be required to perform the legal services properly;

(2) the fee customarily charged in the locality for similar legal services;

(3) the value of property recovered or sought to be recovered by the personal representative under this section;

(4) the benefits to the estate that the attorney will be responsible for securing; and

(5) the experience and ability of the attorney who will be performing the services.

(e) On satisfactory proof to the court, a personal representative of an estate is entitled to all necessary and reasonable expenses incurred by the personal representative in collecting or attempting to collect a claim or debt owed to the estate or in recovering or attempting to recover property to which the estate has a title or claim.

Sec. 234. Exercise of Powers With and Without Court Order.

(a) Powers To Be Exercised Under Order of the Court. The personal representative of the estate of any person may, upon application and order authorizing same, renew or extend any obligation owing by or to such estate. When a personal representative deems it for the interest of the estate, he may, upon written application to the court, and by order granting authority:

(1) Purchase or exchange property;

(2) Take claims or property for the use and benefit of the estate in payment of any debt due or owing to the estate;

(3) Compound bad or doubtful debts due or owing to the estate;

(4) Make compromises or settlements in relation to property or claims in dispute or litigation;

(5) Compromise or pay in full any secured claim which has been allowed and approved as required by law against the estate by conveying to the holder of such claim the real estate or personalty securing the same, in full payment, liquidation, and satisfaction thereof, and in consideration of cancellation of notes, deeds of trust, mortgages, chattel mortgages, or other evidences of liens securing the payment of such claim.

(b) Powers To Be Exercised Without Court Order. The personal representative of the estate of any person may, without application to or order of the court, exercise the powers listed below, provided, however, that a personal representative under court control may apply and obtain an order if doubtful of the propriety of the exercise of any such powers:

(1) Release liens upon payment at maturity of the debt secured thereby;
(2) Vote stocks by limited or general proxy;
(3) Pay calls and assessments;
(4) Insure the estate against liability in appropriate cases;
(5) Insure property of the estate against fire, theft, and other hazards;
(6) Pay taxes, court costs, bond premiums.

PART 6. COMPENSATION, EXPENSES, AND COURT COSTS

Sec. 241. Compensation of Personal Representatives.

(a) Executors, administrators, and temporary administrators shall be entitled to receive a commission of five per cent (5%) on all sums they may actually receive in cash, and the same per cent on all sums they may actually pay out in cash, in the administration of the estate on a finding by the court that the executor or administrator has taken care of and managed the estate in compliance with the standards of this code; provided, no commission shall be allowed for receiving funds belonging to the testator or intestate which were on hand or were held for the testator or intestate at the time of his death in a financial institution or a brokerage firm, including cash or a cash equivalent held in a checking account, savings account, certificate of deposit, or money market account; nor for collecting the proceeds of any life insurance policy; nor for paying out cash to the heirs or legatees as such; provided, further, however, that in no event shall the executor or administrator be entitled in the aggregate to more than five per cent (5%) of the gross fair market value of the estate subject to administration. If the executor or administrator manages a farm, ranch, factory, or other business of the estate, or if the compensation as calculated above is unreasonably low, the court may allow him reasonable compensation for his services, including unusual effort to collect funds or life insurance. For this purpose, the county court shall have jurisdiction to receive, consider, and act on applications from independent executors. The court may, on application of an interested person or on its own motion, deny a commission allowed by this subsection in whole or in part if:
(1) the court finds that the executor or administrator has not taken care of and managed estate property prudently; or
(2) the executor or administrator has been removed under Section 149C or 222 of this code.

(b) Definition. In this section, "financial institution" means an organization authorized to do business under state or federal laws relating to financial institutions, including banks and trust companies, savings banks, building and loan associations, savings and loan companies or associations, and credit unions.

Sec. 242. Expenses Allowed.

Personal representatives of estates shall also be entitled to all necessary and reasonable expenses incurred by them in the preservation, safekeeping, and management of the estate, and in collecting or attempting to collect claims or debts, and in recovering or attempting to recover property to which the estate has a title or claim, and all reasonable attorney's fees, necessarily incurred in connection with the proceedings and management of such estate, on satisfactory proof to the court.

Sec. 244. Expense Accounts.

All expense charges shall be made in writing, showing specifically each item of expense and the date thereof, and shall be verified by affidavit of the representative, filed with the clerk and entered on the claim docket, and shall be acted on by the court in like manner as other claims against the estate.

Sec. 250. Inventory and Appraisement.

Within ninety days after his qualification, unless a longer time shall be granted by the court, the representative shall file with the clerk of court a verified, full and detailed inventory, in one written instrument, of all the property of such estate which has come to his possession or knowledge, which inventory shall include:

(a) all real property of the estate situated in the State of Texas;

(b) all personal property of the estate wherever situated. The representative shall set out in the inventory his appraisement of the fair market value of each item thereof as of the date of death in the case of grant of letters testamentary or of administration, as the case may be; provided that if the court shall appoint an appraiser or appraisers of the estate, the representative shall determine the fair market value of each item of the inventory with the assistance of such appraiser or appraisers and shall set out in the inventory such appraisement. The inventory shall specify what portion of the property, if any, is separate property and what portion, if any, is community property. If any property is owned in common with others, the interest owned by the estate shall be shown, together with the names and relationship, if known, of co-owners. Such inventory, when approved by the court and duly filed with the clerk of court, shall constitute for all purposes the inventory and appraisement of the estate referred to in this Code. The court for good cause shown may require the filing of the inventory and appraisement at a time prior to ninety days after the qualification of the representative.

Sec. 251. List of Claims.

There shall also be made out and attached to said inventory a full and complete list of all claims due or owing to the estate, which shall state:

(a) The name of each person indebted to the estate and his address when known.

(b) The nature of such debt, whether by note, bill, bond, or other written obligation, or by account or verbal contract.

(c) The date of such indebtedness, and the date when the same was or will be due.

(d) The amount of each claim, the rate of interest thereon, and time for which the same bears interest.

(e) In the case of decedent's estate, which of such claims are separate property and which are of the community.

(f) What portion of the claims, if any, is held in common with others, giving the names and the relationships, if any, of other part owners, and the interest of the estate therein.

Sec. 252. Affidavit to be Attached.

The representative of the estate shall also attach to such inventory and list of claims his affidavit subscribed and sworn to before an officer in the county authorized by law to administer oaths, that the said inventory and list of claims are a true and complete statement of the property and claims of the estate that have come to his knowledge.

Sec. 270. Liability of Homestead for Debts.

The homestead shall not be liable for the payment of any of the debts of the estate, except for the purchase money thereof, the taxes due thereon, or work and material used in constructing improvements thereon; and in this last case only when the work and material are contracted for in writing, with the consent of both spouses given in the same manner as required in making a sale and conveyance of the homestead.

Sec. 271. Exempt Property to Be Set Apart.

(a) Unless an affidavit is filed under Subsection (b) of this section, immediately after the inventory, appraisement, and list of claims have been approved, the court shall, by order, set apart for the use and benefit of the surviving spouse and minor children and unmarried children remaining with the family of the deceased, all such property of the estate as is exempt from execution or forced sale by the constitution and laws of the state.

(b) Before the approval of the inventory, appraisement, and list of claims, a surviving spouse, any person who is authorized to act on behalf of minor children of the deceased, or any unmarried children remaining with the family of the deceased may apply to the court to have exempt property set aside by filing an application and a verified affidavit listing all of the property that the applicant claims is exempt. The applicant bears the burden of proof by a preponderance of the evidence at any hearing on the application. The court shall set aside property of the decedent's estate that the court finds is exempt.

Sec. 272. To Whom Delivered.

The exempt property set apart to the surviving spouse and children shall be delivered by the executor or administrator without delay as follows:

(a) If there be a surviving spouse and no children, or if the children be the children of the surviving spouse, the whole of such property shall be delivered to the surviving spouse.

(b) If there be children and no surviving spouse, such property, except the homestead, shall be delivered to such children if they be of lawful age, or to their guardian if they be minors.

(c) If there be children of the deceased of whom the surviving spouse is not the parent, the share of such children in such exempted property, except the homestead, shall be delivered to such children if they be of lawful age, or to their guardian, if they be minors.

(d) In all cases, the homestead shall be delivered to the surviving spouse, if there be one, and if there be no surviving spouse, to the guardian of the minor children and unmarried children, if any, living with the family.

Sec. 273. Allowance in Lieu of Exempt Property.

In case there should not be among the effects of the deceased all or any of the specific articles exempted from execution or forced sale by the Constitution and laws of this state, the court shall make a reasonable allowance in lieu thereof, to be paid to such surviving spouse and children, or such of them as there are, as hereinafter provided. The allowance in lieu of a homestead shall in no case exceed $15,000 and the allowance for other exempted property shall in no case exceed $5,000, exclusive of the allowance for the support of the surviving spouse and minor children which is hereinafter provided for.

Sec. 274. How Allowance Paid.

The allowance made in lieu of any of the exempted property shall be paid either in money out of the funds of the estate that come to the hands of the executor or administrator, or in any property of the deceased that such surviving spouse or children, if they be of lawful age, or their guardian if they be minors, shall choose to take at the appraisement, or a part thereof, or both, as they shall select; provided, however, that property specifically bequeathed or devised to another may be so taken, or may be sold to raise funds for the allowance as hereinafter provided, only if the other available property shall be insufficient to provide the allowance.

Sec. 275. To Whom Allowance Paid.

The allowance in lieu of exempt property shall be paid by the executor or administrator, as follows:

(a) If there be a surviving spouse and no children, or if all the children be the children of the surviving spouse, the whole shall be paid to such surviving spouse.

(b) If there be children and no surviving spouse, the whole shall be paid to and equally divided among them if they be of lawful age, but if any of such children are minors, their shares shall be paid to their guardian or guardians.

(c) If there be a surviving spouse, and children of the deceased, some of whom are not children of the surviving spouse, the surviving spouse shall receive one-half of the whole, plus the shares of the children of whom the survivor is the parent, and the remaining shares shall be paid to the children of whom the survivor is not the parent, or, if they are minors, to their guardian.

Sec. 276. Sale to Raise Allowance.

If there be no property of the deceased that such surviving spouse or children are willing to take for such allowance, or not a sufficiency, and there be no funds, or not sufficient funds, of the estate in the hands of such executor or administrator to pay such allowance, or any part thereof, the court, on the application in writing of such surviving spouse and children, shall order a sale of so much of the estate for cash as will be sufficient to raise the amount of such allowance, or a part thereof, as the case requires.

Sec. 277. Preference of Liens.

If property upon which there is a valid subsisting lien or encumbrance shall be set apart to the surviving spouse or children as exempt property, or appropriated to make up allowances made in lieu of exempt property or for the support of the surviving spouse or children, the debts secured by such lien shall, if necessity requires, be either paid or continued as against such property. This provision applies to all estates, whether solvent or insolvent.

Sec. 278. When Estate Is Solvent.

If, upon a final settlement of the estate, it shall appear that the same is solvent, the exempted property, except the homestead or any allowance in lieu thereof, shall be subject to partition and distribution among the heirs and distributees of such estate in like manner as the other property of the estate.

Sec. 279. When Estate is Insolvent.

Should the estate, upon final settlement, prove to be insolvent, the title of the surviving spouse and children to all the property and allowances set apart or paid to them under the provisions of this Code shall be absolute, and shall not be taken for any of the debts of the estate except as hereinafter provided.

Sec. 280. Exempt Property Not Considered in Determining Solvency.

In ascertaining whether an estate is solvent or insolvent, the exempt property set apart to the surviving spouse or children, or the allowance in lieu thereof, and the family allowance hereinafter provided for, shall not be estimated or considered as assets of the estate.

Sec. 281. Exempt Property Liable for Certain Debts.

The exempt property, other than the homestead or any allowance made in lieu thereof, shall be liable for the payment of the funeral expenses and the expenses of last sickness of the deceased, when claims are presented within the time prescribed therefor, but such property shall not be liable for any other debts of the estate.

Sec. 282. Nature of Homestead Property Immaterial.

The homestead rights of the surviving spouse and children of the deceased are the same whether the homestead be the separate property of the deceased or community property between the surviving spouse and the deceased, and the respective interests of such surviving spouse and children shall be the same in one case as in the other.

Sec. 283. Homestead Rights of Surviving Spouse.

On the death of the husband or wife, leaving a spouse surviving, the homestead shall descend and vest in like manner as other real property of the deceased and shall be governed by the same laws of descent and distribution.

Sec. 284. When Homestead Not Partitioned.

The homestead shall not be partitioned among the heirs of the deceased during the lifetime of the surviving spouse, or so long as the survivor elects to use or occupy the same as a homestead, or so long as the guardian of the minor children of the deceased is permitted, under the order of the proper court having jurisdiction, to use and occupy the same.

Sec. 285. When Homestead Can Be Partitioned.

When the surviving spouse dies or sells his or her interest in the homestead, or elects no longer to use or occupy the same as a homestead, or when the proper court no longer permits the guardian of the minor children to use and occupy the same as a homestead, it may be partitioned among the respective owners thereof in like manner as other property held in common.

Sec. 286. Family Allowance to Surviving Spouses and Minors.

(a) Unless an affidavit is filed under Subsection (b) of this section, immediately after the inventory, appraisement, and list of claims have been approved, the court shall fix a family allowance for the support of the surviving spouse and minor children of the deceased.

(b) Before the approval of the inventory, appraisement, and list of claims, a surviving spouse or any person who is authorized to act on behalf of minor children of the deceased may apply to the court to have the court fix the family allowance by filing an application and a verified affidavit describing the amount necessary for the maintenance of the surviving spouse and minor children for one year after the date of the death of the decedent and describing the spouse's separate property and any property that minor children have in their own right. The applicant bears the burden of proof by a preponderance of the evidence at any hearing on the application. The court shall fix a family allowance for the support of the surviving spouse and minor children of the deceased.

Sec. 287. Amount of Family Allowance.

Such allowance shall be of an amount sufficient for the maintenance of such surviving spouse and minor children for one year from the time of the death of the testator or intestate. The allowance shall be fixed with regard to the facts or circumstances then existing and those anticipated to exist during the first year after such death. The allowance may be paid either in a lump sum or in installments, as the court shall order.

Sec. 288. When Family Allowance Not Made.

No such allowance shall be made for the surviving spouse when the survivor has separate property adequate to the survivor's maintenance; nor shall such allowance be made for the minor children when they have property in their own right adequate to their maintenance.

Sec. 290. Family Allowance Preferred.

The family allowance made for the support of the surviving spouse and minor children of the deceased shall be paid in preference to all other debts or charges against the estate, except expenses of the funeral and last sickness of the deceased.

Sec. 291. To Whom Family Allowance Paid.

The executor or administrator shall apportion and pay the family allowance:

(a) To the surviving spouse, if there be one, for the use of the survivor and the minor children, if such children be the survivor's.

(b) If the surviving spouse is not the parent of such minor children, or of some of them, the portion of such allowance necessary for the support of such minor child or children of which the survivor is not the parent shall be paid to the guardian or guardians of such child or children.

(c) If there be no surviving spouse, the allowance to the minor child or children shall be paid to the guardian or guardians of such minor child or children.

(d) If there be a surviving spouse and no minor child or children, the entire allowance shall be paid to the surviving spouse.

Sec. 292. May Take Property for Family Allowance.

The surviving spouse, or the guardian of the minor children, as the case may be, shall have the right to take in payment of such allowance, or any part thereof, any of the personal property of the estate at its appraised value as shown by the appraisement; provided, however, that property specifically devised or bequeathed to another may be so taken, or may be sold to raise funds for the allowance as hereinafter provided, only if the other available property shall be insufficient to provide the allowance.

Sec. 293. Sale to Raise Funds for Family Allowance.

If there be no personal property of the deceased that the surviving spouse or guardian is willing to take for such allowance, or not a sufficiency of them, and if there be no funds or not sufficient funds in the hands of such executor or administrator to pay such allowance, or any part thereof, then the court, as soon as the inventory, appraisement, and list of claims are returned and approved, shall order a sale of so much of the estate for cash as will be sufficient to raise the amount of such allowance, or a part thereof, as the case requires.

Sec. 294. Notice by Representative of Appointment.

(a) Giving of Notice Required. Within one month after receiving letters, personal representatives of estates shall send to the comptroller of public accounts by certified or registered mail if the decedent remitted or should have remitted taxes administered by the comptroller of public accounts and publish in some newspaper, printed in the county where the letters were issued, if there be one, a notice requiring all persons having claims against the estate being administered to present the same within the time prescribed by law. The notice shall include the date of issuance of letters held by the representative, the address to which claims may be presented, and an instruction of the representative's choice that claims be addressed in care of the representative, in care of the representative's attorney, or in care of "Representative, Estate of _____" (naming the estate).

(b) Proof of Publication. A copy of such printed notice, together with the affidavit of the publisher, duly sworn to and subscribed before a proper officer, to the effect that the notice was published as provided in this Code for the service of citation or notice by publication, shall be filed in the court where the cause is pending.

(c) When No Newspaper Printed in the County. When no newspaper is printed in the county, the notice shall be posted and the return made and filed as required by this Code.

(d) Permissive Notice to Unsecured Creditors. At any time before an estate administration is closed, the personal representative may give notice by certified or registered mail, with return receipt requested, to an unsecured creditor having a claim for money against the estate expressly stating that the creditor must present a claim within four months after the date of the receipt of the notice or the claim is barred, if the claim is not barred by the general statutes of limitation. The notice must include:

(1) the dates of issuance of letters held by the representative;

(2) the address to which claims may be presented; and

(3) an instruction of the representative's choice that the claim be addressed in care of:

(A) the representative;

(B) the representative's attorney; or

(C) "Representative, Estate of " (naming the estate).

Sec. 295. Notice to Holders of Secured Claims.

(a) When notice required for secured claimants. Within two months after receiving letters, the personal representative of an estate shall give notice of the issuance of such letters to each and every person known to the personal representative to have a claim for money against the estate of a decedent that is secured by real or personal property of the estate. Within a reasonable time after the personal representative obtains actual knowledge of the existence of a person having a secured claim for money and to whom notice was not previously given, the personal representative shall give notice to the person of the issuance of letters.

(b) How notice shall be given. The notice stating the original grant of letters shall be given by mailing same by certified or registered mail, with return receipt requested, addressed to the record holder of such indebtedness or claim at the record holder's last known post office address.

(c) Proof of service of notice. A copy of each notice required by Subsection (a) of this section and a copy of the return receipt and an affidavit of the representative, stating that said notice was mailed as required by law, giving the name of the person to whom the notice was mailed, if not shown on the notice or receipt, shall be filed with the clerk of the court from which letters were issued.

Sec. 298. Claims Against Estates of Decedents.

(a) Time for Presentation of Claims. A claim may be presented to the personal representative at any time before the estate is closed if suit on the claim has not been barred by the general statutes of limitation. If a claim of an unsecured creditor for money is not presented within four months after the date of receipt of the notice permitted by Section 294(d), the claim is barred.

(b) Claims Barred by Limitation Not to Be Allowed or Approved. No claims for money against a decedent, or against the estate of the decedent, on which a suit is barred under Subsection (a) of this section, Section 313, or Section 317(a) or by a general statute of limitation applicable thereto shall be allowed by a personal representative. If allowed by the representative and the court is satisfied that the claim is barred or that limitation has run, the claim shall be disapproved.

Sec. 310. Claims for Money Must be Authenticated.

No personal representative of a decedent's estate shall allow, and the court shall not approve, a claim for money against such estate, unless such claim be supported by an affidavit that the claim is just and that all legal offsets, payments, and credits known to the affiant have been allowed. If the claim is not founded on a written instrument or account, the affidavit shall also state the facts upon which the claim is founded. A photostatic copy of any exhibit or voucher necessary to prove a claim may be offered with and attached to the claim in lieu of the original.

Sec. 309. Memorandum of Allowance or Rejection of Claim.

When a duly authenticated claim against an estate is presented to the representative, or deposited with the clerk as heretofore provided, the representative shall, within thirty days after the claim is presented or deposited, endorse thereon, annex thereto, or file with the clerk a memorandum signed by the representative, stating the date of presentation or depositing of the claim, and that the representative allows or rejects it, or what portion thereof the representative allows or rejects.

Sec. 316. Claims Against Personal Representatives.

The naming of an executor in a will shall not operate to extinguish any just claim which the deceased had against the person named as executor; and, in all cases where a personal representative is indebted to the testator or intestate, the representative shall account for the debt in the same manner as if it were cash in the representative's hands; provided, however, that if said debt was not due at the time of receiving letters, the representative shall be required to account for it only from the date when it becomes due.

Sec. 317. Claims by Personal Representatives.

(a) By Executors or Administrators. The foregoing provisions of this Code relative to the presentation of claims against an estate shall not be construed to apply to any claim of a personal representative against the testator or intestate; but a personal representative holding such claim shall file the same in the court granting the letters, verified by affidavit as required in other cases, within six months after the representative has qualified, or such claim shall be barred.

(b) Action on Such Claims. When a claim by a personal representative has been filed with the court within the required time, such claim shall be entered upon the claim docket and acted upon by the court in the same manner as in other cases, and, when the claim has been acted upon by the court, an appeal from the judgment of the court may be taken as in other cases.

(c) Provisions Not Applicable to Certain Claims. The foregoing provisions relative to the presentment of claims shall not be so construed as to apply to the claim of any heir, devisee, or legatee who claims in such capacity, or to any claim that accrues against the estate after the granting of letters for which the representative of the estate has contracted.

Sec. 319. Claims Not to be Paid Unless Approved.

No claim for money against the estate of a decedent, or any part thereof, shall be paid until it has been approved by the court or established by the judgment of a court of competent jurisdiction.

Sec. 320. Order of Payment of Claims.

(a) Priority of Payments. Personal representatives, when they have funds in their hands belonging to the estate, shall pay in the following order:

(1) Funeral expenses and expenses of last sickness, in an amount not to exceed Five Thousand Dollars.

(2) Allowances made to the surviving spouse and children, or to either.

(3) Expenses of administration and the expenses incurred in the preservation, safekeeping, and management of the estate.

(4) Other claims against the estate in the order of their classification.

(b) Sale of Mortgaged Property. If a personal representative has the proceeds of a sale that has been made for the satisfaction of a mortgage, lien, or security interest, and the proceeds, or any part of the proceeds, are not required for the payment of any debts against the estate that have a preference over the mortgage, lien, or security interest, the personal representative shall pay the proceeds to any holder of a mortgage, lien, or security interest. If there is more than one mortgage, lien, or security interest against the property, the personal representative shall pay the holders in the order of the holders' priority. If the personal representative fails to pay proceeds under this subsection, a holder, on proof of the failure to pay, may obtain an order from the court directing the payment to be made.

(c) Claimant's Petition. A claimant whose claim has not been paid may petition the court for determination of his claim at any time before it is barred by the applicable statute of limitations and upon due proof procure an order for its allowance and payment from the estate.

(d) Permissive Order of Payment. After the sixth month after the date letters are granted and on application by the personal representative stating that the personal representative has no actual knowledge of any outstanding enforceable claims against the estate other than the claims already approved and classified by the court, the court may order the personal representative to pay any claim that is allowed and approved.

Sec. 320A. Funeral Expenses.

When personal representatives pay claims for funeral expenses and for items incident thereto, such as tombstones, grave markers, crypts or burial plots, they shall charge the whole of such claims to the decedent's estate and shall charge no part thereof to the community share of a surviving spouse.

Sec. 321. Deficiency of Assets.

When there is a deficiency of assets to pay all claims of the same class, other than secured claims for money, the claims in such class shall be paid pro rata, as directed by the court, and in the order directed. No personal representative shall be allowed to pay the claims, whether the estate is solvent or insolvent, except with the pro rata amount of the funds of the estate that have come to hand.

Sec. 322. Classification of Claims Against Estates of Decedent.

Claims against an estate of a decedent shall be classified and have priority of payment, as follows:

Class 1. Funeral expenses and expenses of last sickness for a reasonable amount to be approved by the court, not to exceed Five Thousand Dollars, with any excess to be classified and paid as other unsecured claims.

Class 2. Expenses of administration and expenses incurred in the preservation, safekeeping, and management of the estate.

Class 3. Secured claims for money under Section 306(a)(1), including tax liens, so far as the same can be paid out of the proceeds of the property subject to such mortgage or other lien, and when more than one mortgage, lien, or security interest shall exist upon the same property, they shall be paid in order of their priority.

Class 4. Claims for taxes, penalties, and interest due under Title 2, Tax Code; Chapter 8, Title 132, Revised Statutes; Section 81.111, Natural Resources Code; the Municipal Sales and Use Tax Act (Chapter 321, Tax Code); Section 11B, Chapter 141, Acts of the 63rd Legislature, Regular Session, 1973 (Article 1118x, Vernon's Texas Civil Statutes); or Section 16, Chapter 683, Acts of the 66th Legislature, Regular Session, 1979 (Article 1118y, Vernon's Texas Civil Statutes).

Class 5. Claims for the cost of confinement established by the institutional division of the Texas Department of Criminal Justice under Section 501.017, Government Code.

Class 6. Claims for repayment of medical assistance payments made by the state under Chapter 32, Human Resources Code, to or for the benefit of the decedent.

Class 7. All other claims.

Sec. 331. Court Must Order Sales.

Except as hereinafter provided, no sale of any property of an estate shall be made without an order of court authorizing the same. The court may order property sold for cash or on credit, at public auction or privately, as it may consider most to the advantage of the estate, except when otherwise specially provided herein.

Sec. 332. Sales Authorized by Will.

Whenever by the terms of a will an executor is authorized to sell any property of the testator, no order of court shall be necessary to authorize the executor to make such sale, and the sale may be made at public auction or privately as the executor deems to be in the best interest of the estate and may be made for cash or upon such credit terms as the executor shall determine; provided, that when particular directions are given by a testator in his will respecting the sale of any property belonging to his estate, the same shall be followed, unless such directions have been annulled or suspended by order of the court.

Sec. 333. Certain Personal Property to Be Sold.

(a) The representative of an estate, after approval of inventory and appraisement, shall promptly apply for an order of the court to sell at public auction or privately, for cash or on credit not exceeding six months, all of the estate that is liable to perish, waste, or deteriorate in value, or that will be an expense or disadvantage to the estate if kept. Property exempt from forced sale, specific legacies, and personal property necessary to carry on a farm, ranch, factory, or any other business which it is thought best to operate, shall not be included in such sales.

(b) In determining whether to order the sale of an asset under Subsection (a) of this section, the court shall consider:

(1) the representative's duty to take care of and manage the estate as a person of ordinary prudence, discretion, and intelligence would exercise in the management of the person's own affairs; and

(2) whether the asset constitutes an asset that a trustee is authorized to invest under Section 113.056 or Subchapter F, Chapter 113, Property Code.

Sec. 334. Sales of Other Personal Property.

Upon application by the personal representative of the estate or by any interested person, the court may order the sale of any personal property of the estate not required to be sold by the preceding Section, including growing or harvested crops or livestock, but not including exempt property or specific legacies, if the court finds that so to do would be in the best interest of the estate in order to pay expenses of administration, funeral expenses, expenses of last illness, allowances, or claims against the estate, from the proceeds of the sale of such property. In so far as possible, applications and orders for the sale of personal property shall conform to the requirements hereinafter set forth for applications and orders for the sale of real estate.

Sec. 341. Application for Sale of Real Estate.

Application may be made to the court for an order to sell property of the estate when it appears necessary or advisable in order to:

(1) Pay expenses of administration, funeral expenses and expenses of last sickness of decedents, and allowances and claims against the estates of decedents.

(2) Dispose of any interest in real property of the estate of a decedent, when it is deemed to the best interest of the estate to sell such interest.

Sec. 342. Contents of Application for Sale of Real Estate.

An application for the sale of real estate shall be in writing, shall describe the real estate or interest in or part thereof sought to be sold, and shall be accompanied by an exhibit, verified by affidavit, showing fully and in detail the condition of the estate, the charges and claims that have been approved or established by suit, or that have been rejected and may yet be established, the amount of each such claim, the property of the estate remaining on hand liable for the payment of such claims, and any other facts tending to show the necessity or advisability of such sale.

Sec. 346. Order of Sale.

If satisfied upon hearing that the sale of the property of the estate described in the application is necessary or advisable, the court shall order the sale to be made; otherwise, the court may deny the application and may, if it deems best, order the sale of other property the sale of which would be more advantageous to the estate. An order for the sale of real estate shall specify:

(a) The property to be sold, giving such description as will identify it; and

(b) Whether the property is to be sold at public auction or at private sale, and, if at public auction, the time and place of such sale; and

(c) The necessity or advisability of the sale and its purpose; and

(d) Except in cases in which no general bond is required, that, having examined the general bond of the representative of the estate, the court finds it to be sufficient as required by law, or finds the same to be insufficient and specifies the necessary or increased bond, as the case may be; and

(e) That the sale shall be made and the report returned in accordance with law; and

(f) The terms of the sale.

Sec. 348. Permissible Terms of Sale of Real Estate.

(a) For Cash or Credit. The real estate may be sold for cash, or for part cash and part credit, or the equity in land securing an indebtedness may be sold subject to such indebtedness, or with an assumption of such indebtedness, at public or private sale, as appears to the court to be for the best interest of the estate. When real estate is sold partly on credit, the cash payment shall not be less than one-fifth of the purchase price, and the purchaser shall execute a note for the deferred payments payable in monthly, quarterly, semi-annual or annual installments, of such amounts as appears to the court to be for the best interest of the estate, to bear interest from date at a rate of not less than four percent (4%) per annum, payable as provided in such note. Default in the payment of principal or interest, or any part thereof when due, shall, at the election of the holder of such note, mature the whole debt. Such note shall be secured by vendor's lien retained in the deed and in the note upon the property sold, and be further secured by deed of trust upon the property sold, with the usual provisions for foreclosure and sale upon failure to make the payments provided in the deed and notes.

(b) Reconveyance Upon Redemption. When an estate owning real estate by virtue of foreclosure of vendor's lien or mortgage belonging to the estate, either by judicial sale or by a foreclosure suit or through sale under deed of trust or by acceptance of a deed in cancellation of a lien or mortgage owned by the estate, and it appears to the court that an application to redeem the property foreclosed upon has been made by the former owner of the real estate to any corporation or agency now created or hereafter to be created by any Act or Acts of the Congress of the United States or of the State of Texas in connection with legislation for the relief of owners of mortgaged or encumbered homes, farms, ranches, or other real estate, and it further appears to the court that it would be to the best interest of the estate to own bonds of one of the above named federal or state corporations or agencies instead of the real estate, then upon proper application and proof, the court may dispense with the provisions of credit sales as provided above, and may order reconveyance of the property to the former mortgage debtor, or former owner, reserving vendor's lien notes for the total amount of the indebtedness due or for the total amount of bonds which the corporation or agency above named is under its rules and regulations allowed to advance, and, upon obtaining such an order, it shall be proper for the representative to indorse and assign the notes so obtained over to any one of the corporations or agencies above named in exchange for bonds of that corporation or agency.

Sec. 353. Reports of Sale.

All sales of real property of an estate shall be reported to the court ordering the same within thirty days after the sales are made. Reports shall be in writing, sworn to, and filed with the clerk, and noted on the probate docket. They shall show:

(a) The date of the order of sale.

(b) The property sold, describing it.

(c) The time and place of sale.

(d) The name of the purchaser.

(e) The amount for which each parcel of property or interest therein was sold.

(f) The terms of the sale, and whether made at public auction or privately.

(g) Whether the purchaser is ready to comply with the order of sale.

Sec. 399. Annual Accounts Required.

(a) Estates of Decedents Being Administered Under Order of Court. The personal representative of the estate of a decedent being administered under order of court shall, upon the expiration of twelve (12) months from the date of qualification and receipt of letters, return to the court an exhibit in writing under oath setting forth a list of all claims against the estate that were presented to him within the period covered by the account, specifying which have been allowed by him, which have been paid, which have been rejected and the date when rejected, which have been sued upon, and the condition of the suit, and show:

(1) All property that has come to his knowledge or into his possession not previously listed or inventoried as property of the estate.

(2) Any changes in the property of the estate which have not been previously reported.

(3) A complete account of receipts and disbursements for the period covered by the account, and the source and nature thereof, with receipts of principal and income to be shown separately.

(4) A complete, accurate and detailed description of the property being administered, the condition of the property and the use being made thereof, and, if rented, the terms upon and the price for which rented.

(5) The cash balance on hand and the name and location of the depository wherein such balance is kept; also, any other sums of cash in savings accounts or other form, deposited subject to court order, and the name and location of the depository thereof.

(6) A detailed description of personal property of the estate, which shall, with respect to bonds, notes, and other securities, include the names of obligor and obligee, or if payable to bearer, so state; the date of issue and maturity; the rate of interest; serial or other identifying numbers; in what manner the property is secured; and other data necessary to identify the same fully, and how and where held for safekeeping.

(7) A statement that, during the period covered by the account, all tax returns due have been filed and that all taxes due and owing have been paid and a complete account of the amount of the taxes, the date the taxes were paid, and the governmental entity to which the taxes were paid.

(8) If any tax return due to be filed or any taxes due to be paid are delinquent on the filing of the account, a description of the delinquency and the reasons for the delinquency.

(b) Annual Reports Continue Until Estate Closed. Each personal representative of the estate of a decedent shall continue to file annual accounts conforming to the essential requirements of those in Subsection (a) hereof as to changes in the assets of the estate after rendition of the former account so that the true condition of the estate, with respect to money, securities, and other property, can be ascertained by the court or by any interested person, by adding to the balances forward the receipts, and then subtracting the disbursements. The description of property sufficiently described in an inventory or previous account may be by reference thereto.

(c) Supporting Vouchers, etc., Attached to Accounts. Annexed to all annual accounts of representatives of estates shall be:

(1) Proper vouchers for each item of credit claimed in the account, or, in the absence of such voucher, the item must be supported by evidence satisfactory to the court. Original vouchers may, upon application, be returned to the representative after approval of his account.

(2) An official letter from the bank or other depository in which the money on hand of the estate is deposited, showing the amounts in general or special deposits.

(3) Proof of the existence and possession of securities owned by the estate, or shown by the accounting, as well as other assets held by a depository subject to orders of the court, the proof to be by one of the following means:

a. By an official letter from the bank or other depository wherein said securities or other assets are held for safekeeping; provided, that if such depository is the representative, the official letter shall be signed by a representative of such depository other than the one verifying the account; or

b. By a certificate of an authorized representative of the corporation which is surety on the representative's bonds; or

c. By a certificate of the clerk or a deputy clerk of a court of record in this State; or

d. By an affidavit of any other reputable person designated by the court upon request of the representative or other interested party.

Such certificate or affidavit shall be to the effect that the affiant has examined the assets exhibited to him by the representative as assets of the estate in which the accounting is made, and shall describe the assets by reference to the account or otherwise sufficiently to identify those so exhibited, and shall state the time when and the place where exhibited. In lieu of using a certificate or an affidavit, the representative may exhibit the securities to the judge of the court who shall endorse on the account, or include in his order with respect thereto, a statement that the securities shown therein as on hand were in fact exhibited to him, and that those so exhibited were the same as those shown in the account, or note any variance. If the securities are exhibited at any place other than where deposited for safekeeping, it shall be at the expense and risk of the representative. The court may require additional evidence as to the existence and custody of such securities and other personal property as in his discretion he shall deem proper; and may require the representative to exhibit them to the court, or any person designated by him, at any time at the place where held for safekeeping.

(d) Verification of Account. The representative filing the account shall attach thereto his affidavit that it contains a correct and complete statement of the matters to which it relates.

Sec. 404. Closing Administration of Estates of Decedents and Guardianship of Wards or Their Estates.

(a) Administration of the estates of decedents and guardianship of the persons and estates of wards shall be settled and closed:

(1) when all the debts known to exist against the estate of a deceased person have been paid, or when they have been paid so far as the assets in the hands of an administrator or executor of such estate will permit, and when there is no further need for administration;

Sec. 404. Closing Administration of Estates of Decedents.

Administration of the estates of decedents shall be settled and closed when all the debts known to exist against the estate of a deceased person have been paid, or when they have been paid so far as the assets in the hands of an administrator or executor of such estate will permit, and when there is no further need for administration.

Sec. 405. Account for Final Settlement of Estates of Decedents and Persons and Estates of Wards.

When administration of the estate of a decedent, or guardianship of person or estate, or of the person and estate of a ward, is to be settled and closed, the personal representative of such estate or of such ward shall present to the court his verified account for final settlement. In such account it shall be sufficient to refer to the inventory without describing each item of property in detail, and to refer to and adopt any and all proceedings had in the administration or guardianship, as the case may be, concerning sales, renting or hiring, leasing for mineral development, or any other transactions on behalf of the estate or of the ward, as the case may be, including exhibits, accounts, and vouchers previously filed and approved, without restating the particular items thereof. Each final account, however, shall be accompanied by proper vouchers in support of each item thereof not already accounted for and shall show, either by reference to any proceedings authorized above or by statement of the facts:

(a) As to Estates of Decedents.

1. The property belonging to the estate which has come into the hands of the executor or administrator.
2. The disposition that has been made of such property.
3. The debts that have been paid.
4. The debts and expenses, if any, still owing by the estate.
5. The property of the estate, if any, still remaining on hand.
6. The persons entitled to receive such estate, their relationship to the decedent, and their residence, if known, and whether adults or minors, and, if minors, the names of their guardians, if any.
7. All advancements or payments that have been made, if any, by the executor or administrator from such estate to any such person.
8. The tax returns due that have been filed and the taxes due and owing that have been paid and a complete account of the amount of taxes, the date the taxes were paid, and the governmental entity to which the taxes were paid.
9. If any tax return due to be filed or any taxes due to be paid are delinquent on the filing of the account, a description of the delinquency and the reasons for the delinquency.

Sec. 405. Account for Final Settlement of Estates of Decedents.

When administration of the estate of a decedent is to be settled and closed, the personal representative of such estate shall present to the court his verified account for final settlement. In such account it shall be sufficient to refer to the inventory without describing each item of property in detail, and to refer to and adopt any and all proceedings had in the administration concerning sales, renting or hiring, leasing for mineral development, or any other transactions on behalf of the estate, including exhibits, accounts, and vouchers previously filed and approved, without restating the particular items thereof. Each final account, however, shall be accompanied by proper vouchers in support of each item thereof not already accounted for and shall show, either by reference to any proceedings authorized above or by statement of the facts:

1. The property belonging to the estate which has come into the hands of the executor or administrator.
2. The disposition that has been made of such property.
3. The debts that have been paid.
4. The debts and expenses, if any, still owing by the estate.
5. The property of the estate, if any, still remaining on hand.
6. The persons entitled to receive such estate, their relationship to the decedent, and their residence, if known, and whether adults or minors, and, if minors, the names of their guardians, if any.
7. All advancements or payments that have been made, if any, by the executor or administrator from such estate to any such person.

Sec. 407. Citation Upon Presentation of Account for Final Settlement.

Upon the filing of an account for final settlement by temporary or permanent personal representatives of the estates of decedents, citation shall contain a statement that such final account has been filed, the time and place when it will be considered by the court, and a statement requiring the person or persons cited to appear and contest the same if they see proper. Such citation shall be issued by the county clerk to the persons and in the manner set out below.

1. In case of the estates of deceased persons, notice shall be given by the personal representative to each heir or beneficiary of the decedent by certified mail, return receipt requested, unless another type of notice is directed by the court by written order. The notice must include a copy of the account for final settlement.
2. If the court deems further additional notice necessary, it shall require the same by written order. In its discretion, the court may allow the waiver of notice of an account for final settlement in a proceeding concerning a decedent's estate.

Sec. 501. Time to File Application for Informal Probate.

(a) An applicant may file an application for the informal probate of a will with the court clerk not earlier than the 30th day after the date of the testator's death.

(b) A will may not be admitted for informal probate after the fourth anniversary of the date of the testator's death unless the applicant shows that the applicant was not aware of the will's existence and did not cause the failure to timely file the will for probate.

Sec. 502. Eligible Applicants for Informal Probate; Venue.

(a) An executor, alternate, devisee, or legatee named in a will may make an application for the informal probate of the will.

(b) The applicant may file the application in the county in which the testator was domiciled on the date of death or in the county in which the estate assets are located.

Sec. 503. Requirements for Informal Probate.

(a) An applicant may file a will for informal probate with the court clerk:

(1) if:

(A) all of the estate's known debts have been satisfied;

(B) all existing and outstanding debts are secured on real or personal property through certificates of title or by Uniform Commercial Code filings; or

(C) the applicant notifies all creditors of the estate by certified or registered mail of the filing; and

(2) if:

(A) an application has not been filed and is not pending under Section 81, 82, 89, or 145 of this code; and

(B) the applicant files an affidavit of a disinterested witness that contains the proof of facts required to probate a will under Sections 88(a) and (b) of this code.

(b) The applicant submits personally to the jurisdiction of the probate court in any proceeding for relief relating to the informal probate proceeding and distribution of assets and to the suit in the probate court for any actions taken while administering estate assets, including a civil action for perjury or fraud relating to the application.

Sec. 504. Contents of Application.

(a) An application for informal probate of a will must be under oath and must establish:

(1) that 30 days have elapsed after the date of the testator's death;

(2) that all debts of the estate have been satisfied or are properly secured or all creditors have received notice of the application's filing;

(3) that the total gross fair market value of the estate, including real and personal property but not including homestead or exempt property, did not exceed $50,000 on the date the application was prepared;

(4) that the court has venue;

(5) to the applicant's knowledge and belief, that the will being offered for informal probate has never been revoked; and

(6) to the applicant's knowledge and belief, that no person named in the will has objected to the offer of the will for informal probate.

(b) The application must contain the social security number and present address of the applicant and the social security number and last known address of the testator.

Sec. 505. Notice.

(a) Before filing an application for informal probate, the applicant shall give notice of the intent to file the application by certified or registered mail to all persons named in the will whose addresses are known or are reasonably ascertainable and to the decedent's surviving spouse and children and shall provide those persons a copy of the will.

(b) If a distributee named in the will is a minor or incompetent, the applicant shall notify the natural guardian of the minor or the guardian of the person of the incompetent distributee.

(c) The applicant shall file the return receipts or original returned notices with the application.

(d) Notice is not required under this section to a person who joins in the application for informal probate or to a person who waives notice if the person's sworn waiver of notice is filed with the application or is filed before the court considers the application.

Sec. 506. Filing of Will or Affidavit; Inventory.

(a) The applicant must file the will. The will remains in the custody of the court clerk unless removed by order of a proper court.

(b) The applicant shall prepare a sworn, full, and complete inventory of all assets required to be included in the testator's estate. The applicant shall list all assets at the assets' fair market value at or about the time the application was prepared without reduction for any outstanding secured debts. If the valuation of an asset is questioned, the court may, on its own motion or on request of an interested person, appoint an appraiser for the asset and order that the applicant deposit the cost of the appraisal in advance with the court clerk. The applicant shall file the inventory with the application. The inventory must:

(1) contain the information required by Sections 250 and 251 of this code; and

(2) if the testator is survived by a spouse, identify the community assets and list the assets' one-half community value.

(c) The court clerk may not present the application to the judge of the court before the 11th day after the date the application is filed. The court shall determine, in its discretion, whether the application meets the requirements for an application for informal probate and may admit the will for informal probate.

(d) If the court determines that the will is not admissible for informal probate, the denial is not a final adjudication of the validity of the will and does not preclude a subsequent application for probate of the will in a formal probate proceeding.

Sec. 507. Limited Letters Testamentary.

(a) An executor, alternate, devisee, or legatee named in a will may request in an application for the informal probate of the will that the clerk of the probate court issue limited letters testamentary to the applicant for the purpose of transferring title to the assets or interests in the assets of the testator's estate, including any increases to the assets that accrued after the date of the testator's death and that are specifically identified and described in the inventory included in the application or any subsequently filed amended or supplemental inventory.

(b) The letters or a certified copy of the inventory attached to the letters must identify the assets subject to transfer under the letters.

(c) A transfer or an attempt to transfer title to assets of the estate not identified in the letters, including any increases to the assets that may have accrued after the date of the testator's death, is void.

(d) Limited letters are valid for one year after the date of the application's approval.

(e) The judge of the court that issued the original letters may order the issuance of additional letters. The order for additional letters must contain the date that those letters expire. Additional letters are not renewable.

Sec. 508. Review of Application for Informal Probate.

(a) The court in which an application for informal probate has been filed shall determine whether:

(1) the application is complete;

(2) the applicant has acknowledged that all statements of fact contained in the application are true and correct;

(3) the applicant is an executor, alternate, devisee, or legatee named in the will;

(4) venue is correct;

(5) an original, duly executed will is filed with the application;

(6) copies of required notices or waivers by persons named in the will and the surviving spouse, children, and creditors are attached to the application;

(7) an objection has not been made to the request for informal probate by any creditor or person named in the will;

(8) the time for applying for an informal probate has not expired;

(9) the application contains the required information; and

(10) an appraiser is necessary to determine the value of any asset.

(b) The court shall deny the application if:

(1) a personal representative has been appointed in another county;

(2) except as provided by Subsection (d) of this section, this or another will of the decedent has been the subject of a previous probate order in this state; or

(3) the court, in its discretion, determines formal probate is necessary.

(c) The court may probate a will that is a self-proved will under Section 59 of this code without further proof. If the will is not self-proving under Section 59 of this code, the court may, in the absence of an objection, presume compliance with Section 59 of this code if the will is filed with a sworn statement or affidavit of a witness to the execution of the will.

(d) A court may informally probate at any time a will that has been probated by the court of another state on the written application of a representative, devisee, or legatee named in the will. The applicant shall file an authenticated copy of the will and foreign proceedings in place of the original will.

Sec. 509. Effect of Informal Probate.

(a) A person who makes a payment or transfers property under the terms of a will admitted to informal probate or under limited letters is released from liability or responsibility to the same extent as if the payment or transfer had been made to the personal representative of an estate. The person is not required to see the application for informal probate or to inquire into the truth of any statement contained in the application for informal probate. The devisee of an asset is liable to a personal representative, a creditor of the testator, or any person having a superior right or claim of possession or ownership to the asset.

(b) A representative or beneficiary under an informally probated will who acquires property under the will may be liable to the extent of the value of the property actually acquired to a person or creditor of the estate with a superior right or claim to the property for damages caused by the transfer of the property to the representative or beneficiary under the terms of the will.

(c) If a person who is entitled to property of the estate, including the representative, a creditor, a beneficiary, or a guardian, makes a written demand by certified or registered mail containing a certified copy of the probated will and order admitting the will or limited letters to a person in possession of estate property and the person refuses or fails to deliver or transfer the property before the 31st day after the date of the demand, the person who is entitled to the property may file a show cause action in the court that probated the will to recover the property. The person entitled to the property may recover the fair market value of the property, reasonable damages for the loss of use of the property, reasonable attorney fees, and costs of court.

(d) If a beneficiary under a will is a minor or an incompetent without a guardian of the minor's or incompetent's estate, all cash, stocks, bonds, or personal property that can be converted to cash to which the beneficiary is entitled may not be distributed to the natural guardian or guardian of the person. The representative of the estate shall convert the assets to cash and deposit the cash in the court registry until a legal guardian of an estate is appointed or shall deposit the cash as provided by Section 144 of this code for the benefit of the ward.

Sec. 510. Time to Contest Validity of Will.

(a) Except as provided by Subsection (b) or (c) of this section, an interested person may file suit to contest the validity of a will admitted to informal probate not later than two years after the date the will was admitted.

(b) An interested person may institute suit to contest the validity of a will admitted to informal probate for forgery or other fraud not later than two years after the date the forgery or fraud is discovered.

(c) A minor or incompetent person may file suit to contest the validity of a will admitted to informal probate not later than two years after the date the disabilities of the minor or incompetent are removed.

Appendix B
Blank Forms

Be sure to read this book carefully before using any of the following forms. If there is anything you do not understand, consult with an attorney. Below is a list of the forms in this appendix, with the page number listed for where each form begins. Each type of probate administration is listed below, with the forms that only pertain to that type. You may need to supplement these forms with some of the forms from the "Miscellaneous Forms" section. Be sure to read the chapter of this book relating to the type of administration you are using, and read the appropriate checklist (checklists are found at the end of chapters).

Many of the forms included in this book have optional provisions. You may either retype the form, omitting the provisions that do not apply to your situation, or you may use the forms in the book and cross out the provisions that do not apply. The optional provisions are highlighted in bold in the text or are separated by the word "**OR**."

Independent Administration

form 1: APPLICATION FOR PROBATE OF WILL AND ISSUANCE OF LETTERS TESTAMENTARY . . 103

form 2: PROOF OF DEATH AND OTHER FACTS 105

form 3: ORDER ADMITTING WILL TO PROBATE AND AUTHORIZING LETTERS TESTAMENTARY . . . 107

form 4: OATH 109

Regular Dependent Administration (RDA)

form 5: APPLICATION FOR LETTERS OF ADMINISTRATION 111

form 6: PROOF OF DEATH AND OTHER FACTS 113

form 7: ORDER AUTHORIZING LETTERS OF ADMINISTRATION 115

form 8: OATH OF ADMINISTRATOR 117

Administration with Will Annexed (AWA)

form 9: APPLICATION FOR PROBATE OF WILL AND ISSUANCE OF
LETTERS TESTAMENTARY WITH WILL ANNEXED 119

form 10: PROOF OF DEATH AND OTHER FACTS 121

form 11: ORDER ADMITTING WILL TO PROBATE AND AUTHORIZING
LETTERS TESTAMENTARY WITH WILL ANNEXED 123

form 12: OATH 125

Administration with Dependent Executor (ADE)

form 13: APPLICATION FOR PROBATE OF WILL AND
ISSUANCE OF LETTERS TESTAMENTARY 127

form 14: PROOF OF DEATH AND OTHER FACTS 129

form 15: ORDER ADMITTING WILL TO PROBATE AND AUTHORIZING
LETTERS TESTAMENTARY 131

form 16: OATH 133

Muniment of Title

form 17: APPLICATION FOR PROBATE OF WILL AS A MUNIMENT OF TITLE 135

form 18: PROOF OF DEATH AND OTHER FACTS 137

form 19: ORDER ADMITTING WILL TO PROBATE AS A MUNIMENT OF TITLE 139

form 20: AFFIDAVIT REGARDING FULFILLMENT OF WILL ADMITTED TO PROBATE AS A
MUNIMENT OF TITLE 141

Heirship Determination

form 21: APPLICATION TO DETERMINE HEIRSHIP 143

form 22: STATEMENT OF FACTS 147

form 23: JUDGMENT DECLARING HEIRSHIP 149

Small Estate

form 24: SMALL ESTATE AFFIDAVIT AND ORDER 151

Miscellaneous Forms

form 25: MOTION TO OPEN SAFE DEPOSIT BOX AND TO EXAMINE PAPERS 157

form 26: APPOINTMENT OF RESIDENT AGENT 159

form 27: PROOF OF SUBSCRIBING WITNESS 161

form 28: NOTICE TO CREDITORS 163

form 29: PROOF OF SERVICE OF NOTICE UPON CLAIMANTS AGAINST ESTATE 165

form 30: PUBLISHER'S AFFIDAVIT 167

form 31: APPLICATION FOR EMPLOYER IDENTIFICATION NUMBER (IRS FORM SS-4) 169

form 32: INVENTORY, APPRAISEMENT AND LIST OF CLAIMS 177

form 33: ORDER APPROVING INVENTORY AND APPRAISEMENT 181

form 34: APPLICATION TO SET ASIDE EXEMPT PROPERTY 183

form 35: ORDER TO SET ASIDE EXEMPT PROPERTY 185

form 36: APPLICATION FOR FAMILY ALLOWANCE 187

form 37: ORDER FOR FAMILY ALLOWANCE 189

form 38: AFFIDAVIT REGARDING DEBTS AND TAXES 191

form 39: ANNUAL ACCOUNT 193

form 40: ORDER APPROVING ANNUAL ACCOUNT. 197

form 41: ACCOUNT FOR FINAL SETTLEMENT 199

form 42: ORDER APPROVING ACCOUNT FOR FINAL SETTLEMENT AND AUTHORIZING
DISTRIBUTION OF ESTATE 203

form 43: RECEIPT AND RELEASE. 205

form 44: APPLICATION TO CLOSE ESTATE AND TO DISCHARGE PERSONAL REPRESENTATIVE . . . 207

form 45: ORDER CLOSING ESTATE AND DISCHARGING PERSONAL REPRESENTATIVE. 209

form 46: NOTICE CONCERNING FIDUCIARY RELATIONSHIP (IRS FORM 56). 211

form 47: AFFIDAVIT OF HEIRSHIP 213

form 48: U.S. INDIVIDUAL INCOME TAX RETURN (IRS FORM 1040) 215

form 1

NO._____

ESTATE OF § IN THE PROBATE COURT
§
_____, § NO. _____ OF
§
DECEASED § _____ COUNTY,
TEXAS

APPLICATION FOR PROBATE OF WILL
AND ISSUANCE OF LETTERS TESTAMENTARY

TO THE HONORABLE JUDGE OF SAID COURT:

_____ ("Applicant") furnishes the following information to the Court for the probate of the written Last Will and Testament of _____ ("Decedent") and for issuance of Letters Testamentary to Applicant:

    1.   Applicant is an individual interested in this Estate, domiciled and residing at _____, _____ County, Texas _____.

    2.   Decedent died _____, _____, in _____ _____, _____ County, Texas, at the age of ____ years.

    3.   Decedent was domiciled and resided at _____ _____, _____ County, Texas _____.

    4.   This Court has jurisdiction and venue because Decedent was domiciled and had a fixed place of residence in this county on the date of death.

    5.   Decedent owned personal property described generally as cash, securities, automobiles, home, household goods, personal effects, etc. of a probable value in excess of $_____.

    6.   Decedent left a valid written will ("Will") dated _____, _____, which was never revoked and is filed herewith.

    7.   The subscribing witnesses to the Will are _____, whose current address is _____, _____, Texas, _____, and _____,

whose current address is _____,
_____, Texas, _____.

    8.   The will was made self proved in the manner prescribed by law.

    9.   No child or children were born to or adopted by Decedent after the date of the Will.

OR

    9.   After the date of the Will, _____, who survived Decedent was born to or adopted by Decedent.

    10.   Decedent was never divorced.

OR

    10.   Decedent was divorced from _____, on _____, _____.

OR

    10.   Decedent was divorced from _____, the date or place of which divorce is not known to Applicant.

    11.   A necessity exists for the administration of this Estate.

    12.   Decedent's Will named Applicant to serve without bond or other security as Independent Executor.

    13.   Applicant would not be disqualified by law from serving as Executor or from accepting Letters Testamentary and Applicant would be entitled to such Letters.

    14.   No state, governmental agency of a state, or charitable organization is named as a devisee in the Will.

    Applicant prays that citation issue as required by law to all persons interested in this Estate; that the Will be admitted to probate; that Letters Testamentary be issued to Applicant; and that all other orders be entered as the Court may deem proper.

    Respectfully submitted,

_____

Print Name:_____

form 2

NO._____

ESTATE OF § IN THE PROBATE COURT
§
_____, § NO. _____ OF
§
DECEASED § _____, COUNTY,
TEXAS

PROOF OF DEATH AND OTHER FACTS

On this day, _____ ("Affiant") personally appeared in Open Court, and after being duly sworn, stated the following:

1. _____ ("Decedent") died on _____, _____ , in _____, Texas, at the age of _____ years, and four years have not elapsed since the date of Decedent's death.

2. Decedent was domiciled and had a fixed place of residence in this County at the date of death.

3. The document dated _____, _____, now shown to me and which purports to be Decedent's Will was never revoked so far as I know.

4. A necessity exists for the administration of this Estate.

5. No child or children were born to or adopted by Decedent after the date of the Will.

OR

5. After the date of the Will, _____ , who survived Decedent was born to or adopted by Decedent.

6. Decedent was never divorced.

OR

6. Decedent was divorced from, _____,
on _____.

OR

6. Decedent was divorced from _____,
the date and place of the divorce is not known to me.

7. The Independent Executor named in the Will is not disqualified by law from accepting Letters Testamentary or from serving as such and is entitled to such Letters.

SIGNED this _____ day of _____, _____.

_____
Print Name:_____
Affiant

SUBSCRIBED AND SWORN TO BEFORE ME by _____
_____this _____ day of _____, _____,
to certify which witness by hand and seal of office.

Clerk of the Probate Court of
_____ County, Texas

By_____
Deputy

form 3

NO._____

ESTATE OF   §   IN THE PROBATE COURT
                                        §
_____, §   NO. _____ OF
                                        §
DECEASED   §   _____ COUNTY, TEXAS

ORDER ADMITTING WILL TO PROBATE AND
AUTHORIZING LETTERS TESTAMENTARY

On this day the Court heard the Application for Probate of Will and Issuance of Letters Testamentary filed by _____ ("Applicant") in the Estate of _____, Deceased ("Decedent").

The Court heard the evidence and reviewed the Will and the other documents filed herein and finds that the allegations contained in the Application are true; that notice and citation have been given in the manner and for the length of time required by law; that Decedent is dead and that four years have not elapsed since the date of Decedent's death; that this Court has jurisdiction and venue of the Decedent's estate; that Decedent left a Will dated _____, _____, which was executed with the formalities and solemnities and under the circumstances required by law to make them a valid Will ("the Will"); that on such date Decedent had attained the age of 18 years and was of sound mind; that the Will was not revoked by Decedent; that no objection to or contest of the probate of the Will has been filed; that all of the necessary proof required for the probate of the Will has been made; that the Will is entitled to probate; that in the Will, Decedent named Applicant as Independent Executor, to serve without bond; that Applicant is duly qualified and not disqualified by law to act as such and to receive Letters Testamentary; that a necessity exists for the administration of this Estate; and that no interested person has applied for the appointment of appraisers and none are deemed necessary by the Court.

It is ORDERED that the valid Will is admitted to probate and the Clerk of this Court is ORDERED to record the Will together with the Application, in the Minutes of the Court.

107

It is ORDERED that no bond or other security is required and that upon the taking and filing of the Oath required by law, Letters Testamentary shall issue to _____ _____ who is appointed as Independent Executor of Decedent's Will and Estate, and no other action shall be had in this Court other than the return of an Inventory, Appraisement, and List of Claims as required by law.

SIGNED this _____ day of _____, _____.

_____
Judge Presiding

form 4

NO._____

ESTATE OF	§	IN THE PROBATE COURT
	§	
_____,	§	NO. _____ OF
	§	
DECEASED	§	_____ COUNTY, TEXAS

OATH

I do solemnly swear that the writing which has been offered for probate is the Will of _____, so far as I know or believe, and that I will well and truly perform all the duties of Independent Executor of the Estate of _____, Deceased.

_____

Print Name:_____

STATE OF)
)
COUNTY OF)

SUBSCRIBED AND SWORN to before me by _____ _____ this _____ day of _____, _____, to certify which, witness my hand and seal of office.

_____

Notary Public in and for
_____ County,
State of_____

My Commission Expires:

This page intentionally left blank.

form 5

NO._____

ESTATE OF	§	IN THE PROBATE COURT
	§	
_____,	§	NO. _____ OF
	§	
DECEASED	§	_____ COUNTY, TEXAS

APPLICATION FOR LETTERS OF ADMINISTRATION

_____ ("Applicant") furnishes the following information to the Court concerning the Estate of _____ _____, Deceased ("Decedent"), and for issuance of Letters of Administration to Applicant:

1. Applicant is an individual interested in this Estate, domiciled in and residing at _____, _____ County, Texas, is entitled to Letters of Administration, is not disqualified by law, and is Decedent's _____.

2. Decedent died intestate on _____ in _____ _____, _____County, _____, at the age of _____ years.

3. This Court has jurisdiction and venue because Decedent was domiciled and had a fixed place of residence in this county on the date of death.

4. Decedent owned real and personal property described generally as_____ _____ _____of a probable value in excess of $ _____.

5. The name, age, marital status, address, and relationship of each heir to Decedent is as follows:

Name	Age	Marital Status	Address	Relationship to Decedent
_____	___	_____	_____	_____
_____	___	_____	_____	_____
_____	___	_____	_____	_____
_____	___	_____	_____	_____

6. No child or children were born to or adopted by Decedent.

OR

6. The children born to or adopted by Decedent were:

Name Date of Birth Place of Birth

_____ _____ _____
_____ _____ _____
_____ _____ _____
_____ _____ _____
_____ _____ _____

7. Decedent was never divorced.

OR

7. Decedent was divorced from _____ on _____.

OR

7. Decedent was divorced from _____, the date or place of which divorce is not known to Applicant.

8. A necessity exists for the administration of this estate.

9. There is no need for the appointment of appraisers.

Applicant prays that citation issue as required by law to all persons interested in this Estate; that Applicant be appointed Administrator of this Estate; that Letters of Administration be issued to Applicant; that appraisers not be appointed; and that all other orders be entered as the Court may deem proper.

 Respectfully submitted,

 _____
 Print Name:_____

form 6

NO._____

ESTATE OF § IN THE PROBATE COURT
§
§
_____, § NO. _____ OF
§
DECEASED § _____ COUNTY, TEXAS

PROOF OF DEATH AND OTHER FACTS

On this day _____ ("Affiant") personally appeared in Open Court, and after being duly sworn, stated the following:

1. _____ ("Decedent") died on _____, in _____, _____ County, _____, at the age of _____ years, and four years have not elapsed since the date of Decedent's death.

2. Decedent was domiciled and had a fixed place of residence in this County at the date of death.

3. So far as I know and believe, Decedent did not leave a Will.

4. A necessity exists for the administration of this Estate.

5. The Applicant for Letters of Administration is not disqualified by law from accepting Letters of Administration or from serving as Administrator of this Estate, and is entitled to such Letters.

SIGNED this _____ day of _____, _____.

_____
Print Name: _____
Affiant

SUBSCRIBED AND SWORN TO BEFORE ME by _____ _____ this _____ day of _____, _____, to certify which witness by hand and seal of office.

Clerk of the Probate Court of
_____County, Texas

By _____
Deputy

113

This page intentionally left blank.

NO. _____

ESTATE OF § IN THE PROBATE COURT
§
_____, § NO. _____ OF
§
DECEASED § _____ COUNTY, TEXAS

ORDER AUTHORIZING LETTERS OF ADMINISTRATION

On this day the Court heard the Application For Letters of Administration filed by _____ ("Applicant") in the Estate of _____, Deceased ("Decedent").

The Court heard the evidence and reviewed the documents filed herein and finds that the allegations contained in the Application are true; that notice and citation have been given in the manner and for the length of time required by law; that Decedent is dead and that four years have not elapsed since the date of Decedent's death; that this Court has jurisdiction and venue of the Decedent's estate; that Decedent died intestate; that there is a necessity for administration of this Estate; that the Application for Letters of Administration should be granted; that Applicant is entitled by law to be appointed Administrator of this Estate and is not disqualified from acting as such Administrator and is qualified to receive Letters of Administration; and that no interested person has applied for the appointment of appraisers and none are deemed necessary by the Court.

It is ORDERED that a bond in the sum of $ _____ payable and conditioned as required by law shall be required, and that upon the taking and filing of the Oath required by law, Letters of Administration shall issue to _____ who is appointed as Administrator of this Estate.

SIGNED, this _____ day of _____, _____.

_____
Judge Presiding

This page intentionally left blank.

NO._____

ESTATE OF § IN THE PROBATE COURT
§
_____, § NO. _____ OF
§
DECEASED § _____ COUNTY, TEXAS

OATH OF ADMINISTRATOR

    I do solemnly swear that _____ ("Decedent") died without leaving any lawful will, so far as I know or believe, and that I will well and truly perform all of the duties of Administrator of Decedent's Estate.

_____

Print Name:_____

STATE OF)
)
COUNTY OF)

    SUBSCRIBED AND SWORN to before me by _____ _____ this _____day of _____, _____, to certify which, witness my hand and seal of office.

_____
Notary Public in and for
_____ County,
State of _____

My Commission Expires:

This page intentionally left blank.

NO._____

ESTATE OF	§	IN THE PROBATE COURT
_____,	§	NO. _____ OF
DECEASED	§	_____ COUNTY, TEXAS

APPLICATION FOR PROBATE OF WILL
AND ISSUANCE OF LETTERS OF ADMINISTRATION WITH WILL ANNEXED

TO THE HONORABLE JUDGE OF SAID COURT:

_____ ("Applicant") furnishes the following information to the Court for the probate of the written Last Will and Testament of _____ ("Decedent") and for issuance of Letters Administration to Applicant:

    1.   Applicant is an individual interested in this Estate, domiciled and residing at _____, _____, _____ County, Texas _____.

    2.   Decedent died _____, _____, in _____, _____, _____ County, Texas, at the age of _____ years.

    3.   Decedent was domiciled and resided at _____ _____, _____, _____ County, Texas _____.

    4.   This Court has jurisdiction and venue because Decedent was domiciled and had a fixed place of residence in this county on the date of death.

    5.   Decedent owned personal property described generally as cash, securities, automobiles, home, household goods, personal effects, etc. of a probable value in excess of $_____.

    6.   Decedent left a valid written will ("Will") dated _____, _____, which was never revoked and is filed herewith.

7. The subscribing witnesses to the Will are _____, whose current address is _____, _____, Texas, _____, and _____ _____, whose current address is _____ _____, _____, Texas, _____.

8. The will was made self proved in the manner prescribed by law.

9. No child or children were born to or adopted by Decedent after the date of the Will.

OR

9. After the date of the Will, _____ _____, who survived Decedent was born to or adopted by Decedent.

10. Decedent was never divorced.

OR

10. Decedent was divorced from _____ on _____, _____.

OR

10. Decedent was divorced from _____, the date or place of which divorce is not known to Applicant.

11. A necessity exists for the administration of this Estate.

12. Decedent's Will named _____ to serve without bond or other security as Executor, but _____ is unable or not qualified to serve as such.

13. Applicant is Decedent's _____, is qualified to be appointed as Administrator With Will Annexed of the Estate, and is not disqualified by law to act as such.

14. No state, governmental agency of a state, or charitable organization is named as a devisee in the Will.

Applicant prays that citation issue as required by law to all persons interested in this Estate; that the Will be admitted to probate; that Letters of Administration be issued to Applicant; and that all other orders be entered as the Court may deem proper.

Respectfully submitted,

_____
Print Name:_____

form 10

NO._____

ESTATE OF	§	IN THE PROBATE COURT
	§	
_____,	§	NO. _____ OF
	§	
DECEASED	§	_____ COUNTY, TEXAS

PROOF OF DEATH AND OTHER FACTS

On this day, _____ ("Affiant") personally appeared in Open Court, and after being duly sworn, stated the following:

1. _____ ("Decedent") died on _____, _____, in _____, Texas, at the age of _____ years and four years have not elapsed since the date of Decedent's death.

2. Decedent was domiciled and had a fixed place of residence in this County at the date of death.

3. The document, dated _____, _____, now shown to me and which purports to be Decedent's Will was never revoked so far as I know.

4. A necessity exists for the administration of this Estate.

5. No child or children were born to or adopted by Decedent after the date of the Will.

OR

5. After the date of the Will, _____ _____, who survived Decedent was born to or adopted by Decedent.

6. Decedent was never divorced.

OR

6. Decedent was divorced from _____ on_____, _____.

OR

6. Decedent was divorced from _____, the date and place of the divorce is not known to me.

121

7. The Independent Executor named in the Will is unable or not qualified to serve as such.

8. _____ , Applicant herein, is not disqualified by law from accepting Letters of Administration or from serving as Administrator With Will Annexed of this Estate, and is entitled to such Letters.

SIGNED this _____ day of _____, _____.

_____

_____
Print Name:_____
Affiant

SUBSCRIBED AND SWORN TO BEFORE ME by _____ this _____ day of _____, _____, to certify which witness by hand and seal of office.

Clerk of the Probate Court of
_____ County, Texas

By _____
Deputy

form 11

NO. _____

ESTATE OF	§	IN THE PROBATE COURT
	§	
_____,	§	NO. _____ OF
	§	
DECEASED	§	_____ COUNTY, TEXAS

ORDER ADMITTING WILL TO PROBATE AND AUTHORIZING LETTERS OF ADMINISTRATION WITH WILL ANNEXED

On this day the Court heard the Application for Probate of Will and Issuance of Letters of Administration filed by _____ ("Applicant") in the Estate of _____, Deceased ("Decedent").

The Court heard the evidence and reviewed the Will and the other documents filed herein and finds that the allegations contained in the Application are true; that notice and citation have been given in the manner and for the length of time required by law; that Decedent is dead and that four years have not elapsed since the date of Decedent's death; that this Court has jurisdiction and venue of the Decedent's estate; that Decedent left a Will dated _____, _____, which was executed with the formalities and solemnities and under the circumstances required by law to make them a valid Will ("the Will"); that on such date Decedent had attained the age of 18 years and was of sound mind; that the Will was not revoked by Decedent; that no objection to or contest of the probate of the Will has been filed; that all of the necessary proof required for the probate of the Will has been made; that the Will is entitled to probate; that in the Will, Decedent named _____ as Independent Executor, to serve without bond, but _____ is not able or qualified to serve as such and Letters Testamentary cannot be authorized; that Applicant is not disqualified by law, but is qualified to be Administrator With Will Annexed and to receive Letters of Administration; that a necessity exists for the administration of this Estate; and that no interested person has applied for the appointment of appraisers and none are deemed necessary by the Court.

It is ORDERED that the valid Will is admitted to probate and the Clerk of this Court is ORDERED to record the Will together with the Application, in the Minutes of the Court.

It is ORDERED a bond in the sum of $ _____ payable and conditioned as required by law shall be required and that upon the taking and filing of the Oath required by law, Letters of Administration shall issue to _____ who is appointed as Administrator With Will Annexed of this Estate.

SIGNED this _____ day of _____ , _____.

_____
Judge Presiding

123

This page intentionally left blank.

form 12

NO._____

ESTATE OF § IN THE PROBATE COURT
§
_____, § NO. _____ OF
§
DECEASED § _____ COUNTY, TEXAS

OATH

I do solemnly swear that the writing which has been offered for probate is the Will of _____, so far as I know or believe, and that I will well and truly perform all the duties of Administrator With Will Annexed of the Estate of _____, Deceased.

_____
Print Name:_____

STATE OF)
)
COUNTY OF)

SUBSCRIBED AND SWORN to before me by _____ _____ this _____ day of _____, _____, to certify which, witness my hand and seal of office.

_____
Notary Public in and for
_____ County,
State of_____

My Commission Expires:

125

This page intentionally left blank.

NO._____

ESTATE OF § IN THE PROBATE COURT
§
§
_____, § NO. _____ OF
§
§
DECEASED § _____ COUNTY, TEXAS

APPLICATION FOR PROBATE OF WILL
AND ISSUANCE OF LETTERS TESTAMENTARY

TO THE HONORABLE JUDGE OF SAID COURT:

_____ ("Applicant") furnishes the following information to the Court for the probate of the written Last Will and Testament of _____ ("Decedent") and for issuance of Letters Testamentary to Applicant:

    1.   Applicant is an individual interested in this Estate, domiciled and residing at _____, _____, _____ County, Texas _____.

    2.   Decedent died _____, _____, in _____ _____, _____ County, Texas, at the age of _____ years.

    3.   Decedent was domiciled and resided at _____ _____, _____, _____ County, Texas _____.

    4.   This Court has jurisdiction and venue because Decedent was domiciled and had a fixed place of residence in this county on the date of death.

    5.   Decedent owned personal property described generally as cash, securities, automobiles, home, household goods, personal effects, etc. of a probable value in excess of $_____.

    6.   Decedent left a valid written will ("Will") dated _____, _____, which was never revoked and is filed herewith.

    7.   The subscribing witnesses to the Will are _____, whose current address is _____,

_____, Texas, _____ and _____, whose current address is _____, _____, Texas, _____.

8. The will was made self proved in the manner prescribed by law.

9. No child or children were born to or adopted by Decedent after the date of the Will.

OR

9. After the date of the Will, _____, who survived Decedent was born to or adopted by Decedent.

10. Decedent was never divorced.

OR

10. Decedent was divorced from _____ on _____, _____.

OR

10. Decedent was divorced from _____, the date or place of which divorce is not known to Applicant.

11. A necessity exists for the administration of this Estate.

12. Decedent's Will named Applicant to serve without bond or other security as Executor but did not specify that Applicant would be Independent nor did Decedent specify that no action shall be had in any court in relation to the settlement of the estate other than the probating and recording of the Will, and the return of an inventory, appraisement and list of claims of the estate.

13. Applicant would not be disqualified by law from serving as Executor or from accepting Letters Testamentary and Applicant would be entitled to such Letters.

14. No state, governmental agency of a state, or charitable organization is named as a devisee in the Will.

Applicant prays that citation issue as required by law to all persons interested in this Estate; that the Will be admitted to probate; that Letters Testamentary be issued to Applicant; and that all other orders be entered as the Court may deem proper.

Respectfully submitted,

_____
Print Name:_____

form 14

NO._____

ESTATE OF	§	IN THE PROBATE COURT
	§	
_____,	§	NO. _____ OF
	§	
DECEASED	§	_____ COUNTY, TEXAS

PROOF OF DEATH AND OTHER FACTS

On this day, _____ ("Affiant") personally appeared in Open Court, and after being duly sworn, stated the following:

1. _____ ("Decedent") died on _____, 20_____, in _____, Texas, at the age of _____ years and four years have not elapsed since the date of Decedent's death.

2. Decedent was domiciled and had a fixed place of residence in this County at the date of death.

3. The document dated _____, _____, now shown to me and which purports to be Decedent's Will was never revoked so far as I know.

4. A necessity exists for the administration of this Estate.

5. No child or children were born to or adopted by Decedent after the date of the Will.

OR

5. After the date of the Will, _____, who survived Decedent was born to or adopted by Decedent.

6. Decedent was never divorced.

OR

6. Decedent was divorced from _____ on _____, _____.

OR

6. Decedent was divorced from _____, the date and place of the divorce is not known to me.

129

7. _____, Applicant herein, is not disqualified by law from accepting Letters Testamentary or from serving as Executor of this Estate and is entitled to such Letters.

SIGNED this _____ day of _____, _____.

_____
Print Name:_____
Affiant

SUBSCRIBED AND SWORN TO BEFORE ME by _____ this _____ day of _____, _____, to certify which witness by hand and seal of office.

Clerk of the Probate Court of
_____ County, Texas

By_____
   Deputy

form 15

NO._____

ESTATE OF	§	IN THE PROBATE COURT
	§	
_____,	§	NO. _____ OF
	§	
DECEASED	§	_____ COUNTY, TEXAS

ORDER ADMITTING WILL TO PROBATE AND AUTHORIZING LETTERS TESTAMENTARY

On this day the Court heard the Application for Probate of Will and Issuance of Letters Testamentary filed by _____ ("Applicant") in the Estate of _____, Deceased ("Decedent").

The Court heard the evidence and reviewed the Will and the other documents filed herein and finds that the allegations contained in the Application are true; that notice and citation have been given in the manner and for the length of time required by law; that Decedent is dead and that four years have not elapsed since the date of Decedent's death; that this Court has jurisdiction and venue of the Decedent's estate; that Decedent left a Will dated _____, _____, which was executed with the formalities and solemnities and under the circumstances required by law to make them a valid Will ("the Will"); that on such date Decedent had attained the age of 18 years and was of sound mind; that the Will was not revoked by Decedent; that no objection to or contest of the probate of the Will has been filed; that all of the necessary proof required for the probate of the Will has been made; that the Will is entitled to probate; that in the Will, Decedent named Applicant as Executor, to serve without bond but did not specify that Applicant would be Independent or otherwise provide for an independent administration of the estate; that Applicant is duly qualified and not disqualified by law to act as such and to receive Letters Testamentary; that a necessity exists for the administration of this Estate; and that no interested person has applied for the appointment of appraisers and none are deemed necessary by the Court.

It is ORDERED that the valid Will is admitted to probate and the Clerk of this Court is ORDERED to record the Will together with the Application, in the Minutes of the Court.

It is ORDERED that no bond or other security is required and that upon the taking and filing of the Oath required by law, Letters Testamentary shall issue to _____ who is appointed as Executor of Decedent's Will and Estate.

SIGNED this _____ day of _____, _____.

_____
Judge Presiding

This page intentionally left blank.

form 16

NO._____

ESTATE OF	§	IN THE PROBATE COURT
	§	
	§	
_____,	§	NO. _____ OF
	§	
DECEASED	§	_____ COUNTY, TEXAS

OATH

I do solemnly swear that the writing which has been offered for probate is the Will of _____, so far as I know or believe, and that I will well and truly perform all the duties of Executor of the Estate of _____, Deceased.

_____

Print Name:_____

STATE OF   )
)
COUNTY OF   )

SUBSCRIBED AND SWORN to before me by _____
_____ this _____ day of _____, _____, to certify which, witness my hand and seal of office.

_____
Notary Public in and for
_____ County,
State of_____

My Commission Expires:

This page intentionally left blank.

form 17

NO._____

ESTATE OF	§	IN THE PROBATE COURT
	§	
_____,	§	NO. _____ OF
	§	
DECEASED	§	_____ COUNTY, TEXAS

APPLICATION FOR PROBATE OF WILL
AS A MUNIMENT OF TITLE

TO THE HONORABLE JUDGE OF SAID COURT:

_____ ("Applicant") furnishes the following information to the Court for the probate of the written Last Will and Testament of _____ ("Decedent") as a Muniment of Title:

1. Applicant is an individual interested in this Estate, domiciled and residing at _____, _____, _____ County, Texas _____.

2. Decedent died _____, _____, in _____, _____ County, Texas, at the age of _____ years.

3. Decedent was domiciled and resided at _____ _____, _____, _____ County, Texas _____.

4. This Court has jurisdiction and venue because Decedent was domiciled and had a fixed place of residence in this county on the date of death.

5. Decedent owned personal property described generally as cash, securities, automobiles, home, household goods, personal effects, etc. of a probable value in excess of $_____.

6. Decedent left a valid written will ("Will") dated _____, _____, which was never revoked and is filed herewith.

7. The subscribing witnesses to the Will are _____, whose current address is _____, _____, Texas, _____ , and _____,

135

whose current address is _____,
_____, Texas, _____.

    8.   The will was made self proved in the manner prescribed by law.

    9.   No child or children were born to or adopted by Decedent after the date of the Will.

OR

    9.   After the date of the Will, _____
_____,
who survived Decedent are children born to or adopted by Decedent.

    10.   Decedent was never divorced.

OR

    10.   Decedent was divorced from _____
on _____, _____.

OR

    10.   Decedent was divorced from _____,
the date or place of which divorce is not known to Applicant.

    11.   There are no debts owed by Decedent which are not secured by liens upon real estate and there is no necessity for any administration of this Estate.

    12.   Decedent's Will named Applicant to serve without bond or other security as Independent Executor.

    13.   Applicant would not be disqualified by law from serving as Executor or from accepting Letters Testamentary and Applicant would be entitled to such Letters.

    14.   No state, governmental agency of a state, or charitable organization is named as a devisee in the Will.

Applicant prays that citation issue as required by law to all persons interested in this Estate; that the Will be admitted to probate as a Muniment of Title and without any administration thereon; and that all other orders be entered as the Court may deem proper.

    Respectfully submitted,

_____
Print Name:_____

form 18

NO. _____

ESTATE OF	§	IN THE PROBATE COURT
	§	
_____,	§	NO. _____ OF
	§	
DECEASED	§	_____ COUNTY, TEXAS

PROOF OF DEATH AND OTHER FACTS

On this day, _____ ("Affiant") personally appeared in Open Court, and after being duly sworn, stated the following:

1. _____ ("Decedent") died on _____, _____, in _____, Texas, at the age of _____ years, and four years have not elapsed since the date of Decedent's death.

2. Decedent was domiciled and had a fixed place of residence in this County at the date of death.

3. The document dated _____, _____, now shown to me and which purports to be Decedent's Will was never revoked so far as I know.

4. No child or children were born to or adopted by Decedent after the date of the Will.
OR
4. After the date of the Will, _____ who survived Decedent was born to or adopted by Decedent.

5. Decedent was never divorced.
OR
5. Decedent was divorced from _____ on _____, _____.
OR
5. Decedent was divorced from _____, but the date and place of the divorce is not known to me.

6. I have personal knowledge of the financial affairs of Decedent. There is no necessity for any administration of Decedent's estate because there are no debts owed by Decedent which are not secured by liens on real estate.

7. Citation has been served and returned as required by the Texas Probate Code.

SIGNED this _____ day of _____, _____.

                                                                         _____
                                                                          Print Name:_____
                                                                          Affiant

SUBSCRIBED AND SWORN TO BEFORE ME by _____ this _____ day of _____, _____, to certify which witness by hand and seal of office.

                                                                          _____
                                                                          Clerk of the Probate Court of
                                                                          _____ County, Texas

                                                                          By _____
                                                                                    Deputy

form 19

NO._____

ESTATE OF	§	IN THE PROBATE COURT
	§	
_____,	§	NO. _____ OF
	§	
DECEASED	§	_____ COUNTY, TEXAS

ORDER ADMITTING WILL TO PROBATE
AS A MUNIMENT OF TITLE

On this day the Court heard the Application for Probate of Will as a Muniment of Title filed by _____ ("Applicant") in the Estate of _____, Deceased ("Decedent").

The Court heard the evidence and reviewed the Will and the other documents filed herein and finds that the allegations contained in the Application are true; that notice and citation have been given in the manner and for the length of time required by law; that Decedent is dead and that four years have not elapsed since the date of Decedent's death; that this Court has jurisdiction and venue of the Decedent's estate; that Decedent left a Will dated _____, _____, which was executed with the formalities and solemnities and under the circumstances required by law to make them a valid Will ("the Will"); that on such date Decedent had attained the age of 18 years and was of sound mind; that the Will was not revoked by Decedent; that no objection to or contest of the probate of the Will has been filed; that all of the necessary proof required for the probate of the Will has been made; that the Will is entitled to probate; that there are no unpaid debts owing by the Estate of Decedent other than those secured by liens on real estate; and that there is no necessity for the administration of this Estate.

It is ORDERED that the valid Will is admitted to probate as a Muniment of Title only, and the Clerk of this Court is ORDERED to record the Will together with the Application, in the Minutes of the Court, and this Order shall constitute sufficient legal authority to all persons purchasing from or otherwise dealing with Decedent's estate and to those persons owing any money, having custody of any property, or acting as registrar or transfer agent of any evidence of interest, indebtedness, property, or right belonging to Decedent's estate, for payment or transfer by them to the persons described in such Will.

It is ORDERED that upon the payment of taxes, if any are due, and the filing of an Inventory and the filing with the Clerk of the Court before the 181st day after this date, a sworn affidavit stating specifically the terms of the Will that have been fulfilled and the terms of the Will that have been unfulfilled, this Estate shall be dropped from the Docket.

SIGNED this _____ day of _____, _____.

_____

Judge Presiding

This page intentionally left blank.

form 20

NO._____

ESTATE OF	§	IN THE PROBATE COURT
_____,	§	NO. _____ OF
DECEASED	§	_____ COUNTY, TEXAS

AFFIDAVIT REGARDING FULFILLMENT OF WILL ADMITTED TO PROBATE AS A MUNIMENT OF TITLE

STATE OF _____)
)
COUNTY OF _____)

BEFORE ME, the undersigned authority, on this day personally appeared _____ and after being duly sworn, stated that:

"My name is _____. I was the Applicant for the admission to probate of the Last Will and Testament of _____ Deceased ("Decedent") as a Muniment of Title, and I do hereby make the following declaration:

1. The following terms of the Will of Decedent have been fulfilled:

2. The following terms of the Will of Decedent have not been fulfilled:

_____
Print Name:_____

SUBSCRIBED AND SWORN to before me by _____ _____ this _____ day of _____, _____, to certify which, witness my hand and seal of office.

_____
Notary Public in and for
_____ County,
State of_____
My Commission Expires:

This page intentionally left blank.

form 21

NO._____

ESTATE OF	§	IN THE PROBATE COURT
	§	
_____,	§	NO. _____ OF
	§	
DECEASED	§	_____ COUNTY, TEXAS

APPLICATION TO DETERMINE HEIRSHIP

_____ ("Applicant"), who resides at _____, _____, Texas furnishes the following information to the Court:

    1. _____ ("Decedent") died on _____, _____, at _____, _____ _____, County, Texas.

    2. No administration is pending upon Decedent's Estate and none appears necessary. It is necessary and in the best interest of the Estate for the Court to determine who are the heirs and only heirs of Decedent.

    3. Applicant claims to be the owner of a part of Decedent's Estate. The names and residences of all of Decedent's heirs, the relationship of each heir to Decedent, and the true interest of the Applicant and of each of the heirs in the Estate of Decedent are as follows:

Names and Residences	Relationship	True Interest

    4. At the time of Decedent's death, Decedent owned the following property:

5. Decedent was married to _____ who survived Decedent.

OR

5. Decedent was never married.

OR

5. Decedent was not married on the date of death but had been married and divorced from _____ on _____, and such divorced spouse of Decedent has no interest in Decedent's property.

6. No child or children were born to or adopted by Decedent.

OR

6. Only one child, _____, was born to or adopted by Decedent.

OR

6. Only _____ children, _____
_____ were born to or adopted by Decedent.

7. All children born to or adopted by Decedent have been listed. Each marriage of Decedent has been listed.

8. To the best of my knowledge, Decedent died intestate.

9. This Application does not omit any information required by Probate Code Section 49.

10. There are no debts owed by Decedent that are not secured by liens upon real estate and there is no necessity for administration of this Estate.

Applicant prays that citation issue as required by law; that an attorney ad litem be appointed to represent Decedent's living heirs whose names and whereabouts are unknown; that upon hearing hereof, this Court determine who are the heirs and only heirs of Decedent and their respective shares and interests in this Estate and that no necessity exists for an administration of Decedent's Estate.

Respectfully submitted,

_____
Print Name:_____

AFFIDAVIT

STATE OF _____)
) KNOW ALL MEN BY THESE PRESENTS:
COUNTY OF_____)

      BEFORE ME, the undersigned authority, on this day personally appeared _____ and after being duly sworn stated that:

      Insofar as is known to me, all the allegations of the foregoing Application are true in substance and in fact and that no material fact or circumstance has, within my knowledge, been omitted from the Application.

                                                           _____
                                                           Print Name:

      SUBSCRIBED AND SWORN to before me by _____ _____ this _____ day of _____, _____, to certify which, witness my hand and seal of office.

                                                           _____
                                                           Notary Public in and for
                                                           _____ County,
                                                           State of_____

                                                           My Commission Expires:

This page intentionally left blank.

form 22

NO._____

ESTATE OF	§	IN THE PROBATE COURT
	§	
_____,	§	NO. _____ OF
	§	
DECEASED	§	_____ COUNTY, TEXAS

STATEMENT OF FACTS

On this day _____ ("Affiant") personally appeared in open Court and, after being duly sworn, stated that:

I am well acquainted with the family history of _____ ("Decedent") who died in _____, _____ County, Texas, on _____, _____. To the best of my knowledge, Decedent died intestate.

Decedent was married to _____ who survived Decedent.
OR
Decedent was never married.
OR
Decedent was not married on the date of death but had been married and divorced from _____ on _____, and such divorced spouse of Decedent has no interest in Decedent's property.

No child or children were born to or adopted by Decedent.
OR
Only one child, _____, was born to or adopted by Decedent.
OR
Only _____ children, _____ _____ were born to or adopted by Decedent.

All children born to or adopted by Decedent have been listed. Each marriage of Decedent has been listed.

There are no debts owed by Decedent that are not secured by liens upon real estate and there is no necessity for administration of this Estate.

I have no interests in the estate of Decedent.

SIGNED this _____ day of _____, _____.

_____
Print Name:_____
Affiant

SUBSCRIBED AND SWORN TO BEFORE ME by _____ in open Court this _____ day of _____, _____, to certify which witness my hand seal of office.

Clerk of the _____ Court of _____County, Texas

By_____
Deputy

form 23

NO._____

ESTATE OF	§	IN THE PROBATE COURT
	§	
_____,	§	NO. _____ OF
	§	
DECEASED	§	_____ COUNTY, TEXAS

JUDGMENT DECLARING HEIRSHIP

On this day came on to be heard the sworn Application to Determine Heirship of the Estate of _____, Deceased ("Decedent"), wherein _____ is the Applicant and Decedent's living heirs whose names are known are Respondents and Decedent's living heirs whose names and/or whereabouts are unknown and heirs suffering legal disability are Defendants, and it appears to the Court, and the Court so finds that all parties interested in the Estate of Decedent have been made parties to the Application, have filed written waivers of service of citation, have appeared and answered herein, or have been duly and legally served with citation as required by law; that the Court appointed an attorney ad litem to appear and answer and to represent Defendants and such attorney ad litem did so appear and filed an answer for Defendants; that this Court has jurisdiction of the subject matter and all persons and parties; that the evidence presented and admitted fully and satisfactorily proves each and every issue presented to the Court; that Decedent died intestate and that the heirship of Decedent has been fully and satisfactorily proved as well as the identity of the nature of Decedent's property as being separate or community and the interest and shares of each of the heirs therein; and that no administration is necessary.

The Court finds and it is ORDERED by the Court that the names and places of residence of the heirs of Decedent and their respective shares and interests in the real and personal property of Decedent are as follows:

Name and Place of Residence	Share and Description of Real Property	Share and Description of Personal Property

It is ORDERED that the attorney ad litem appointed to represent the interests of the Defendants is allowed a fee of $_____ to be paid out of the assets of Decedent.

The Court finds that there exists no necessity for administration of the Estate of Decedent, none is ordered, and upon payment of all costs of Court no further proceedings be had in this cause.

SIGNED this _____ day of _____ , _____ .

_____
Judge Presiding

form 24

NO._____

ESTATE OF	§	IN THE PROBATE COURT
	§	
_____,	§	NO._____OF
	§	
DECEASED	§	_____COUNTY, TEXAS

SMALL ESTATE AFFIDAVIT AND ORDER

STATE OF   )
)
COUNTY OF   )

    Each of the undersigned ("Distributees"), being first duly sworn, states on oath and furnishes the following information to the Court:

    1.   I have personal knowledge of all facts set forth herein and they are true and correct.

    2.   _____ ("Decedent") died on _____, in _____, _____ County, _____. To the best of my knowledge, Decedent died intestate.

    3.   Decedent's domicile was in _____ County, Texas, where the principal part of Decedent's property at the time of death was situated.

    4.   Decedent was married to and was survived by _____ on the date of Decedent's death.

OR

    4.   Decedent was not married on the date of Decedent's death.

    5.   No child was born to or adopted by Decedent.

OR

    5.   Only one child, _____, who survived Decedent, was born to or adopted by Decedent.

OR

    5.   Only one child, _____, who predeceased Decedent, was born to or adopted by Decedent. No children were born to or adopted by this child.

OR

    5.   Only _____ children, _____ _____, who survived Decedent, were born to or adopted by Decedent.

    6.   No petition for the appointment of a personal representative is pending or has been granted for Decedent's Estate.

    7.   More than thirty days have elapsed since the death of Decedent.

8. The value of the entire assets of Decedent as of the date of death, exclusive of homestead and exempt property, does not exceed $50,000.00 and those non-exempt assets exceed the known liabilities of the Estate.

9. The names and addresses of all the distributees, heirs, devisees, or assignees of the money or property of the Estate of Decedent, and their right to receive the same are as follows:

Name	Residence	Relationship to Decedent	Share of Estate

10. The known assets and liabilities of Decedent's Estate are as follows:

ASSETS		
Description	Estimated Value	Encumbrances

LIABILITIES	
Creditor	Amount of Claim
[Set forth a complete listing and description of each debt]	

11. Distributees pray that this Affidavit and Application be approved by the Court and recorded in the Small Estate Records; and that the Clerk issue certified copies thereof in order to allow the Distributees to present the same to persons owing money to the Estate, having custody or possession of property of the Estate, or acting as registrar, fiduciary, or transfer agent of anyone having evidences of interest, indebtedness, property, or other right belonging to said Estate in order for such persons to pay, deliver, issue, or transfer such property.

[Repeat signature line and notary provision for each adult distributee]

_____
Distributee
SSN:_____

SUBSCRIBED AND SWORN TO BEFORE ME by _____ _____, on this _____ day of _____, _____, to certify which witness my hand and seal of office.

_____
Name (Print):_____
Notary Public, State of _____
My commission expires:_____

[Repeat signature line and notary provision for each distributee who is a minor.]

_____
Distributee
SSN:_____
By: _____,
natural guardian and next of kin

SUBSCRIBED AND SWORN TO BEFORE ME by _____, natural guardian and next of kin of _____, Distributee, on this _____ day of _____, _____, to certify which witness my hand and seal of office.

_____
Name (Print):_____
Notary Public, State of _____
My commission expires:_____

The undersigned witness, being first duly sworn, states on oath that:

"I have no financial or beneficial interest in the Estate of Decedent under the laws of descent and distribution or otherwise. I have read the document to which my affidavit is attached and have personal knowledge of all matters set forth therein and the facts therein set forth are true."

_____
, Witness

SUBSCRIBED AND SWORN TO BEFORE ME by the said _____
_____, on this _____ day of _____, _____, to certify which witness my hand and seal of office.

_____
Name (Print):_____
Notary Public, State of _____
My commission expires:_____

"I have no financial or beneficial interest in the Estate of Decedent under the laws of descent and distribution or otherwise. I have read the document to which my affidavit is attached and have personal knowledge of all matters set forth therein and the facts therein set forth are true."

_____
, Witness

SUBSCRIBED AND SWORN TO BEFORE ME by the said _____
_____, on this _____ day of _____, _____, to certify which witness my hand and seal of office.

_____
Name (Print):_____
Notary Public, State of _____
My commission expires:_____

ORDER

On this day the Court considered the Affidavit of the Distributee(s) of this Estate and the Court finds that the above Affidavit complies with the terms and provisions of the Texas Probate Code, that this Court has jurisdiction and venue, that this Estate qualifies under the provisions of the Probate Code as a Small Estate, that the appointment of a personal representative is not necessary, and that the Affidavit should be approved.

It is ORDERED that the foregoing Affidavit be and the same is hereby APPROVED, and shall forthwith be recorded in the Small Estate Records of this County, that each of the Distributee(s) named therein is entitled to that portion of Decedent's Estate, and the Clerk of this Court shall issue certified copies thereof to all persons entitled thereto.

SIGNED this _____ day of _____, _____.

_____
JUDGE PRESIDING

This page intentionally left blank.

NO._____

ESTATE OF § IN THE PROBATE COURT
§
_____, § NO. _____ OF
§
DECEASED § _____ COUNTY, TEXAS

MOTION TO OPEN SAFE DEPOSIT BOX AND TO EXAMINE PAPERS

TO THE HONORABLE JUDGE OF SAID COURT:

_____ ("Movant") furnishes the following information to the Court for authorization to examine the safe deposit box of _____, Deceased ("Decedent"):

1. Decedent died on _____.

2. This Court has jurisdiction and venue of the estate of Decedent.

3. Decedent had leased a safe deposit box from _____ _____ ("Respondent").

4. The box may contain Decedent's Will, a deed to a burial plot in which Decedent is to be buried, or an insurance policy issued in Decedent's name and payable to a beneficiary named in the policy.

Movant prays that Respondent be ordered to permit Movant to examine the box and remove those items as may be directed by the Court.

Respectfully submitted,

_____
Print Name:_____

ORDER

On this day came on to be heard the foregoing Motion, and the Court having heard the evidence finds that the allegations contained in such Motion are true and that it should be granted.

Respondent, _____, is ORDERED to permit Movant to examine such safe deposit box in the presence of an officer of Respondent, who is appointed as an agent of this Court, and if such documents are found therein, upon proper receipt, Respondent is directed to deliver to Movant any purported Will of Decedent, a deed to a burial plot in which Decedent is to be buried, and all insurance policies issued in Decedent's name and payable to a beneficiary named in the policy.

SIGNED this ___ day of _____, _____.

_____
Judge Presiding

This page intentionally left blank.

NO._____

ESTATE OF   §   IN THE PROBATE COURT
                               §
_____, §   NO. _____ OF
                               §
DECEASED   §   _____ COUNTY, TEXAS

APPOINTMENT OF RESIDENT AGENT

     The undersigned has and does by these presents appoint _____ _____, whose address is _____, _____, Texas _____, to be resident agent to accept service of process in all actions or proceedings with respect to his Estate pursuant to the provisions of Section 78(d) of the Texas Probate Code and in anticipation of the appointment of the undersigned as Executor of this Estate.

     SIGNED this _____ day of _____, _____.

                                                    _____
                                                    Print Name:_____

STATE OF   )
)
COUNTY OF   )

     SUBSCRIBED AND SWORN to before me by _____ _____ this _____ day of _____, _____, to certify which, witness my hand and seal of office.

                                                    _____
                                                  Notary Public in and for
                                                  _____ County,
                                                  State of _____

                                                  My Commission Expires:

This page intentionally left blank.

NO._____

ESTATE OF   §   IN THE PROBATE COURT
                                       §
_____,   §   NO._____ OF
                                       §
DECEASED   §   _____ COUNTY, TEXAS

PROOF BY SUBSCRIBING WITNESS

On this day _____ ("Affiant") personally appeared in Open Court, and after being duly sworn, stated the following:

On the same day that the Will is dated, I was present and saw _____ _____ ("Decedent") sign the document now shown to me and which purports to be Decedent's Will, and Decedent published and declared to _____ and to me that this document was Decedent's Will. At Decedent's request, _____ and I, then each being credible witnesses above the age of fourteen years, subscribed our names to this document in the presence of Decedent and of each other. On such date, Decedent was of sound mind and had attained the age of eighteen years.

SIGNED this _____ day of _____, _____ .

_____
Print Name:_____
Affiant

SUBSCRIBED AND SWORN TO BEFORE ME by _____
_____ this _____ day of _____, _____, to certify which, witness my hand and seal of office.

Clerk of the Probate Court
of _____County, Texas

By_____
         Deputy

This page intentionally left blank.

form 28

NOTICE TO CREDITORS

      Notice is hereby given that original Letters _____ for the Estate of _____, Deceased were issued on the _____ day of _____, _____, in Cause No. _____, pending in the Probate Court No. _____ of _____ County, Texas, to _____.

      Claims may be presented in care of the Executor/Administrator of the Estate addressed as follows:

                    Estate of_____, Deceased
                    _____
                    _____

      All persons having claims against this Estate which is currently being administered are required to present them within the time and the manner prescribed by law.

      DATED the _____ day of _____, _____.

By:_____
Executor or Administrator

form **163**

This page intentionally left blank.

form 29

NO._____

ESTATE OF	§	IN THE PROBATE COURT
_____,	§ § §	NO. _____ OF
DECEASED	§ §	_____ COUNTY, TEXAS

PROOF OF SERVICE OF NOTICE UPON CLAIMANTS AGAINST ESTATE

STATE OF)
)
COUNTY OF)

    BEFORE ME, the undersigned authority, on this day personally appeared _____, and after being duly sworn, stated that:

    The attached notice is a copy of the notice which was sent by _____ Mail, Return Receipt Requested, to the last known post office address of _____ in compliance with Section 295 of the Texas Probate Code. The Return Receipt is attached to the notice.

_____

Print Name:_____

    SUBSCRIBED AND SWORN to before me by _____ _____ this _____ day of _____, _____, to certify which, witness my hand and seal of office.

_____
Notary Public in and for
_____ County,
State of_____
My Commission Expires:

This page intentionally left blank.

form 31

Form **SS-4**
(Rev. December 2001)
Department of the Treasury
Internal Revenue Service

Application for Employer Identification Number

(For use by employers, corporations, partnerships, trusts, estates, churches, government agencies, Indian tribal entities, certain individuals, and others.)
· See separate instructions for each line.   · Keep a copy for your records.

EIN

OMB No. 1545-0003

Type or print clearly.

1 Legal name of entity (or individual) for whom the EIN is being requested

2 Trade name of business (if different from name on line 1)

3 Executor, trustee, "care of" name

4a Mailing address (room, apt., suite no. and street, or P.O. box)

5a Street address (if different) (Do not enter a P.O. box.)

4b City, state, and ZIP code

5b City, state, and ZIP code

6 County and state where principal business is located

7a Name of principal officer, general partner, grantor, owner, or trustor

7b SSN, ITIN, or EIN

8a Type of entity (check only one box)
☐ Sole proprietor (SSN) _____
☐ Partnership
☐ Corporation (enter form number to be filed) · _____
☐ Personal service corp.
☐ Church or church-controlled organization
☐ Other nonprofit organization (specify) · _____
☐ Other (specify) ·

☐ Estate (SSN of decedent) _____
☐ Plan administrator (SSN) _____
☐ Trust (SSN of grantor) _____
☐ National Guard   ☐ State/local government
☐ Farmers' cooperative ☐ Federal government/military
☐ REMIC   ☐ Indian tribal governments/enterprises
Group Exemption Number (GEN) · _____

8b If a corporation, name the state or foreign country (if applicable) where incorporated

State

Foreign country

9 **Reason for applying** (check only one box)
☐ Started new business (specify type) · _____
☐ Hired employees (Check the box and see line 12.)
☐ Compliance with IRS withholding regulations
☐ Other (specify) ·

☐ Banking purpose (specify purpose) · _____
☐ Changed type of organization (specify new type) · _____
☐ Purchased going business
☐ Created a trust (specify type) · _____
☐ Created a pension plan (specify type) · _____

10 Date business started or acquired (month, day, year)

11 Closing month of accounting year

12 First date wages or annuities were paid or will be paid (month, day, year). **Note:** *If applicant is a withholding agent, enter date income will first be paid to nonresident alien. (month, day, year)* . . . .

13 Highest number of employees expected in the next 12 months. **Note:** *If the applicant does not expect to have any employees during the period, enter "-0-."* . . . .

Agricultural | Household | Other

14 Check **one** box that best describes the principal activity of your business.
☐ Construction ☐ Rental & leasing ☐ Transportation & warehousing ☐ Health care & social assistance ☐ Wholesale–agent/broker
☐ Real estate   ☐ Manufacturing   ☐ Finance & insurance   ☐ Accommodation & food service ☐ Wholesale–other   ☐ Retail
                                                                     ☐ Other (specify)

15 Indicate principal line of merchandise sold; specific construction work done; products produced; or services provided.

16a Has the applicant ever applied for an employer identification number for this or any other business? . . . . . ☐ Yes ☐ No
Note: *If "Yes," please complete lines 16b and 16c.*

16b If you checked "Yes" on line 16a, give applicant's legal name and trade name shown on prior application if different from line 1 or 2 above.
Legal name ·   Trade name ·

16c Approximate date when, and city and state where, the application was filed. Enter previous employer identification number if known.
Approximate date when filed (mo., day, year) | City and state where filed | Previous EIN

Third Party Designee

Complete this section **only** if you want to authorize the named individual to receive the entity's EIN and answer questions about the completion of this form.

Designee's name

Designee's telephone number (include area code)
( )

Address and ZIP code

Designee's fax number (include area code)
( )

Under penalties of perjury, I declare that I have examined this application, and to the best of my knowledge and belief, it is true, correct, and complete.

Applicant's telephone number (include area code)
( )

Name and title (type or print clearly) ·

Applicant's fax number (include area code)
( )

Signature ·   Date ·

For Privacy Act and Paperwork Reduction Act Notice, see separate instructions.   Cat. No. 16055N   Form **SS-4** (Rev. 12-2001)

Form SS-4 (Rev. 12-2001) Page **2**

Do I Need an EIN?

File Form SS-4 if the applicant entity does not already have an EIN but is required to show an EIN on any return, statement, or other document.[1] **See also the separate instructions for each line on Form SS-4.**

IF the applicant...	AND...	THEN...
Started a new business	Does not currently have (nor expect to have) employees	Complete lines 1, 2, 4a-6, 8a, and 9-16c.
Hired (or will hire) employees, including household employees	Does not already have an EIN	Complete lines 1, 2, 4a-6, 7a-b (if applicable), 8a, 8b (if applicable), and 9-16c.
Opened a bank account	Needs an EIN for banking purposes only	Complete lines 1-5b, 7a-b (if applicable), 8a, 9, and 16a-c.
Changed type of organization	Either the legal character of the organization or its ownership changed (e.g., you incorporate a sole proprietorship or form a partnership)[2]	Complete lines 1-16c (as applicable).
Purchased a going business[3]	Does not already have an EIN	Complete lines 1-16c (as applicable).
Created a trust	The trust is other than a grantor trust or an IRA trust[4]	Complete lines 1-16c (as applicable).
Created a pension plan as a plan administrator[5]	Needs an EIN for reporting purposes	Complete lines 1, 2, 4a-6, 8a, 9, and 16a-c.
Is a foreign person needing an EIN to comply with IRS withholding regulations	Needs an EIN to complete a Form W-8 (other than Form W-8ECI), avoid withholding on portfolio assets, or claim tax treaty benefits[6]	Complete lines 1-5b, 7a-b (SSN or ITIN optional), 8a-9, and 16a-c.
Is administering an estate	Needs an EIN to report estate income on Form 1041	Complete lines 1, 3, 4a-b, 8a, 9, and 16a-c.
Is a withholding agent for taxes on non-wage income paid to an alien (i.e., individual, corporation, or partnership, etc.)	Is an agent, broker, fiduciary, manager, tenant, or spouse who is required to file **Form 1042**, Annual Withholding Tax Return for U.S. Source Income of Foreign Persons	Complete lines 1, 2, 3 (if applicable), 4a-5b, 7a-b (if applicable), 8a, 9, and 16a-c.
Is a state or local agency	Serves as a tax reporting agent for public assistance recipients under Rev. Proc. 80-4, 1980-1 C.B. 581[7]	Complete lines 1, 2, 4a-5b, 8a, 9, and 16a-c.
Is a single-member LLC	Needs an EIN to file **Form 8832**, Classification Election, for filing employment tax returns, **or** for state reporting purposes[8]	Complete lines 1-16c (as applicable).
Is an S corporation	Needs an EIN to file **Form 2553**, Election by a Small Business Corporation[9]	Complete lines 1-16c (as applicable).

[1] For example, a sole proprietorship or self-employed farmer who establishes a qualified retirement plan, or is required to file excise, employment, alcohol, tobacco, or firearms returns, must have an EIN. **A partnership, corporation, REMIC (real estate mortgage investment conduit), nonprofit organization (church, club, etc.), or farmers' cooperative must use an EIN for any tax-related purpose even if the entity does not have employees.**

[2] However, **do not** apply for a new EIN if the existing entity only **(a)** changed its business name, **(b)** elected on Form 8832 to change the way it is taxed (or is covered by the default rules), or **(c)** terminated its partnership status because at least 50% of the total interests in partnership capital and profits were sold or exchanged within a 12-month period. (The EIN of the terminated partnership should continue to be used. See Regulations section 301.6109-1(d)(2)(iii).)

[3] Do not use the EIN of the prior business unless you became the "owner" of a corporation by acquiring its stock.

[4] However, IRA trusts that are required to file **Form 990-T**, Exempt Organization Business Income Tax Return, must have an EIN.

[5] A plan administrator is the person or group of persons specified as the administrator by the instrument under which the plan is operated.

[6] Entities applying to be a Qualified Intermediary (QI) need a QI-EIN even if they already have an EIN. **See Rev. Proc. 2000-12.**

[7] See also *Household employer* on page 4. (**Note:** State or local agencies may need an EIN for other reasons, e.g., hired employees.)

[8] Most LLCs **do not** need to file Form 8832. See **Limited liability company (LLC)** on page 4 for details on completing Form SS-4 for an LLC.

[9] An existing corporation that is electing or revoking S corporation status should use its previously-assigned EIN.

170

Instructions for Form SS-4
(Rev. December 2001)
Application for Employer Identification Number

Department of the Treasury
Internal Revenue Service

Section references are to the Internal Revenue Code unless otherwise noted.

General Instructions

Use these instructions to complete **Form SS-4,** Application for Employer Identification Number. Also see **Do I Need an EIN?** on page 2 of Form SS-4.

Purpose of Form

Use Form SS-4 to apply for an employer identification number (EIN). An EIN is a nine-digit number (for example, 12-3456789) assigned to sole proprietors, corporations, partnerships, estates, trusts, and other entities for tax filing and reporting purposes. The information you provide on this form will establish your business tax account.

*An EIN is for use in connection with your business activities only. Do **not** use your EIN in place of your social security number (SSN).*

File only one Form SS-4. Generally, a sole proprietor should file only one Form SS-4 and needs only one EIN, regardless of the number of businesses operated as a sole proprietorship or trade names under which a business operates. However, if the proprietorship incorporates or enters into a partnership, a new EIN is required. Also, each corporation in an affiliated group must have its own EIN.

EIN applied for, but not received. If you do not have an EIN by the time a **return** is due, write "Applied For" and the date you applied in the space shown for the number. **Do not** show your social security number (SSN) as an EIN on returns.

If you do not have an EIN by the time a **tax deposit** is due, send your payment to the Internal Revenue Service Center for your filing area as shown in the instructions for the form that you are are filing. Make your check or money order payable to the **"United States Treasury"** and show your name (as shown on Form SS-4), address, type of tax, period covered, and date you applied for an EIN.

Related Forms and Publications

The following **forms** and **instructions** may be useful to filers of Form SS-4:
- **Form 990-T,** Exempt Organization Business Income Tax Return
- **Instructions for Form 990-T**
- **Schedule C (Form 1040),** Profit or Loss From Business
- **Schedule F (Form 1040),** Profit or Loss From Farming
- **Instructions for Form 1041 and Schedules A, B, D, G, I, J, and K-1,** U.S. Income Tax Return for Estates and Trusts
- **Form 1042,** Annual Withholding Tax Return for U.S. Source Income of Foreign Persons
- **Instructions for Form 1065,** U.S. Return of Partnership Income
- **Instructions for Form 1066,** U.S. Real Estate Mortgage Investment Conduit (REMIC) Income Tax Return
- **Instructions for Forms 1120 and 1120-A**
- **Form 2553,** Election by a Small Business Corporation
- **Form 2848,** Power of Attorney and Declaration of Representative
- **Form 8821,** Tax Information Authorization
- **Form 8832,** Entity Classification Election

For more **information** about filing Form SS-4 and related issues, see:
- **Circular A,** Agricultural Employer's Tax Guide (Pub. 51)
- **Circular E,** Employer's Tax Guide (Pub. 15)
- **Pub. 538,** Accounting Periods and Methods
- **Pub. 542,** Corporations
- **Pub. 557,** Exempt Status for Your Organization
- **Pub. 583,** Starting a Business and Keeping Records
- **Pub. 966,** EFTPS: Now a Full Range of Electronic Choices to Pay All Your Federal Taxes
- **Pub. 1635,** Understanding Your EIN
- **Package 1023,** Application for Recognition of Exemption
- **Package 1024,** Application for Recognition of Exemption Under Section 501(a)

How To Get Forms and Publications

Phone. You can order forms, instructions, and publications by phone 24 hours a day, 7 days a week. Just call 1-800-TAX-FORM (1-800-829-3676). You should receive your order or notification of its status within 10 workdays.

Personal computer. With your personal computer and modem, you can get the forms and information you need using the IRS Web Site at **www.irs.gov** or File Transfer Protocol at **ftp.irs.gov.**

CD-ROM. For small businesses, return preparers, or others who may frequently need tax forms or publications, a CD-ROM containing over 2,000 tax products (including many prior year forms) can be purchased from the National Technical Information Service (NTIS).

To order **Pub. 1796,** Federal Tax Products on CD-ROM, call **1-877-CDFORMS** (1-877-233-6767) toll free or connect to **www.irs.gov/cdorders.**

Cat. No. 62736F

Tax Help for Your Business

IRS-sponsored Small Business Workshops provide information about your Federal and state tax obligations. For information about workshops in your area, call 1-800-829-1040 and ask for your Taxpayer Education Coordinator.

How To Apply

You can apply for an EIN by telephone, fax, or mail depending on how soon you need to use the EIN.

Application by Tele-TIN. Under the Tele-TIN program, you can receive your EIN by telephone and use it immediately to file a return or make a payment. To receive an EIN by telephone, IRS suggests that you complete Form SS-4 so that you will have all relevant information available. Then call the Tele-TIN number at 1-866-816-2065. (International applicants must call 215-516-6999.) Tele-TIN hours of operation are 7:30 a.m. to 5:30 p.m. The person making the call must be authorized to sign the form or be an authorized designee. See **Signature** and **Third Party Designee** on page 6. Also see the **TIP** below.

An IRS representative will use the information from the Form SS-4 to establish your account and assign you an EIN. Write the number you are given on the upper right corner of the form and sign and date it. Keep this copy for your records.

If requested by an IRS representative, mail or fax (facsimile) the signed Form SS-4 (including any Third Party Designee authorization) **within 24 hours** to the Tele-TIN Unit at the service center address provided by the IRS representative.

*Taxpayer representatives can use Tele-TIN to apply for an EIN on behalf of their client and request that the EIN be faxed to their **client** on the same day. (**Note:** By utilizing this procedure, you are authorizing the IRS to fax the EIN without a cover sheet.)*

Application by Fax-TIN. Under the Fax-TIN program, you can receive your EIN by fax within 4 business days. Complete and fax Form SS-4 to the IRS using the Fax-TIN number listed below for your state. A long-distance charge to callers outside of the local calling area will apply. Fax-TIN numbers can only be used to apply for an EIN. **The numbers may change without notice.** Fax-TIN is available 24 hours a day, 7 days a week.

Be sure to provide your fax number so that IRS can fax the EIN back to you. (**Note:** By utilizing this procedure, you are authorizing the IRS to fax the EIN without a cover sheet.)

Do not call Tele-TIN for the same entity because duplicate EINs may be issued. See **Third Party Designee** on page 6.

Application by mail. Complete Form SS-4 at least 4 to 5 weeks before you will need an EIN. Sign and date the application and mail it to the service center address for your state. You will receive your EIN in the mail in approximately 4 weeks. See also **Third Party Designee** on page 6.

Call 1-800-829-1040 to verify a number or to ask about the status of an application by mail.

If your principal business, office or agency, or legal residence in the case of an individual, is located in:	Call the Tele-TIN or Fax-TIN number shown or file with the "Internal Revenue Service Center" at:
Connecticut, Delaware, District of Columbia, Florida, Georgia, Maine, Maryland, Massachusetts, New Hampshire, New Jersey, New York, North Carolina, Ohio, Pennsylvania, Rhode Island, South Carolina, Vermont, Virginia, West Virginia	Attn: EIN Operation Holtsville, NY 00501 Tele-TIN 866-816-2065 Fax-TIN 631-447-8960
Illinois, Indiana, Kentucky, Michigan	Attn: EIN Operation Cincinnati, OH 45999 Tele-TIN 866-816-2065 Fax-TIN 859-669-5760
Alabama, Alaska, Arizona, Arkansas, California, Colorado, Hawaii, Idaho, Iowa, Kansas, Louisiana, Minnesota, Mississippi, Missouri, Montana, Nebraska, Nevada, New Mexico, North Dakota, Oklahoma, Oregon, Puerto Rico, South Dakota, Tennessee, Texas, Utah, Washington, Wisconsin, Wyoming	Attn: EIN Operation Philadelphia, PA 19255 Tele-TIN 866-816-2065 Fax-TIN 215-516-3990
If you have no legal residence, principal place of business, or principal office or agency in any state:	Attn: EIN Operation Philadelphia, PA 19255 Tele-TIN 215-516-6999 Fax-TIN 215-516-3990

Specific Instructions

Print or type all entries on Form SS-4. Follow the instructions for each line to expedite processing and to avoid unnecessary IRS requests for additional information. Enter "N/A" (nonapplicable) on the lines that do not apply.

Line 1—Legal name of entity (or individual) for whom the EIN is being requested. Enter the legal name of the entity (or individual) applying for the EIN exactly as it appears on the social security card, charter, or other applicable legal document.

Individuals. Enter your first name, middle initial, and last name. If you are a sole proprietor, enter your individual name, not your business name. Enter your business name on line 2. Do not use abbreviations or nicknames on line 1.

Trusts. Enter the name of the trust.

Estate of a decedent. Enter the name of the estate.

Partnerships. Enter the legal name of the partnership as it appears in the partnership agreement.

Corporations. Enter the corporate name as it appears in the corporation charter or other legal document creating it.

Plan administrators. Enter the name of the plan administrator. A plan administrator who already has an EIN should use that number.

Line 2—Trade name of business. Enter the trade name of the business if different from the legal name. The trade name is the "doing business as " (DBA) name.

*Use the full legal name shown on line 1 on all tax returns filed for the entity. (However, if you enter a trade name on line 2 and choose to use the trade name instead of the legal name, enter the trade name on **all returns** you file.) To prevent processing delays and errors, **always** use the legal name only (or the trade name only) on **all** tax returns.*

Line 3—Executor, trustee, "care of" name. Trusts enter the name of the trustee. Estates enter the name of the executor, administrator, or other fiduciary. If the entity applying has a designated person to receive tax information, enter that person's name as the "care of" person. Enter the individual's first name, middle initial, and last name.

Lines 4a-b—Mailing address. Enter the mailing address for the entity's correspondence. If line 3 is completed, enter the address for the executor, trustee or "care of" person. Generally, this address will be used on all tax returns.

*File **Form 8822**, Change of Address, to report any subsequent changes to the entity's mailing address.*

Lines 5a-b—Street address. Provide the entity's physical address **only** if different from its mailing address shown in lines 4a-b. **Do not** enter a P.O. box number here.

Line 6—County and state where principal business is located. Enter the entity's primary **physical** location.

Lines 7a-b—Name of principal officer, general partner, grantor, owner, or trustor. Enter the first name, middle initial, last name, and SSN of **(a)** the principal officer if the business is a corporation, **(b)** a general partner if a partnership, **(c)** the owner of an entity that is disregarded as separate from its owner (disregarded entities owned by a corporation enter the corporation's name and EIN), or **(d)** a grantor, owner, or trustor if a trust.

If the person in question is an **alien individual** with a previously assigned individual taxpayer identification number (ITIN), enter the ITIN in the space provided and submit a copy of an official identifying document. If necessary, complete **Form W-7,** Application for IRS Individual Taxpayer Identification Number, to obtain an ITIN.

You are **required** to enter an SSN, ITIN, or EIN unless the only reason you are applying for an EIN is to make an entity classification election (see Regulations section 301.7701-1 through 301.7701-3) and you are a nonresident alien with no effectively connected income from sources within the United States.

Line 8a—Type of entity. Check the box that best describes the type of entity applying for the EIN. If you are an alien individual with an ITIN previously assigned to you, enter the ITIN in place of a requested SSN.

This is not an election for a tax classification of an entity. See "Limited liability company (LLC)" on page 4.

Other. If not specifically mentioned, check the "Other" box, enter the type of entity and the type of return, if any, that will be filed (for example, "Common Trust Fund, Form 1065" or "Created a Pension Plan"). Do not enter "N/A." If you are an alien individual applying for an EIN, see the **Lines 7a-b** instructions above.

● **Household employer.** If you are an individual, check the "Other" box and enter "Household Employer" and your SSN. If you are a state or local agency serving as a tax reporting agent for public assistance recipients who become household employers, check the "Other" box and enter "Household Employer Agent." If you are a trust that qualifies as a household employer, you do not need a separate EIN for reporting tax information relating to household employees; use the EIN of the trust.

● **QSub.** For a qualified subchapter S subsidiary (QSub) check the "Other" box and specify "QSub."

● **Withholding agent.** If you are a withholding agent required to file Form 1042, check the "Other" box and enter "Withholding Agent."

Sole proprietor. Check this box if you file Schedule C, C-EZ, or F (Form 1040) and have a qualified plan, or are required to file excise, employment, or alcohol, tobacco, or firearms returns, or are a payer of gambling winnings. Enter your SSN (or ITIN) in the space provided. If you are a nonresident alien with no effectively connected income from sources within the United States, you do not need to enter an SSN or ITIN.

Corporation. This box is for any corporation **other than a personal service corporation.** If you check this box, enter the income tax form number to be filed by the entity in the space provided.

*If you entered "1120S" after the "Corporation" checkbox, the corporation **must** file Form 2553 **no later than the 15th day of the 3rd month of the tax year the election is to take effect.** Until Form 2553 has been received and approved, you will be considered a Form 1120 filer. See the Instructions for Form 2553.*

Personal service corp. Check this box if the entity is a personal service corporation. An entity is a personal service corporation for a tax year only if:
● The principal activity of the entity during the testing period (prior tax year) for the tax year is the performance of personal services substantially by employee-owners, and
● The employee-owners own at least 10% of the fair market value of the outstanding stock in the entity on the last day of the testing period.

Personal services include performance of services in such fields as health, law, accounting, or consulting. For more information about personal service corporations, see the Instructions for Forms 1120 and 1120-A and Pub. 542.

Other nonprofit organization. Check this box if the nonprofit organization is other than a church or church-controlled organization and specify the type of nonprofit organization (for example, an educational organization).

 *If the organization also seeks tax-exempt status, you **must** file either Package 1023 or Package 1024. See Pub. 557 for more information.*

If the organization is covered by a group exemption letter, enter the four-digit **group exemption number (GEN).** (Do not confuse the GEN with the nine-digit EIN.) If you do not know the GEN, contact the parent organization. Get Pub. 557 for more information about group exemption numbers.

Plan administrator. If the plan administrator is an individual, enter the plan administrator's SSN in the space provided.

REMIC. Check this box if the entity has elected to be treated as a real estate mortgage investment conduit (REMIC). See the Instructions for Form 1066 for more information.

Limited liability company (LLC). An LLC is an entity organized under the laws of a state or foreign country as a limited liability company. For Federal tax purposes, an LLC may be treated as a partnership or corporation or be disregarded as an entity separate from its owner.

By **default,** a domestic LLC with only one member is **disregarded** as an entity separate from its owner and must include all of its income and expenses on the owner's tax return (e.g., **Schedule C (Form 1040)**). Also by default, a domestic LLC with two or more members is treated as a partnership. A domestic LLC may file Form 8832 to avoid either default classification and elect to be classified as an association taxable as a corporation. For more information on entity classifications (including the rules for foreign entities), see the instructions for Form 8832.

 *Do not file Form 8832 if the LLC accepts the default classifications above. **However, if the LLC will be electing S Corporation status, it must timely file both Form 8832 and Form 2553.***

Complete Form SS-4 for LLCs as follows:
• A single-member, domestic LLC that accepts the default classification (above) does not need an EIN and generally should not file Form SS-4. Generally, the LLC should use the name and EIN of its **owner** for all Federal tax purposes. However, the reporting and payment of employment taxes for employees of the LLC may be made using the name and EIN or **either** the owner or the LLC as explained in Notice 99-6, 1999-1 C.B. 321. You can find Notice 99-6 on page 12 of Internal Revenue Bulletin 1999-3 at **www.irs.gov. (Note:** If the LLC-applicant indicates in box 13 that it has employees or expects to have employees, the owner (whether an individual or other entity) of a single-member domestic LLC will also be assigned its own EIN (if it does not already have one) even if the LLC will be filing the employment tax returns.)

• A single-member, domestic LLC that accepts the default classification (above) and wants an EIN for filing employment tax returns (see above) or non-Federal purposes, such as a state requirement, must check the "Other" box and write "Disregarded Entity" or, when applicable, "Disregarded Entity—Sole Proprietorship" in the space provided.

• A multi-member, domestic LLC that accepts the default classification (above) must check the "Partnership" box.

• A domestic LLC that will be filing Form 8832 to elect corporate status must check the "Corporation" box and write in "Single-Member" or "Multi-Member" immediately below the "form number" entry line.

Line 9—Reason for applying. Check only **one** box. Do not enter "N/A."

Started new business. Check this box if you are starting a new business that requires an EIN. If you check this box, enter the type of business being started. **Do not** apply if you already have an EIN and are only adding another place of business.

Hired employees. Check this box if the existing business is requesting an EIN because it has hired or is hiring employees and is therefore required to file employment tax returns. **Do not** apply if you already have an EIN and are only hiring employees. For information on employment taxes (e.g., for family members), see Circular E.

 You may be required to make electronic deposits of all depository taxes (such as employment tax, excise tax, and corporate income tax) using the Electronic Federal Tax Payment System (EFTPS). See section 11, Depositing Taxes, of Circular E and Pub. 966.

Created a pension plan. Check this box if you have created a pension plan and need an EIN for reporting purposes. Also, enter the type of plan in the space provided.

Check this box if you are applying for a trust EIN when a new pension plan is established. In addition, check the "Other" box in line 8a and write "Created a Pension Plan" in the space provided.

Banking purpose. Check this box if you are requesting an EIN for banking purposes only, and enter the banking purpose (for example, a bowling league for depositing dues or an investment club for dividend and interest reporting).

Changed type of organization. Check this box if the business is changing its type of organization for example, the business was a sole proprietorship and has been incorporated or has become a partnership. If you check this box, specify in the space provided (including available space immediately below) the type of change made. For example, "From Sole Proprietorship to Partnership."

Purchased going business. Check this box if you purchased an existing business. **Do not** use the former owner's EIN unless you became the "owner" of a corporation by acquiring its stock.

Created a trust. Check this box if you created a trust, and enter the type of trust created. For example, indicate if the trust is a nonexempt charitable trust or a split-interest trust.

Exception. Do **not** file this form for certain grantor-type trusts. The trustee does not need an EIN for the trust if the trustee furnishes the name and TIN of the grantor/owner and the address of the trust to all payors. See the Instructions for Form 1041 for more information.

 Do not check this box if you are applying for a trust EIN when a new pension plan is established. Check "Created a pension plan."

Other. Check this box if you are requesting an EIN for any other reason; and enter the reason. For example, a newly-formed state government entity should enter "Newly-Formed State Government Entity" in the space provided.

Line 10—Date business started or acquired. If you are starting a new business, enter the starting date of the business. If the business you acquired is already operating, enter the date you acquired the business. Trusts should enter the date the trust was legally created. Estates should enter the date of death of the decedent whose name appears on line 1 or the date when the estate was legally funded.

Line 11—Closing month of accounting year. Enter the last month of your accounting year or tax year. An accounting or tax year is usually 12 consecutive months, either a calendar year or a fiscal year (including a period of 52 or 53 weeks). A calendar year is 12 consecutive months ending on December 31. A fiscal year is either 12 consecutive months ending on the last day of any month other than December or a 52-53 week year. For more information on accounting periods, see Pub. 538.

Individuals. Your tax year generally will be a calendar year.

Partnerships. Partnerships must adopt one of the following tax years:
- The tax year of the majority of its partners,
- The tax year common to all of its principal partners,
- The tax year that results in the least aggregate deferral of income, or
- In certain cases, some other tax year.

See the Instructions for Form 1065 for more information.

REMICs. REMICs must have a calendar year as their tax year.

Personal service corporations. A personal service corporation generally must adopt a calendar year unless:
- It can establish a business purpose for having a different tax year, or
- It elects under section 444 to have a tax year other than a calendar year.

Trusts. Generally, a trust must adopt a calendar year except for the following:
- Tax-exempt trusts,
- Charitable trusts, and
- Grantor-owned trusts.

Line 12—First date wages or annuities were paid or will be paid. If the business has or will have employees, enter the date on which the business began or will begin to pay wages. If the business does not plan to have employees, enter "N/A."

Withholding agent. Enter the date you began or will begin to pay income (including annuities) to a nonresident alien. This also applies to individuals who are required to file Form 1042 to report alimony paid to a nonresident alien.

Line 13—Highest number of employees expected in the next 12 months. Complete each box by entering the number (including zero ("-0-")) of "Agricultural," "Household," or "Other" employees expected by the applicant in the next 12 months. For a definition of agricultural labor (farmwork), see Circular A.

Lines 14 and 15. Check the **one** box in line 14 that best describes the principal activity of the applicant's business. Check the "Other" box (and specify the applicant's principal activity) if none of the listed boxes applies.

Use line 15 to describe the applicant's principal line of business in more detail. For example, if you checked the "Construction" box in line 14, enter additional detail such as "General contractor for residential buildings" in line 15.

 Do not complete lines 14 and 15 if you entered zero "(-0-)" in line 13.

Construction. Check this box if the applicant is engaged in erecting buildings or other structures, (e.g., streets, highways, bridges, tunnels). The term "Construction" also includes special trade contractors, (e.g., plumbing, HVAC, electrical, carpentry, concrete, excavation, etc. contractors).

Real estate. Check this box if the applicant is engaged in renting or leasing real estate to others; managing, selling, buying or renting real estate for others; or providing related real estate services (e.g., appraisal services).

Rental and leasing. Check this box if the applicant is engaged in providing tangible goods such as autos, computers, consumer goods, or industrial machinery and equipment to customers in return for a periodic rental or lease payment.

Manufacturing. Check this box if the applicant is engaged in the mechanical, physical, or chemical transformation of materials, substances, or components into new products. The assembling of component parts of manufactured products is also considered to be manufacturing.

Transportation & warehousing. Check this box if the applicant provides transportation of passengers or cargo; warehousing or storage of goods; scenic or sight-seeing transportation; or support activities related to these modes of transportation.

Finance & insurance. Check this box if the applicant is engaged in transactions involving the creation, liquidation, or change of ownership of financial assets and/or facilitating such financial transactions;

underwriting annuities/insurance policies; facilitating such underwriting by selling insurance policies; or by providing other insurance or employee-benefit related services.

Health care and social assistance. Check this box if the applicant is engaged in providing physical, medical, or psychiatric care using licensed health care professionals or providing social assistance activities such as youth centers, adoption agencies, individual/family services, temporary shelters, etc.

Accommodation & food services. Check this box if the applicant is engaged in providing customers with lodging, meal preparation, snacks, or beverages for immediate consumption.

Wholesale–agent/broker. Check this box if the applicant is engaged in arranging for the purchase or sale of goods owned by others or purchasing goods on a commission basis for goods traded in the wholesale market, usually between businesses.

Wholesale–other. Check this box if the applicant is engaged in selling goods in the wholesale market generally to other businesses for resale on their own account.

Retail. Check this box if the applicant is engaged in selling merchandise to the general public from a fixed store; by direct, mail-order, or electronic sales; or by using vending machines.

Other. Check this box if the applicant is engaged in an activity not described above. Describe the applicant's principal business activity in the space provided.

Lines 16a-c. Check the applicable box in line 16a to indicate whether or not the entity (or individual) applying for an EIN was issued one previously. Complete lines 16b and 16c **only** if the "Yes" box in line 16a is checked. If the applicant previously applied for **more than one** EIN, write "See Attached" in the empty space in line 16a and attach a separate sheet providing the line 16b and 16c information for each EIN previously requested.

Third Party Designee. Complete this section **only** if you want to authorize the named individual to receive the entity's EIN and answer questions about the completion of Form SS-4. The designee's authority terminates at the time the EIN is assigned and released to the designee. **You must complete the signature area for the authorization to be valid.**

Signature. When required, the application must be signed by **(a)** the individual, if the applicant is an individual, **(b)** the president, vice president, or other principal officer, if the applicant is a corporation, **(c)** a responsible and duly authorized member or officer having knowledge of its affairs, if the applicant is a partnership, government entity, or other unincorporated organization, or **(d)** the fiduciary, if the applicant is a trust or an estate. Foreign applicants may have any duly-authorized person, (e.g., division manager), sign Form SS-4.

Privacy Act and Paperwork Reduction Act Notice.
We ask for the information on this form to carry out the Internal Revenue laws of the United States. We need it to comply with section 6109 and the regulations thereunder which generally require the inclusion of an employer identification number (EIN) on certain returns, statements, or other documents filed with the Internal Revenue Service. If your entity is required to obtain an EIN, you are required to provide all of the information requested on this form. Information on this form may be used to determine which Federal tax returns you are required to file and to provide you with related forms and publications.

We disclose this form to the Social Security Administration for their use in determining compliance with applicable laws. We may give this information to the Department of Justice for use in civil and criminal litigation, and to the cities, states, and the District of Columbia for use in administering their tax laws. We may also disclose this information to Federal, state, or local agencies that investigate or respond to acts or threats of terrorism or participate in intelligence or counterintelligence activities concerning terrorism.

We will be unable to issue an EIN to you unless you provide all of the requested information which applies to your entity. Providing false information could subject you to penalties.

You are not required to provide the information requested on a form that is subject to the Paperwork Reduction Act unless the form displays a valid OMB control number. Books or records relating to a form or its instructions must be retained as long as their contents may become material in the administration of any Internal Revenue law. Generally, tax returns and return information are confidential, as required by section 6103.

The time needed to complete and file this form will vary depending on individual circumstances. The estimated average time is:

Recordkeeping	6 min.
Learning about the law or the form	22 min.
Preparing the form	46 min.
Copying, assembling, and sending the form to the IRS	20 min.

If you have comments concerning the accuracy of these time estimates or suggestions for making this form simpler, we would be happy to hear from you. You can write to the Tax Forms Committee, Western Area Distribution Center, Rancho Cordova, CA 95743-0001. **Do not** send the form to this address. Instead, see **How To Apply** on page 2.

form 32

NO._____

ESTATE OF	§	IN THE PROBATE COURT
	§	
	§	
_____,	§	NO. _____ OF
	§	
DECEASED	§	_____ COUNTY, TEXAS

INVENTORY, APPRAISEMENT AND LIST OF CLAIMS

Date of Death:

TO THE HONORABLE JUDGE OF SAID COURT:

    The following is a full, true and complete inventory of all real property of this Estate situated in the State of Texas, and all personal property of this Estate, wherever situated, which has come to the possession or knowledge of the undersigned personal representative of the Estate, an appraisement of the fair market value of each item of that property as of _____, and a full and complete list of all claims due or owing to the Estate. All of the property is the community property of the Decedent unless otherwise noted.

INVENTORY AND APPRAISEMENT

Real Property   Value   Total

    Separate Estate:

    Community Estate:

TOTAL REAL PROPERTY:

Personal Property   Value   Total

    Stocks and Bonds:

        Separate Estate:

        Community Estate:

    TOTAL STOCKS AND BONDS:

    Mortgages, Notes and Cash:

        Separate Estate:

        Community Estate:

    TOTAL MORTGAGES, NOTES AND CASH:

    Miscellaneous Personal Property:

        Separate Estate:

        Community Estate:

    TOTAL MISCELLANEOUS PERSONAL PROPERTY:

    TOTAL PERSONAL PROPERTY:

LIST OF CLAIMS

There are no claims due or owing to the Estate other than those shown on the foregoing Inventory and Appraisement.

RECAPITULATION:

Real Property

    Separate:

    Community:

Less one-half community interest of
_____, as surviving spouse.

    TOTAL REAL PROPERTY:

Personal Property

    Separate:

    Community:

Less one-half community interest of
_____, as surviving spouse.

    TOTAL PERSONAL PROPERTY:

    TOTAL VALUE OF DECEDENT'S ESTATE:

The undersigned requests that this Inventory, Appraisement and List of Claims be approved and ordered entered of record.

Respectfully submitted,

_____
Independent Executor of the Estate of
_____, Deceased

STATE OF _____)
) KNOW ALL MEN BY THESE PRESENTS THAT:
COUNTY OF _____)

I, _____, having been duly sworn, hereby state on oath that the foregoing Inventory, Appraisement, and List of Claims is a true and complete statement of all the property and claims of the Estate that have come to my knowledge.

_____

SUBSCRIBED AND SWORN to before me by _____ this _____ day of _____, _____, to certify which, witness my hand and seal of office.

_____
Notary Public in and for
_____ County,
State of_____

My Commission Expires:

NO._____

ESTATE OF	§	IN THE PROBATE COURT
	§	
_____,	§	NO._____ OF
	§	
DECEASED	§	_____ COUNTY, TEXAS

ORDER APPROVING INVENTORY AND APPRAISEMENT

On this _____ day of _____, _____, came to be examined the Inventory and Appraisement of the above styled estate filed on _____, _____, and the same is hereby approved.

Signed this _____ day of _____, _____.

_____
JUDGE PRESIDING

This page intentionally left blank.

form 34

NO._____

ESTATE OF _____ §   IN THE PROBATE COURT
                                §
_____, §   NO. _____ OF
DECEASED   §   _____ COUNTY, TEXAS

APPLICATION TO SET ASIDE EXEMPT PROPERTY

_____, _____ of this Estate ("Applicant"), furnishes the following information to the Court:

 1. The Inventory, Appraisement, and List of Claims of this Estate has been approved.

 2. _____ ("Decedent") was survived by [(____, **Decedent's Surviving Spouse)(and by)(**____**, children)]**.

 3. The following described property ("the Property") belonging to the Estate is exempt from executive or forced sale under the Constitution and laws of Texas:

 4. The Property should be set apart for the use and benefit of Decedent's **[(Surviving Spouse)(and)(children)]** pursuant to Section 271 of the Texas Probate Code.

 5. The Property should be delivered to **[(Decedent's Surviving Spouse)(and)(the guardian of Decedent's minor children)(Decedent's unmarried children of lawful age)]**.

Applicant requests the Court to enter an Order setting apart the Property for the use and benefit of Decedent's **[(Surviving Spouse)(and)(children)]**.

          Respectfully submitted,

          _____
          Print Name:_____

This page intentionally left blank.

form 35

NO._____

ESTATE OF	§	IN THE PROBATE COURT
	§	
_____,	§	NO. _____ OF
	§	
DECEASED	§	_____ COUNTY, TEXAS

ORDER TO SET ASIDE EXEMPT PROPERTY

On this day the Application to Set Aside Exempt Property was heard by this Court, and the court finds that such Application is true and correct and should be granted.

It is ORDERED that the following described property is hereby set apart for the use and benefit of Decedent's **[(Surviving Spouse)(and)(children)]**:

Such property shall be delivered by the _____, without delay, as follows:

SIGNED this _____ day of _____, _____.

_____
Judge Presiding

185

This page intentionally left blank.

form 36

NO._____

ESTATE OF	§	IN THE PROBATE COURT
_____,	§ § §	NO. _____ OF
DECEASED	§ §	_____ COUNTY, TEXAS

APPLICATION FOR FAMILY ALLOWANCE

_____, _____ of this Estate ("Applicant"), furnishes the following information to the Court:

    1. The Inventory, Appraisement, and List of Claims of this Estate has been approved.

    2. _____ ("Decedent") was survived by _____ ("Decedent's Surviving Spouse") and ____ minor children. Decedent's Surviving Spouse and minor children do not have separate property adequate for their maintenance.

    3. The amount of the family allowance should be determined by the facts and circumstances now existing and those anticipated to exist during the first year after Decedent's death, and such allowance should be in the amount of $_____, payable **[(in a lump sum)(in monthly installments of $_____ each)]**.

    Applicant requests the Court to enter an Order to set the amount of the family allowance and specify the fund or other property from which such allowance should be paid.

    Respectfully submitted,

_____
Print Name:_____

This page intentionally left blank.

form 37

NO._____

ESTATE OF	§	IN THE PROBATE COURT
_____,	§	NO. _____ OF
DECEASED	§	_____ COUNTY, TEXAS

ORDER FOR FAMILY ALLOWANCE

On this day the Application For Family Allowance was heard and considered by this Court, and the Court finds that a fair and reasonable allowance should be paid for the support of Decedent's Surviving Spouse and minor children, based upon the facts now existing and those expected to exist during the first year after the death of the Decedent, is the sum of $_____.

It is ORDERED that a family allowance of $_____ shall be paid **[(in a lump sum)(in monthly installments of $_____ each)]** to Decedent's Surviving Spouse, and minor children and that the _____ pay such allowance from the funds belonging to the Estate.

SIGNED this _____ day of _____, _____.

_____
Judge Presiding

This page intentionally left blank.

form 38

NO._____

ESTATE OF	§	IN PROBATE COURT
_____, §	NO. _____ OF	
DECEASED	§	_____ COUNTY, TEXAS

AFFIDAVIT REGARDING DEBTS AND TAXES

STATE OF)
)
COUNTY OF)

BEFORE ME, the undersigned authority, a Notary Public in and for the State of Texas, on this day personally appeared _____, and after being duly sworn, stated that:

My name is _____. I am familiar with the Estate of _____, Deceased, who died on _____, _____.

There are sufficient funds for the payment of all debts, expenses and taxes including Texas inheritance taxes and federal estate taxes due in connection with this estate.

EXECUTED on this _____ day of _____, _____.

_____
Print Name:_____

SUBSCRIBED AND SWORN to before me by _____ this _____ day of _____, _____, to certify which, witness my hand and seal of office.

_____
Notary Public in and for
_____ County,
State of_____
My Commission Expires:

This page intentionally left blank.

form 39

NO._____

ESTATE OF	§	IN THE PROBATE COURT
	§	
_____,	§	NO. _____ OF
	§	
DECEASED	§	_____ COUNTY, TEXAS

ANNUAL ACCOUNT

_____, _____
of this Estate, presents this verified exhibit pursuant to the provisions of Section 399 of the Texas Probate Code:

    1.   This Account covers the twelve month period from _____ to _____.

    2.   The following claims against the Estate have been presented and the following action has been taken with respect to each:

Claim   **Accepted or Rejected**

    3.   The following property which has come to my knowledge or into my possession and which was not previously listed or inventoried is as follows:

Property   **Value**

4. The following changes have occurred in property of the Estate but have not been reported:

5. The receipts of the Estate are as follows:

6. The disbursements of the Estate have been as follows:

7. The description of the property being administered is the same property shown in the Inventory previously filed herein except as otherwise specified herein.

8. The following cash belonging to the Estate is on hand:

9. Attached to this Account are proper vouchers for each item of credit claimed in this Account.

10. Attached to this Account are Verifications from all depositories where money or other personal property belonging to this Estate are being held in safekeeping.

11. During the period covered by this Account, all tax returns have been filed and all taxes due and owing have been paid and the date the taxes were paid and the governmental entity to which the taxes were paid are as follows:

12. All required bond premiums have been paid for the accounting period.

The undersigned requests the Court to hear and approve this Annual Account and enter such other orders as may be proper.

Respectfully submitted,

_____
Print Name:_____

AFFIDAVIT

STATE OF   )
)
COUNTY OF   )

BEFORE ME, the undersigned authority, on this day personally appeared _____, known to me to be the _____ of the Estate of _____, Deceased, and to be the person whose name is subscribed to the foregoing Annual Account, and after being duly sworn by me, stated that the Annual Account and all vouchers and other attachments thereto are true, correct, and complete in every respect.

_____
Print Name:_____

SUBSCRIBED AND SWORN to before me by _____ _____ this _____day of _____, _____, to certify which, witness my hand and seal of office.

_____
Notary Public in and for
_____ County,
State of_____
My Commission Expires:

This page intentionally left blank.

NO._____

ESTATE OF	§	IN THE PROBATE COURT
_____,	§ § §	NO. _____ OF
DECEASED	§ §	_____ COUNTY, TEXAS

ORDER APPROVING ANNUAL ACCOUNT

On this day the Annual Account for the Estate of _____ was heard and considered by the Court and the Court finds that it has jurisdiction and venue of this proceeding; that such Annual Account has remained on file for a full ten (10) days before being considered; that the Court is fully advised as to all the items of such Account, possession of cash and other assets kept in safekeeping, as well as those on deposit, that all vouchers were produced and filed for each item of credit claimed in such Account and that satisfactory evidence has been presented as to the status and existence of the assets of this estate; and that the facts stated in such Account are true, correct and complete and that this Account should be approved.

It is ORDERED that the foregoing Annual Account is APPROVED.

SIGNED this _____ day of _____, _____.

_____
Judge Presiding

This page intentionally left blank.

form 41

NO._____

ESTATE OF	§	IN THE PROBATE COURT
_____,	§	NO. _____ OF
DECEASED	§	_____ COUNTY, TEXAS

ACCOUNT FOR FINAL SETTLEMENT

_____, _____
of this Estate, presents this verified Account for Final Settlement pursuant to the provisions of the Texas Probate Code:

    1.   There is no further need for administration of this Estate. Except as may be provided below, all debts known to exist against this Estate have been paid.

    2.   The property belonging to the Estate which has come into my hands is that property listed and described in the Inventory, Appraisement and List of Claims previously filed herein, reference to which is here made for all purposes.

    3.   The following debts of the estate have been paid by authorization of the Court and are as follows:

    4.   The previously unreported receipts of the estate are as follows:

    5.   The previously unreported disbursements of the estate have been as follows:

6. The debts and expenses still owing by the estate are as follows:

7. The property of the estate remaining on hand is as follows:

8. Attached to this Account are proper vouchers for each item of credit claimed in this Account.

9. Attached to this Account are Verifications from all depositories where money or other personal property belonging to this Estate are being held in safekeeping.

10. With respect to Inheritance Taxes due and owing to the State of Texas, **[(all such taxes have been paid) (none are due).]** The tax returns that have been filed, the taxes due and owing that have been paid, the date the taxes were paid, and the government entity to which taxes were paid, are as follows:

11. All required bond premiums have been paid for the accounting period.

12. The persons entitled to receive the property remaining on hand after the payment of all debts and expenses are as follows:

13. All advances or payments made to persons entitled to receive portions of Decedent's Estate are as follows:

14. Notice has been or will be given to all heirs and beneficiaries as required by law or by the Court.

Applicant prays that citation be served as required by law, following which, the Court audit, settle, and approve this Account and authorize the payment of all unpaid debts and expenses and the distribution of the property remaining on hand to the persons entitled to receive such property, and enter such orders as may be proper.

Respectfully submitted,

_____

Print Name:_____

AFFIDAVIT

STATE OF   )
)
COUNTY OF   )

BEFORE ME, the undersigned authority, on this day personally appeared _____, known to me to be the _____ of the Estate of _____, Deceased, and to be the person whose name is subscribed to the foregoing Account for Final Settlement, and after being duly sworn by me, stated that the Account and all vouchers and other attachments thereto are true, correct, and complete in every respect.

_____

Print Name:_____

SUBSCRIBED AND SWORN to before me by _____ _____ this _____ day of _____, _____, to certify which, witness my hand and seal of office.

_____
Notary Public in and for
_____ County,
State of_____
My Commission Expires:

201

This page intentionally left blank.

form 42

NO._____

ESTATE OF	§	IN THE PROBATE COURT
_____,	§	NO. _____ OF
DECEASED	§	_____ COUNTY, TEXAS

ORDER APPROVING ACCOUNT FOR FINAL SETTLEMENT AND AUTHORIZING DISTRIBUTION OF ESTATE

On this day, the Account For Final Settlement of this Estate was heard and considered by the Court, and after examining the Account and the vouchers accompanying the same and hearing the evidence in support of same, the Court finds that citation has been duly served upon all persons interested in this Estate; that the Court has jurisdiction of this proceeding and of the subject matter as required by law; that the Account For Final Settlement has been audited and settled by the Court, complies with the law in every respect, and should be approved as filed; that all claims, debts and expenses have been paid or are approved and should be paid; that all inheritance taxes due and owing to the State of Texas have been paid; that this Estate has been fully administered; that the property remaining on hand in this Estate should be delivered to the persons names in the Account For Final Settlement, and that these persons are the persons entitled to receive such property.

It is ORDERED that the Account For Final Settlement is hereby APPROVED, that the debts and expenses remaining unpaid, as set forth in the Account For Final Settlement shall be paid, and that all of the property belonging to the Estate and still remaining on hand after payment of all debts and expenses shall be delivered to the following persons who are entitled to receive such property from Decedent's Estate:

It is ORDERED that upon the distribution of the estate to such persons and the filing of proper receipts therefor, the [Executor or Administrator] of this Estate shall apply to this Court for an Order of Discharge and for a declaration that this Estate is closed.

SIGNED this _____ day of _____, _____ .

_____
Judge Presiding

This page intentionally left blank.

form 43

NO._____

ESTATE OF	§	IN THE PROBATE COURT
_____,	§ § §	NO. _____ OF
DECEASED	§ §	_____ COUNTY, TEXAS

RECEIPT AND RELEASE

The undersigned hereby acknowledges receipt of the following, in full and complete satisfaction of that portion of this Estate to which the undersigned is entitled:

This receipt is also a RELEASE of the Estate and all persons acting for or on behalf of such Estate with respect to any and all claims or demands which the undersigned may have with respect to the Estate or any of its assets.

DATED this _____ day of _____, _____.

_____
[Name of heir or beneficiary]

STATE OF   )
)
COUNTY OF   )

SUBSCRIBED AND SWORN to before me by _____
_____ this _____ day of _____, _____, to certify which, witness my hand and seal of office.

_____
Notary Public in and for
_____ County,
State of_____
My Commission Expires:

205

This page intentionally left blank.

form 44

NO._____

ESTATE OF　　　　　　　　　　　§　　IN THE PROBATE COURT
　　　　　　　　　　　　　　　　§
_____,　§　　NO. _____ OF
　　　　　　　　　　　　　　　　§
DECEASED　　　　　　　　　　　§　　_____ COUNTY, TEXAS

APPLICATION TO CLOSE ESTATE AND TO DISCHARGE PERSONAL REPRESENTATIVE

_____, _____ of this Estate ("Applicant"), furnishes the following information to the Court:

　　1.　　This Court has previously entered its Order approving the Account for Final Settlement of this Estate and ordering Applicant to deliver the property remaining on hand to the persons entitled to receive such property.

　　2.　　Applicant has fully complied with such Order and there is no property belonging to this Estate remaining in the hands of Applicant.

　　Applicant requests this Court to enter an Order discharging Applicant from this trust, discharging the **[(Surety)(Sureties)]** on Applicant's Bond from further liability, and declaring this Estate closed.

　　　　　　　　　　　　　　　　　　　　　　　Respectfully submitted,

　　　　　　　　　　　　　　　　　　　_____
　　　　　　　　　　　　　　　　　　　Print Name:_____

This page intentionally left blank.

form 45

NO._____

ESTATE OF	§	IN THE PROBATE COURT
	§	
_____,	§	NO. _____ OF
	§	
DECEASED	§	_____ COUNTY, TEXAS

ORDER CLOSING ESTATE AND DISCHARGING PERSONAL REPRESENTATIVE

On this day the Court heard and considered the Application To Close Estate and Discharge Personal Representative, filed by _____, _____ of this Estate, and after hearing the evidence in support of such Application, the Court finds that this Estate has been fully administered; that the Account For Final Settlement has previously been approved; that the **[(Executor)(Administrator)]** has delivered all of the property of the Estate remaining on hand to the persons entitled to receive the same; and that this Estate should be closed.

It is ORDERED that _____, _____ of this Estate, is hereby discharged from this trust; that _____, **[(Surety)(Sureties)]** on the Bond of the _____, **[(is)(are)]** hereby discharged from further liability under such Bond; and this Estate is hereby declared to be closed.

SIGNED this _____ day of _____, _____.

_____
Judge Presiding

This page intentionally left blank.

Form **56**
(Rev. August 1997)
Department of the Treasury
Internal Revenue Service

Notice Concerning Fiduciary Relationship

(Internal Revenue Code sections 6036 and 6903)

form 46

OMB No. 1545-0013

Part I — Identification

Name of person for whom you are acting (as shown on the tax return)

Identifying number

Decedent's social security no.

Address of person for whom you are acting (number, street, and room or suite no.)

City or town, state, and ZIP code (If a foreign address, see instructions.)

Fiduciary's name

Address of fiduciary (number, street, and room or suite no.)

City or town, state, and ZIP code

Telephone number (optional)
( )

Part II — Authority

1 Authority for fiduciary relationship. Check applicable box:
- a(1) ☐ Will and codicils or court order appointing fiduciary. Attach certified copy . . . (2) Date of death ....
- b(1) ☐ Court order appointing fiduciary. Attach certified copy . . . . (2) Date (see instructions) ....
- c ☐ Valid trust instrument and amendments. Attach copy
- d ☐ Other. Describe ▶ ....

Part III — Tax Notices

Send to the fiduciary listed in Part I all notices and other written communications involving the following tax matters:

2 Type of tax (estate, gift, generation-skipping transfer, income, excise, etc.) ▶ ....
3 Federal tax form number (706, 1040, 1041, 1120, etc.) ▶ ....
4 Year(s) or period(s) (if estate tax, date of death) ▶

Part IV — Revocation or Termination of Notice

Section A—Total Revocation or Termination

5 Check this box if you are revoking or terminating all prior notices concerning fiduciary relationships on file with the Internal Revenue Service for the same tax matters and years or periods covered by this notice concerning fiduciary relationship . ▶ ☐
Reason for termination of fiduciary relationship. Check applicable box:
- a ☐ Court order revoking fiduciary authority. Attach certified copy.
- b ☐ Certificate of dissolution or termination of a business entity. Attach copy.
- c ☐ Other. Describe ▶

Section B—Partial Revocation

6a Check this box if you are revoking earlier notices concerning fiduciary relationships on file with the Internal Revenue Service for the same tax matters and years or periods covered by this notice concerning fiduciary relationship . . . . ▶ ☐
b Specify to whom granted, date, and address, including ZIP code, or refer to attached copies of earlier notices and authorizations
▶ ....

Section C—Substitute Fiduciary

7 Check this box if a new fiduciary or fiduciaries have been or will be substituted for the revoking or terminating fiduciary(ies) and specify the name(s) and address(es), including ZIP code(s), of the new fiduciary(ies) . . . . ▶ ☐

Part V — Court and Administrative Proceedings

Name of court (if other than a court proceeding, identify the type of proceeding and name of agency)

Date proceeding initiated

Address of court

Docket number of proceeding

City or town, state, and ZIP code

Date | Time a.m. p.m. | Place of other proceedings

Please Sign Here ▶

I certify that I have the authority to execute this notice concerning fiduciary relationship on behalf of the taxpayer.

Fiduciary's signature | Title, if applicable | Date

Fiduciary's signature | Title, if applicable | Date

For Paperwork Reduction Act and Privacy Act Notice, see back page. Cat. No. 16375I Form **56** (Rev. 8-97)

Form 56 (Rev. 8-97) Page **2**

General Instructions

Section references are to the Internal Revenue Code unless otherwise noted.

Purpose of Form

You may use Form 56 to notify the IRS of the creation or termination of a fiduciary relationship under section 6903 and to give notice of qualification under section 6036.

Who Should File

The fiduciary (see **Definitions** below) uses Form 56 to notify the IRS of the creation, or termination, of a fiduciary relationship under section 6903. For example, if you are acting as fiduciary for an individual, a decedent's estate, or a trust, you may file Form 56. If notification is not given to the IRS, notices sent to the last known address of the taxable entity, transferee, or other person subject to tax liability are sufficient to satisfy the requirements of the Internal Revenue Code.

Receivers and assignees for the benefit of creditors also file Form 56 to give notice of qualification under section 6036. However, a bankruptcy trustee, debtor in possession, or other like fiduciary in a bankruptcy proceeding is not required to give notice of qualification under section 6036. Trustees, etc., in bankruptcy proceedings are subject to the notice requirements under title 11 of the United States Code (Bankruptcy Rules).

Definitions

Fiduciary. A fiduciary is any person acting in a fiduciary capacity for any other person (or terminating entity), such as an administrator, conservator, designee, executor, guardian, receiver, trustee of a trust, trustee in bankruptcy, personal representative, person in possession of property of a decedent's estate, or debtor in possession of assets in any bankruptcy proceeding by order of the court.

Person. A person is any individual, trust, estate, partnership, association, company or corporation.

Decedent's estate. A decedent's estate is a taxable entity separate from the decedent that comes into existence at the time of the decedent's death. It generally continues to exist until the final distribution of the assets of the estate is made to the heirs and other beneficiaries.

Terminating entities. A terminating entity, such as a corporation, partnership, trust, etc., only has the legal capacity to establish a fiduciary relationship while it is in existence. Establishing a fiduciary relationship prior to termination of the entity allows the fiduciary to represent the entity on all tax matters after it is terminated.

When and Where To File

Notice of fiduciary relationship. Generally, you should file Form 56 when you create (or terminate) a fiduciary relationship. To receive tax notices upon creation of a fiduciary relationship, file Form 56 with the Internal Revenue Service Center where the person for whom you are acting is required to file tax returns. However, when a fiduciary relationship is first created, a fiduciary who is required to file a return can file Form 56 with the first tax return filed.

Proceedings (other than bankruptcy) and assignments for the benefit of creditors. A fiduciary who is appointed or authorized to act as:

- A receiver in a receivership proceeding or similar fiduciary (including a fiduciary in aid of foreclosure), or
- An assignee for the benefit of creditors,

must file Form 56 on, or within 10 days of, the date of appointment with the Chief, Special Procedures Staff, of the district office of the IRS having jurisdiction over the person for whom you are acting.

The receiver or assignee may also file a separate Form 56 with the service center where the person for whom the fiduciary is acting is required to file tax returns to provide the notice required by section 6903.

Specific Instructions

Part I—Identification

Provide all the information called for in this part.

Identifying number. If you are acting for an individual, an individual debtor, or other person whose assets are controlled, the identifying number is the social security number (SSN). If you are acting for a person other than an individual, including an estate or trust, the identifying number is the employer identification number (EIN).

Decedent's SSN. If you are acting on behalf of a decedent, enter the decedent's SSN shown on his or her final Form 1040 in the space provided.

Address. Include the suite, room, or other unit number after the street address.

If the postal service does not deliver mail to the street address and the fiduciary (or person) has a P.O. box, show the box number instead of the street address.

For a foreign address, enter the information in the following order: city, province or state, and country. Follow the country's practice for entering the postal code. Please **do not** abbreviate the country name.

Part II—Authority

Line 1a. Check the box on line 1a if the decedent died **testate** (i.e., having left a valid will) and enter the decedent's date of death.

Line 1b. Check the box on line 1b if the decedent died **intestate** (i.e., without leaving a valid will). Also, enter the decedent's date of death and write "Date of Death" next to the date.

Assignment for the benefit of creditors. Enter the date the assets were assigned to you and write "Assignment Date" after the date.

Proceedings other than bankruptcy. Enter the date you were appointed or took possession of the assets of the debtor or other person whose assets are controlled.

Part III—Tax Notices

Complete this part if you want the IRS to send you tax notices regarding the person for whom you are acting.

Line 2. Specify the type of tax involved. This line should also identify a transferee tax liability under section 6901 or fiduciary tax liability under 31 U.S.C. 3713(b) when either exists.

Part IV—Revocation or Termination of Notice

Complete this part only if you are revoking or terminating a prior notice concerning a fiduciary relationship. Completing this part will relieve you of any further duty or liability as a fiduciary if used as a notice of termination.

Part V—Court and Administrative Proceedings

Complete this part only if you have been appointed a receiver, trustee, or fiduciary by a court or other governmental unit in a proceeding other than a bankruptcy proceeding.

If proceedings are scheduled for more than one date, time, or place, attach a separate schedule of the proceedings.

Assignment for the benefit of creditors.— You must attach the following information:

1. A brief description of the assets that were assigned, and

2. An explanation of the action to be taken regarding such assets, including any hearings, meetings of creditors, sale, or other scheduled action.

Signature

Sign Form 56 and enter a title describing your role as a fiduciary (e.g., assignee, executor, guardian, trustee, personal representative, receiver, or conservator).

Paperwork Reduction Act and Privacy Act Notice. We ask for the information on this form to carry out the Internal Revenue laws of the United States. Form 56 is provided for your convenience and its use is voluntary. Under section 6109 you must disclose the social security number or employer identification number of the individual or entity for which you are acting. The principal purpose of this disclosure is to secure proper identification of the taxpayer. We also need this information to gain access to the tax information in our files and properly respond to your request. If you do not disclose this information, we may suspend processing the notice of fiduciary relationship and not consider this as proper notification until you provide the information.

You are not required to provide the information requested on a form that is subject to the Paperwork Reduction Act unless the form displays a valid OMB control number. Books or records relating to a form or its instructions must be retained as long as their contents may become material in the administration of any Internal Revenue law. Generally, tax returns and return information are confidential as required by section 6103.

The time needed to complete and file this form will vary depending on individual circumstances. The estimated average time is:

Recordkeeping . . . . 8 min.
Learning about the law or the form . . . . . 32 min.
Preparing the form . . . . . 46 min.
Copying, assembling, and sending the form to the IRS . . 15 min.

If you have comments concerning the accuracy of these time estimates or suggestions for making this form simpler, we would be happy to hear from you. You can write to the Tax Forms Committee, Western Area Distribution Center, Rancho Cordova, CA 95743-0001. **DO NOT** send Form 56 to this address. Instead, see **When and Where To File** on this page.

form 47

AFFIDAVIT OF HEIRSHIP-STATUTORY FORM
AFFIDAVIT OF FACTS CONCERNING THE IDENTITY OF HEIRS

Before me, the undersigned authority, on this day personally appeared _____ ("Affiant") (insert name of affiant) who, being first duly sworn, upon his/her oath states:

1. My name is_____(insert name of an affiant), and I live at_____ (insert address of affiant's residence). I am personally familiar with the family and marital history of _____ ("Decedent") (insert name of decedent), and I have personal knowledge of the facts stated in this affidavit.

2. I knew decedent from _____ (insert date) until _____ (insert date). Decedent died on _____ (insert date of death). Decedent's place of death was _____ _____ (insert place of death). At the time of decedent's death, decedent's residence was _____ (insert address of decedent's residence.

3. Decedent's marital history was as follows: _____ (insert marital history and, if decedent's spouse is deceased, insert date and place of spouse's death).

4. Decedent had the following children: _____(insert name, birth date, name of other parent, and current address of child or date of death of child and descendants of deceased child, as applicable, for each child).

5. Decedent did not have or adopt any other children and did not take any other children into decedent's home or raise any other children, except:_____ (insert name of child or names of children, or state "none").

6. (Include if decedent was not survived by descendants.) Decedent's mother was _____ _____ (insert name, birth date, and current address or date of death of mother, as applicable).

7. (Include if decedent was not survived by descendants.) Decedent's father was _____ _____ (insert name, birth date, and current address or date of death of father, as applicable).

8. (Include if decedent was not survived by descendants or by both mother and father.) Decedent had the following siblings:_____ _____ (insert name, birth date, and current address or date of death of each sibling and parents of each sibling and descendants of each deceased sibling, as applicable, or state "none").

9. (Optional.) The following persons have knowledge regarding the decedent, the identity of decedent's children, if any, parents, or siblings, if any:_____ (insert names of persons with knowledge, or state "none").

10. Decedent died without leaving a written will. (Modify statement if decedent left a written will.)

11. There has been no admission of decedent's estate. (Modify statement if there has been administration of decedent's estate.)

12. Decedent left no debts that are unpaid, except: _____ (insert list of debts, or state "none").

13. There are no unpaid estate or inheritance taxes except: _____ (insert list of unpaid taxes, or state "none").

14. To the best of my knowledge, decedent owned an interest in the following real property: _____ (insert list of real property in which decedent owned an interest, or state "none").

15. (Optional.) The following were the heirs of decedent: _____ _____ (insert names of heirs).

16. (Insert additional information as appropriate, such as size of the decedent's estate.) Signed this _____ day of _____, _____.

_____
(signature of affiant)

State of _____
County of _____

Sworn to and subscribed to before me on _____ (date) by _____.

_____
(signature of notarial officer)

(Seal, if any, of notary)

_____
(printed name)
My commission expires: _____

form 48

Form 1040

Department of the Treasury—Internal Revenue Service

U.S. Individual Income Tax Return 2001 (99) IRS Use Only—Do not write or staple in this space.

For the year Jan. 1–Dec. 31, 2001, or other tax year beginning , 2001, ending , 20 | OMB No. 1545-0074

Label (See instructions on page 19.)
Use the IRS label. Otherwise, please print or type.

Your first name and initial | Last name | Your social security number

If a joint return, spouse's first name and initial | Last name | Spouse's social security number

Home address (number and street). If you have a P.O. box, see page 19. | Apt. no.

City, town or post office, state, and ZIP code. If you have a foreign address, see page 19.

Important! You **must** enter your SSN(s) above.

Presidential Election Campaign (See page 19.)

Note. Checking "Yes" will not change your tax or reduce your refund.
Do you, or your spouse if filing a joint return, want $3 to go to this fund? . . . . .

You: ☐ Yes ☐ No   Spouse: ☐ Yes ☐ No

Filing Status

Check only one box.

1 ☐ Single
2 ☐ Married filing joint return (even if only one had income)
3 ☐ Married filing separate return. Enter spouse's social security no. above and full name here. •
4 ☐ Head of household (with qualifying person). (See page 19.) If the qualifying person is a child but not your dependent, enter this child's name here. •
5 ☐ Qualifying widow(er) with dependent child (year spouse died •). (See page 19.)

Exemptions

6a ☐ **Yourself.** If your parent (or someone else) can claim you as a dependent on his or her tax return, **do not** check box 6a . . . . •

b ☐ **Spouse**

c **Dependents:**

(1) First name Last name	(2) Dependent's social security number	(3) Dependent's relationship to you	(4) ✓ if qualifying child for child tax credit (see page 20)
			☐
			☐
			☐
			☐
			☐
			☐

If more than six dependents, see page 20.

No. of boxes checked on 6a and 6b ___
No. of your children on 6c who:
• lived with you ___
• did not live with you due to divorce or separation (see page 20) ___
Dependents on 6c not entered above ___
Add numbers entered on lines above • ___

d Total number of exemptions claimed . . . .

Income

Attach Forms W-2 and W-2G here. Also attach Form(s) 1099-R if tax was withheld.

If you did not get a W-2, see page 21.

Enclose, but do not attach, any payment. Also, please use Form 1040-V.

7 Wages, salaries, tips, etc. Attach Form(s) W-2 . . . . | 7
8a **Taxable** interest. Attach Schedule B if required . . . . | 8a
b Tax-exempt interest. **Do not** include on line 8a . . . | 8b |
9 Ordinary dividends. Attach Schedule B if required . . . . | 9
10 Taxable refunds, credits, or offsets of state and local income taxes (see page 22) . . | 10
11 Alimony received . . . . | 11
12 Business income or (loss). Attach Schedule C or C-EZ . . . . | 12
13 Capital gain or (loss). Attach Schedule D if required. If not required, check here • ☐ | 13
14 Other gains or (losses). Attach Form 4797 . . . . | 14
15a Total IRA distributions . | 15a | b Taxable amount (see page 23) | 15b
16a Total pensions and annuities | 16a | b Taxable amount (see page 23) | 16b
17 Rental real estate, royalties, partnerships, S corporations, trusts, etc. Attach Schedule E | 17
18 Farm income or (loss). Attach Schedule F . . . . | 18
19 Unemployment compensation . . . . | 19
20a Social security benefits | 20a | b Taxable amount (see page 25) | 20b
21 Other income. List type and amount (see page 27) _____ | 21
22 Add the amounts in the far right column for lines 7 through 21. This is your **total income** • | 22

Adjusted Gross Income

23 IRA deduction (see page 27) . . . . | 23
24 Student loan interest deduction (see page 28) . . | 24
25 Archer MSA deduction. Attach Form 8853 . . . | 25
26 Moving expenses. Attach Form 3903 . . . . . | 26
27 One-half of self-employment tax. Attach Schedule SE | 27
28 Self-employed health insurance deduction (see page 30) | 28
29 Self-employed SEP, SIMPLE, and qualified plans . | 29
30 Penalty on early withdrawal of savings . . . . | 30
31a Alimony paid   b Recipient's SSN • _____ | 31a
32 Add lines 23 through 31a . . . . | 32
33 Subtract line 32 from line 22. This is your **adjusted gross income** . . . . . . • | 33

For Disclosure, Privacy Act, and Paperwork Reduction Act Notice, see page 72.   Cat. No. 11320B   Form **1040** (2001)

Form 1040 (2001) Page 2

Tax and Credits

Standard Deduction for—
- People who checked any box on line 35a or 35b **or** who can be claimed as a dependent, see page 31.
- All others:
Single, $4,550
Head of household, $6,650
Married filing jointly or Qualifying widow(er), $7,600
Married filing separately, $3,800

34	Amount from line 33 (adjusted gross income)	34
35a	Check if: ☐ **You** were 65 or older, ☐ Blind; ☐ **Spouse** was 65 or older, ☐ Blind. Add the number of boxes checked above and enter the total here ▶ 35a	
b	If you are married filing separately and your spouse itemizes deductions, or you were a dual-status alien, see page 31 and check here ▶ 35b ☐	
36	**Itemized deductions** (from Schedule A) **or** your **standard deduction** (see left margin)	36
37	Subtract line 36 from line 34	37
38	If line 34 is $99,725 or less, multiply $2,900 by the total number of exemptions claimed on line 6d. If line 34 is over $99,725, see the worksheet on page 32	38
39	**Taxable income.** Subtract line 38 from line 37. If line 38 is more than line 37, enter -0-	39
40	Tax (see page 33). Check if any tax is from **a** ☐ Form(s) 8814 **b** ☐ Form 4972	40
41	**Alternative minimum tax** (see page 34). Attach Form 6251	41
42	Add lines 40 and 41 ▶	42
43	Foreign tax credit. Attach Form 1116 if required	43
44	Credit for child and dependent care expenses. Attach Form 2441	44
45	Credit for the elderly or the disabled. Attach Schedule R	45
46	Education credits. Attach Form 8863	46
47	Rate reduction credit. See the worksheet on page 36	47
48	Child tax credit (see page 37)	48
49	Adoption credit. Attach Form 8839	49
50	Other credits from: **a** ☐ Form 3800 **b** ☐ Form 8396 **c** ☐ Form 8801 **d** ☐ Form (specify) _____	50
51	Add lines 43 through 50. These are your **total credits**	51
52	Subtract line 51 from line 42. If line 51 is more than line 42, enter -0- ▶	52

Other Taxes

53	Self-employment tax. Attach Schedule SE	53
54	Social security and Medicare tax on tip income not reported to employer. Attach Form 4137	54
55	Tax on qualified plans, including IRAs, and other tax-favored accounts. Attach Form 5329 if required	55
56	Advance earned income credit payments from Form(s) W-2	56
57	Household employment taxes. Attach Schedule H	57
58	Add lines 52 through 57. This is your **total tax** ▶	58

Payments

If you have a qualifying child, attach Schedule EIC.

59	Federal income tax withheld from Forms W-2 and 1099	59
60	2001 estimated tax payments and amount applied from 2000 return	60
61a	**Earned income credit (EIC)**	61a
b	Nontaxable earned income 61b	
62	Excess social security and RRTA tax withheld (see page 51)	62
63	Additional child tax credit. Attach Form 8812	63
64	Amount paid with request for extension to file (see page 51)	64
65	Other payments. Check if from **a** ☐ Form 2439 **b** ☐ Form 4136	65
66	Add lines 59, 60, 61a, and 62 through 65. These are your **total payments** ▶	66

Refund

Direct deposit? See page 51 and fill in 68b, 68c, and 68d.

67	If line 66 is more than line 58, subtract line 58 from line 66. This is the amount you **overpaid**	67
68a	Amount of line 67 you want **refunded to you** ▶	68a
b	Routing number	
	c Type: ☐ Checking ☐ Savings	
d	Account number	
69	Amount of line 67 you want **applied to your 2002 estimated tax** ▶ 69	

Amount You Owe

70	**Amount you owe.** Subtract line 66 from line 58. For details on how to pay, see page 52 ▶	70
71	Estimated tax penalty. Also include on line 70 71	

Third Party Designee

Do you want to allow another person to discuss this return with the IRS (see page 53)? ☐ **Yes.** Complete the following. ☐ No

Designee's name ▶   Phone no. (   )   Personal identification number (PIN) ▶

Sign Here

Joint return? See page 19.
Keep a copy for your records.

Under penalties of perjury, I declare that I have examined this return and accompanying schedules and statements, and to the best of my knowledge and belief, they are true, correct, and complete. Declaration of preparer (other than taxpayer) is based on all information of which preparer has any knowledge.

Your signature   Date   Your occupation   Daytime phone number (   )

Spouse's signature. If a joint return, **both** must sign.   Date   Spouse's occupation

Paid Preparer's Use Only

Preparer's signature   Date   Check if self-employed ☐   Preparer's SSN or PTIN

Firm's name (or yours if self-employed), address, and ZIP code   EIN   Phone no. (   )

Form **1040** (2001)

INDEX

A

accountants, 8
account for final settlement, 199
ADE. *See* Administration with Dependent Executor
Administration with Dependent Executor, 3, 32, 33-34, 36, 38, 39, 53
Administration with Will Annexed, 3, 32-33, 36, 38, 39, 52
administrator, 1, 2, 6, 6-7, 31, 32, 35, 40, 47, 56
    court appointed, 7
affidavit of heirship, 213
affidavit regarding debts and taxes, 191
affidavit regarding fulfillment of will admitted to probate as a muniment of title, 141
ancillary administration, 9
annual account, 193
application for employer identification number (IRS Form SS-4), 169
application for family allowance, 187
application for letters of administration, 111
application for probate of will and issuance of letters testamentary, 103, 127
application for probate of will and issuance of letters testamentary with will annexed, 119
application for probate of will as a muniment of title, 135
application to close estate and to discharge personal representative, 207
application to determine heirship, 143
application to set aside exempt property, 183
appointment of resident agent, 159
assets, 1, 9, 10, 13, 15, 21, 22, 23, 24, 25, 28, 29, 30, 40, 42, 44, 45, 46, 49, 60
attorneys, 2, 8, 11, 11-12
    costs, 12
    fees, 12, 15
AWA. *See* Administration with Will Annexed

B

bank accounts, 22, 42, 56
    checking, 21-22, 30, 42
beneficiaries, 1, 2, 5, 10, 22, 42, 49, 56, 57, 58
bond, 20, 30, 39-40, 47

C

charities, 21, 33, 34, 41
children, 16, 25, 26, 33, 34, 35, 45, 46, 48
court, 6
credit cards, 13
creditors, 1, 7, 10, 11, 13, 20-21, 25, 26, 27, 40, 45, 48, 57, 61
    notice to, 20-21, 40-41
    secured, 20, 21, 40, 41
    unsecured, 20, 40, 41

D

death certificate, 5, 6
debt, 10, 25, 26-27, 28, 34, 42, 43, 45, 47-48, 50, 55, 61
decedent, 1, 7
dependent administration, 15, 16, 29, 31-51

E

estate, 1, 25
    insolvent, 25, 45
    solvent, 25, 45
executor, 1, 2, 3, 6-7, 8, 12, 13, 15, 21, 31, 33, 37, 39, 47, 48, 55, 56
    independent, 15, 19, 33, 56
expenses, 26-27, 47-48, 56

F

family allowance, 25, 46
fees, 9, 37

H

heirs, 1, 2, 5, 10, 57-59, 60, 61
homestead, 24-25, 28, 45, 50, 60

I

independent administration, 3, 15-29, 30, 33, 59
insurance, 14, 30
    life, 6, 8, 12, 23, 44
intestate, 2, 6, 31, 34, 35, 57
inventory, appraisement, and list of claims, 177

J

joint tenancy with rights of survivorship, 4, 5
judgment declaring heirship, 149

L

lawyers. *See* attorneys
legal forms
    form 1, 16-17, 18, 30, 103
    form 2, 18, 30, 105
    form 3, 19, 30, 107
    form 4, 19, 30, 109
    form 5, 35, 54, 111
    form 6, 38, 54, 113
    form 7, 38, 54, 115
    form 8, 39, 54, 117
    form 9, 32-33, 52, 119
    form 10, 38, 52, 121
    form 11, 38, 52, 123
    form 12, 39, 52, 125
    form 13, 33-34, 53, 127
    form 14, 38, 53, 129
    form 15, 38, 53, 131
    form 16, 39, 53, 133
    form 17, 56, 62, 135
    form 18, 56, 62, 137
    form 19, 56-57, 62, 139
    form 20, 57, 62, 141
    form 21, 58, 59, 63, 143
    form 22, 59, 63, 147
    form 23, 59, 63, 149
    form 24, 60-61, 151
    form 25, 13, 157
    form 26, 17, 30, 36, 52, 53, 54, 159
    form 27, 17-18, 30, 36, 37, 52, 53, 161
    form 28, 20, 30, 40-41, 52, 53, 54, 163
    form 29, 21, 41, 165
    form 30, 21, 41, 167
    form 31, 22-23, 30, 43, 52, 53, 54, 62, 63, 169
    form 32, 23-24, 30, 40, 44-45, 46, 52, 53, 54, 57, 177
    form 33, 24, 30, 45, 52, 53, 54, 181
    form 34, 25, 46, 183
    form 35, 25, 185
    form 36, 25, 46, 187
    form 37, 25, 46, 189
    form 38, 29, 30, 52, 53, 54, 191
    form 39, 46-47, 193
    form 40, 46, 197
    form 41, 50-51, 199
    form 42, 50, 203
    form 43, 51, 205
    form 44, 51, 207
    form 45, 51, 209
    form 46, 8, 30, 52, 53, 54, 62, 63, 211
    form 47, 61, 213
    form 48, 8, 27-28, 49, 215
letters of administration, 32, 38, 39, 40, 41, 47
letters testamentary, 19, 20, 21, 26, 30, 32, 33, 38, 39, 40, 41, 47, 48, 57
liabilities, 15, 43, 60

M

mail, 13
military, 14
motion to open safe deposit box and to examine papers, 157
Muniment of Title, 3, 55-57, 59, 62

N

notary, 9, 17, 19, 36
notice concerning fiduciary relationship (IRS Form 56), 211
notice to creditors, 163

O

oath, 109, 125, 133
oath of administrator, 117
order admitting will to probate and authorizing letters testamentary, 107, 131

index

order admitting will to probate and authorizing letters testamentary with will annexed, 123
order admitting will to probate as a muniment of title, 139
order approving account for final settlement and authorizing distribution of estate, 203
order approving annual account, 197
order approving inventory and appraisement, 181
order authorizing letters of administration, 115
order closing estate and discharging personal representative, 209
order for family allowance, 189
order to set aside exempt property, 185

P

pension, 14
proceeding to determine heirship, 4, 55, 57-59, 63
proof of death and other facts, 105, 113, 121, 129, 137
proof of service of notice upon claimants against estate, 165
proof of subscribing witness, 161
property, 50, 56, 60
    community, 5, 8, 24, 59, 60
    distribution of, 1, 22, 42, 50
    exempt, 25, 45-46, 60
    joint, 24
    personal, 7, 16, 19, 22, 32, 34, 35, 40, 42, 44, 45, 60
    probate, 2, 4-6, 8
    real, 4, 7, 16, 22, 24, 28, 32, 34, 35, 42, 44, 50, 55, 60, 61
    separate, 5, 24, 25, 46, 59
publisher's affidavit, 167

R

RDA. *See* Regular Dependent Administration
real estate. *See* property
receipt and release, 205
Regular Dependent Administration, 3, 34-35, 38, 39, 54
resident agent, 7, 17, 36

S

safe deposit boxes, 12-13
small estate affidavit and order, 151
small estates, 4, 55, 59-61
Social Security, 13, 14
Social Security Administration, 13
sole ownership, 4, 5
spouse, 7, 13, 25, 45, 46
    surviving, 25, 26, 27, 35, 45, 48
statement of facts, 147
stocks, 22, 30, 40, 42, 43, 56

T

taxes, 25, 26, 43, 45, 48
    estate, 1, 8, 27, 28, 49
    federal, 8, 49
    income, 8, 27
    inheritance, 1, 8, 27, 28
    returns, 27-28, 49, 49-50
tenancy by the entireties, 4
tenancy in common, 4-5
testate, 2, 31, 59
Texas Probate Code, 2, 15, 16, 18, 19, 25, 26, 27, 31, 37, 38, 39, 42, 43, 44, 46, 47, 48, 50, 57, 59, 61

U

U.S. individual income tax return (IRS Form 1040), 215

V

veteran's benefits, 14

W

will, 1, 2, 3, 12, 16, 31, 55
    self-proved, 17-18, 36
witnesses, 16, 17, 18, 30, 32, 34, 36, 37, 61

SPHINX® PUBLISHING'S NATIONAL TITLES
Valid in All 50 States

LEGAL SURVIVAL IN BUSINESS

The Complete Book of Corporate Forms	$24.95
How to Form a Delaware Corporation from Any State	$24.95
How to Form a Limited Liability Company	$22.95
Incorporate in Nevada from Any State	$24.95
How to Form a Nonprofit Corporation	$24.95
How to Form Your Own Corporation (3E)	$24.95
How to Form Your Own Partnership	$22.95
How to Register Your Own Copyright (4E)	$24.95
How to Register Your Own Trademark (3E)	$21.95
Most Valuable Business Legal Forms You'll Ever Need (3E)	$21.95

LEGAL SURVIVAL IN COURT

Crime Victim's Guide to Justice (2E)	$21.95
Grandparents' Rights (3E)	$24.95
Help Your Lawyer Win Your Case (2E)	$14.95
Jurors' Rights (2E)	$12.95
Legal Research Made Easy (2E)	$16.95
Winning Your Personal Injury Claim (2E)	$24.95
Your Rights When You Owe Too Much	$16.95

LEGAL SURVIVAL IN REAL ESTATE

Essential Guide to Real Estate Contracts	$18.95
Essential Guide to Real Estate Leases	$18.95
How to Buy a Condominium or Townhome (2E)	$19.95

LEGAL SURVIVAL IN PERSONAL AFFAIRS

Cómo Hacer su Propio Testamento	$16.95
Guía de Inmigración a Estados Unidos (3E)	$24.95
Guía de Justicia para Víctimas del Crimen	$21.95
Cómo Solicitar su Propio Divorcio	$24.95
How to File Your Own Bankruptcy (5E)	$21.95
How to File Your Own Divorce (4E)	$24.95
How to Make Your Own Will (2E)	$16.95
How to Write Your Own Living Will (2E)	$16.95
How to Write Your Own Premarital Agreement (3E)	$24.95
How to Win Your Unemployment Compensation Claim	$21.95
Living Trusts and Other Ways to Avoid Probate (3E)	$24.95
Manual de Beneficios para el Seguro Social	$18.95
Mastering the MBE	$16.95
Most Valuable Personal Legal Forms You'll Ever Need	$24.95
Neighbor v. Neighbor (2E)	$16.95
The Nanny and Domestic Help Legal Kit	$22.95
The Power of Attorney Handbook (3E)	$19.95
Repair Your Own Credit and Deal with Debt	$18.95
The Social Security Benefits Handbook (3E)	$18.95
Unmarried Parents' Rights	$19.95
U.S.A. Immigration Guide (3E)	$19.95
Your Right to Child Custody, Visitation and Support (2E)	$24.95

Legal Survival Guides are directly available from Sourcebooks, Inc., or from your local bookstores.
Prices are subject to change without notice.

For credit card orders call 1–800–432–7444, write P.O. Box 4410, Naperville, IL 60567-4410
or fax 630-961-2168

SPHINX® PUBLISHING ORDER FORM

BILL TO:		SHIP TO:	
Phone #	Terms	F.O.B. Chicago, IL	Ship Date

Charge my: ☐ VISA ☐ MasterCard ☐ American Express

☐ Money Order or Personal Check

Credit Card Number　　　　　　　Expiration Date

Qty	ISBN	Title	Retail	Ext.
	SPHINX PUBLISHING NATIONAL TITLES			
	1-57248-148-X	Cómo Hacer su Propio Testamento	$16.95	
	1-57248-147-1	Cómo Solicitar su Propio Divorcio	$24.95	
	1-57248-166-8	The Complete Book of Corporate Forms	$24.95	
	1-57248-163-3	Crime Victim's Guide to Justice (2E)	$21.95	
	1-57248-159-5	Essential Guide to Real Estate Contracts	$18.95	
	1-57248-160-9	Essential Guide to Real Estate Leases	$18.95	
	1-57248-139-0	Grandparents' Rights (3E)	$24.95	
	1-57248-188-9	Guía de Inmigración a Estados Unidos (3E)	$24.95	
	1-57248-187-0	Guía de Justicia para Víctimas del Crimen	$21.95	
	1-57248-103-X	Help Your Lawyer Win Your Case (2E)	$14.95	
	1-57248-164-1	How to Buy a Condominium or Townhome (2E)	$19.95	
	1-57248-191-9	How to File Your Own Bankruptcy (5E)	$21.95	
	1-57248-132-3	How to File Your Own Divorce (4E)	$24.95	
	1-57248-100-5	How to Form a DE Corporation from Any State	$24.95	
	1-57248-083-1	How to Form a Limited Liability Company	$22.95	
	1-57248-099-8	How to Form a Nonprofit Corporation	$24.95	
	1-57248-133-1	How to Form Your Own Corporation (3E)	$24.95	
	1-57071-343-X	How to Form Your Own Partnership	$22.95	
	1-57248-119-6	How to Make Your Own Will (2E)	$16.95	
	1-57248-200-1	How to Register Your Own Copyright (4E)	$24.95	
	1-57248-104-8	How to Register Your Own Trademark (3E)	$21.95	
	1-57071-349-9	How to Win Your Unemployment Compensation Claim	$21.95	
	1-57248-118-8	How to Write Your Own Living Will (2E)	$16.95	
	1-57248-156-0	How to Write Your Own Premarital Agreement (3E)	$24.95	
	1-57248-158-7	Incorporate in Nevada from Any State	$24.95	
	1-57071-333-2	Jurors' Rights (2E)	$12.95	
	1-57071-400-2	Legal Research Made Easy (2E)	$16.95	
	1-57248-165-X	Living Trusts and Other Ways to Avoid Probate (3E)	$24.95	
	1-57248-186-2	Manual de Beneficios para el Seguro Social	$18.95	
	1-57248-220-6	Mastering the MBE	$16.95	
	1-57248-167-6	Most Valuable Bus. Legal Forms You'll Ever Need (3E)	$21.95	
	1-57248-130-7	Most Valuable Personal Legal Forms You'll Ever Need	$24.95	
	1-57248-098-X	The Nanny and Domestic Help Legal Kit	$22.95	
	1-57248-089-0	Neighbor v. Neighbor (2E)	$16.95	
	1-57071-348-0	The Power of Attorney Handbook (3E)	$19.95	
	1-57248-149-8	Repair Your Own Credit and Deal with Debt	$18.95	
	1-57248-168-4	The Social Security Benefits Handbook (3E)	$18.95	
	1-57071-399-5	Unmarried Parents' Rights	$19.95	
	1-57071-354-5	U.S.A. Immigration Guide (3E)	$19.95	
	1-57248-138-2	Winning Your Personal Injury Claim (2E)	$24.95	
	1-57248-162-5	Your Right to Child Custody, Visitation and Support (2E)	$24.95	
	1-57248-157-9	Your Rights When You Owe Too Much	$16.95	
	CALIFORNIA TITLES			
	1-57248-150-1	CA Power of Attorney Handbook (2E)	$18.95	
	1-57248-151-X	How to File for Divorce in CA (3E)	$26.95	
	1-57071-356-1	How to Make a CA Will	$16.95	
	1-57248-145-5	How to Probate and Settle an Estate in California	$26.95	
	1-57248-146-3	How to Start a Business in CA	$18.95	
	1-57071-358-8	How to Win in Small Claims Court in CA	$16.95	
	1-57248-196-X	The Landlord's Legal Guide in CA	$24.95	
	FLORIDA TITLES			
	1-57071-363-4	Florida Power of Attorney Handbook (2E)	$16.95	
	1-57248-176-5	How to File for Divorce in FL (7E)	$26.95	
	1-57248-177-3	How to Form a Corporation in FL (5E)	$24.95	
	1-57248-203-6	How to Form a Limited Liability Co. in FL (2E)	$24.95	
	1-57071-401-0	How to Form a Partnership in FL	$22.95	

Form Continued on Following Page　　　**SUBTOTAL**

To order, call Sourcebooks at 1-800-432-7444 or FAX (630) 961-2168 (Bookstores, libraries, wholesalers—please call for discount)

Prices are subject to change without notice.

SPHINX® PUBLISHING ORDER FORM

Qty	ISBN	Title	Retail	Ext.
___	1-57248-113-7	How to Make a FL Will (6E)	$16.95	___
___	1-57248-088-2	How to Modify Your FL Divorce Judgment (4E)	$24.95	___
___	1-57248-144-7	How to Probate and Settle an Estate in FL (4E)	$26.95	___
___	1-57248-081-5	How to Start a Business in FL (5E)	$16.95	___
___	1-57071-362-6	How to Win in Small Claims Court in FL (6E)	$16.95	___
___	1-57248-123-4	Landlords' Rights and Duties in FL (8E)	$21.95	___

GEORGIA TITLES

Qty	ISBN	Title	Retail	Ext.
___	1-57248-137-4	How to File for Divorce in GA (4E)	$21.95	___
___	1-57248-180-3	How to Make a GA Will (4E)	$21.95	___
___	1-57248-140-4	How to Start a Business in Georgia (2E)	$16.95	___

ILLINOIS TITLES

Qty	ISBN	Title	Retail	Ext.
___	1-57071-405-3	How to File for Divorce in IL (2E)	$21.95	___
___	1-57248-170-6	How to Make an IL Will (3E)	$16.95	___
___	1-57071-416-9	How to Start a Business in IL (2E)	$18.95	___
___	1-57248-078-5	Landlords' Rights & Duties in IL	$21.95	___

MASSACHUSETTS TITLES

Qty	ISBN	Title	Retail	Ext.
___	1-57248-128-5	How to File for Divorce in MA (3E)	$24.95	___
___	1-57248-115-3	How to Form a Corporation in MA	$24.95	___
___	1-57248-108-0	How to Make a MA Will (2E)	$16.95	___
___	1-57248-106-4	How to Start a Business in MA (2E)	$18.95	___
___	1-57248-209-5	The Landlord's Legal Guide in MA	$24.95	___

MICHIGAN TITLES

Qty	ISBN	Title	Retail	Ext.
___	1-57071-409-6	How to File for Divorce in MI (2E)	$21.95	___
___	1-57248-182-X	How to Make a MI Will (3E)	$16.95	___
___	1-57248-183-8	How to Start a Business in MI (3E)	$18.95	___

MINNESOTA TITLES

Qty	ISBN	Title	Retail	Ext.
___	1-57248-142-0	How to File for Divorce in MN	$21.95	___
___	1-57248-179-X	How to Form a Corporation in MN	$24.95	___
___	1-57248-178-1	How to Make a MN Will (2E)	$16.95	___

NEW YORK TITLES

Qty	ISBN	Title	Retail	Ext.
___	1-57248-141-2	How to File for Divorce in NY (2E)	$26.95	___
___	1-57248-105-6	How to Form a Corporation in NY	$24.95	___
___	1-57248-095-5	How to Make a NY Will (2E)	$16.95	___
___	1-57071-185-2	How to Start a Business in NY	$18.95	___
___	1-57071-187-9	How to Win in Small Claims Court in NY	$16.95	___
___	1-57071-186-0	Landlords' Rights and Duties in NY	$21.95	___
___	1-57071-188-7	New York Power of Attorney Handbook	$19.95	___
___	1-57248-122-6	Tenants' Rights in NY	$21.95	___

NORTH CAROLINA TITLES

Qty	ISBN	Title	Retail	Ext.
___	1-57248-185-4	How to File for Divorce in NC (3E)	$22.95	___
___	1-57248-129-3	How to Make a NC Will (3E)	$16.95	___
___	1-57248-184-6	How to Start a Business in NC (3E)	$18.95	___
___	1-57248-091-2	Landlords' Rights & Duties in NC	$21.95	___

OHIO TITLES

Qty	ISBN	Title	Retail	Ext.
___	1-57248-190-0	How to File for Divorce in OH (2E)	$24.95	___
___	1-57248-174-9	How to Form a Corporation in OH	$24.95	___
___	1-57248-173-0	How to Make an OH Will	$16.95	___

PENNSYLVANIA TITLES

Qty	ISBN	Title	Retail	Ext.
___	1-57248-211-7	How to File for Divorce in PA (3E)	$26.95	___
___	1-57248-094-7	How to Make a PA Will (2E)	$16.95	___
___	1-57248-112-9	How to Start a Business in PA (2E)	$18.95	___
___	1-57071-179-8	Landlords' Rights and Duties in PA	$19.95	___

TEXAS TITLES

Qty	ISBN	Title	Retail	Ext.
___	1-57248-171-4	Child Custody, Visitation, and Support in TX	$22.95	___
___	1-57248-172-2	How to File for Divorce in TX (3E)	$24.95	___
___	1-57248-114-5	How to Form a Corporation in TX (2E)	$24.95	___
___	1-57071-417-7	How to Make a TX Will (2E)	$16.95	___
___	1-57248-214-1	How to Probate and Settle an Estate in TX (3E)	$26.95	___
___	1-57248-228-1	How to Start a Business in TX (3E)	$18.95	___
___	1-57248-111-0	How to Win in Small Claims Court in TX (2E)	$16.95	___
___	1-57248-110-2	Landlords' Rights and Duties in TX (2E)	$21.95	___

SUBTOTAL THIS PAGE ___

SUBTOTAL PREVIOUS PAGE ___

Shipping— $5.00 for 1st book, $1.00 each additional ___

Illinois residents add 6.75% sales tax ___

Connecticut residents add 6.00% sales tax ___

TOTAL ___

To order, call Sourcebooks at 1-800-432-7444 or FAX (630) 961-2168 (Bookstores, libraries, wholesalers—please call for discount)

Prices are subject to change without notice.